The CPM Silver Yearbook, 2006

The CPM Silver Yearbook, 2006

CPM Group

WILEY

John Wiley & Sons, Inc.

Published by John Wiley & Sons, Inc., Hoboken, New Jersey
Published simultaneously in Canada

ISBN-13 978-0-471-77733-5
ISBN-10 0-471-77733-1

Printed in the United States of America

10 9 8 7 6 5 4 3 2 1

Founded in 1807, John Wiley & Sons is the oldest independent publishing company in the United States. With offices in North America, Europe, Australia and Asia, Wiley is globally committed to developing and marketing print and electronic products and services for our customers' professional and personal knowledge and understanding.

The Wiley Trading series features books by traders who have survived the market's ever changing temperament and have prospered-some by reinventing systems, others by getting back to basics. Whether a novice trader, professional or somewhere in-between, these books will provide the advice and strategies needed to prosper today and well into the future.

For a list of available titles, please visit our Web site at www.WileyFinance.com.

CPM Group's Silver Yearbook 2006

April 2006
Volume 20, Number 1

CPM Group
30 Broad Street
37th Floor
New York, NY 10004
USA

Telephone:	212-785-8320
Telefax:	212-785-8325
E-mail:	info@cpmgroup.com
Website:	www.cpmgroup.com

Jeffrey M. Christian, Managing Director
Mark Hansen, Executive Vice President
Doug Sherrod, Director
Ralph Mizrahi, Director
Andy Hecht, Director
Phillip Barkett, Director of Marketing
Adam J. Crown, Vice President, Sales & Marketing
Carlos Sanchez, Associate Director, Research
Catherine Virga, Research Analyst
Rohit Savant, Research Analyst
Lennys Ramos, Administrator
Madhusudan Daga, Consultant

CPM Group provides a range of research and consulting services related to precious metals and commodities. These range from research studies on individual markets and market segments to materials management services. In addition to publishing precious metals and commodities research, CPM Group produces special reports. In 2005 CPM Group produced special reports on topics which have piqued investor interests, such as Uranium and Fuel Cells.

The core of CPM Group's product is its consulting services. These include specific projects related to the special needs of individual producers, refiners, fabricators, institutional investors, financial institutions, governments, central banks, and others. CPM Group provides advisory services related to hedging production and raw materials requirements, and manages positions for producers, consumers, and institutional investors. CPM Group's financial engineering includes impartial advice, structuring, placements, and management of hedging and investment positions.

CPM Group provides investment banking advisory programs for commodities-oriented corporations, and metals, materials, and asset management services for producers, consumers and institutional investors.

Annual Research Reports

- **The CPM Gold Yearbook (published by John Wiley & Sons)**
- **The CPM Silver Yearbook (published by John Wiley & Sons)**
- **The CPM Platinum Yearbook (published by John Wiley & Sons)**
- **Gold Supply, Demand, and Prices: Ten Year Projections**
- **Silver Supply, Demand, and Prices: Ten Year Projections**
- **Platinum Group Metals Supply, Demand, and Prices: Ten Year Projections**

Monthly Research Reports

- **Precious Metals Advisory**

Weekly Research Reports

- **Market Views**
- **CPM Soft Commodities News**

Specialized Reports

Preface

Welcome to the **CPM Silver Yearbook 2006**. The Preface to last year's **Silver Survey** discussed changes that were being made to this series of reports. Today's **Silver Yearbook** is the result of these changes. CPM Group has entered into an agreement with the John Wiley & Sons publishing company in which CPM's annual surveys of the gold, silver, and platinum group metals markets have been transformed into annual **Yearbooks**. The reports now are published as hard-cover volumes, companions to Wiley's famous **CRB Commodities Yearbook**, and distributed through bookstores, websites, and retail book outlets worldwide.

Last year's Survey also discussed broader changes that were underway in the silver market. Specifically, that report focused on the influx of new investors into the silver market, which was seen as of growing importance to the market. Many of these investors are familiar with the equity and fixed income markets, and are seeking greater detail and transparency in the silver market. These trends have accelerated in the silver market over the course of 2005 and early 2006, a fact that has been the basis for the sharp increase in silver prices since early 2005. The present report serves to further explicate the many changes now underway in the silver market, from mine production increasing to lower fabrication demand and rising investor demand.

These reports have undergone many transformations since our group began publishing annual reviews of the gold and silver markets in the early 1970s. Some traditions have persisted throughout this period, however. Among them, these reports are intended to provide the best estimates of supply, demand, inventories, and other market conditions available. They also are intended to provide the best possible analysis of market trends. The purpose is not to provide readers with a price conclusion, but rather to outline the most reliable and accurate portrait of the market that is possible, so that each reader may reach his or her own conclusions about the future.

Another tradition that we maintain is our reliance on the contributions, assistance, and support of innumerable companies around the world for the maintenance of our data and analytical base for these precious metals markets. There are 27 companies which have provided major assistance in the production of this year's **Silver Yearbook**. They are Apex Silver Mines, Apogee Minerals, Avino Silver & Gold Mines, Bear Creek Mining, Commodities Now, Endeavor Silver, Excellon Resources, First Majestic Resource, Great Panther Resources, Hecla Mining, IMA Exploration, Kimber Resources, Macmin Silver, Minera Andes, Mines Management, Noah Financial Innovation, Orko Silver, Sabina Silver, Scorpio Mining, Silver Dragon, Silver Standard Resources, Silver Users Association, Silver Wheaton, Silvercorp Metals, the Institute of Scrap Recycling Industries, the Prospector Exploration and Investment Newspaper, and US Resources. In addition to these companies, hundreds of companies provide information, statistics, and insights that allow us to compile the statistical portrait and analysis of the silver market presented here.

We hope you enjoy the **Silver Yearbook 2006**, and find its contents useful, valuable, and informative.

The Following Organizations Assisted in the Preparation of the Silver Yearbook

Apex Silver Mines Ltd.

Apex Silver Mines Limited is a mining development and exploration company. It has assumed an increasingly important profile within the silver sector since it was formed in 1993 and went public in 1997. The company is currently developing its flagship 100%-owned San Cristobal silver-zinc project, one of the world's largest open-pit silver-zinc-lead deposits. Located in southwestern Bolivia, it hosts an orebody which contains approximately 470 million ounces of silver, eight billion pounds of zinc and three billion pounds of lead in proven and probable reserves. Production at San Cristobal is expected to commence in 2007. Once in production, San Cristobal has sufficient reserves to operate for about 16 years, at the current design capacity of 40,000 tonnes of ore per day, and should become one of the world's largest producers of all three metals. Apex Silver also holds an extensive portfolio of exploration properties of highly prospective land located primarily in Bolivia, Peru, Mexico and Argentina. The company has a strong cash and equivalent position. The shares of Apex Silver trade on the American Stock Exchange under the symbol SIL.

Apogee Minerals Ltd.

Apogee Minerals Ltd. is a Canadian mining and exploration company developing advanced Silver-Zinc projects in South America. Apogee's experienced management team is focused on projects that offer significant exploration upside along with the potential to be rapidly developed into producing assets. Projects that fit this profile will typically have past production and/or significant, quality exploration data from previous work. Apogee adds value by investing capital, and modernizing mining and exploration techniques to advance projects quickly. The company currently has a focus in the historic silver producing regions of Bolivia. All of the company's projects fit this "advanced exploration and development" model.

Apogee is currently focusing work on the La Solucion mine and the Pulacayo-Paca project, a Joint Venture with Apex Silver Mines.

The La Solucion Mine has been producing for the past 14 years and the company is currently in the midst of an exploration program focused on the existing mine. The objective is to outline 2 million tonnes of historic production-grade ore. This would allow for a major production expansion to be undertaken. Apogee's objective is to identify a NI 43-101 compliant resource estimate at La Solucion in 2006, with the goal of further expansion as additional drilling is completed.

The Pulacayo-Paca is a Joint Venture with Apex Silver of Denver, Colorado to develop the Pulacayo Mine, the second-largest silver mine in the history of Bolivia with over 600 million ounces of past production, and the Paca project, a large open-pit target. A Phase II drilling program has commenced, with the objectives of outlining a NI 43-101 compliant resource estimate and completing a bankable Feasibility Study in 2006.

Avino Silver & Gold Mines Ltd.

Avino Silver & Gold Mines, founded in 1968, has established a long record of mining and exploration. The company's focus is the acquisition and exploration of top silver prospects throughout North America, and it currently manages three properties in western Canada and two in central Mexico.

Avino's flagship venture has been the Avino Mine near Durango Mexico. The mine opened in 1974 and, over its 27-year history, produced 497 tonnes of silver, 3 tonnes of gold and 11,000 tonnes of copper as well as significant quantities of lead and zinc. Operations were suspended in 2001 due to low metals prices and a smelter closure. However, with metals now in a bull market, management is examining options for re-opening the mine and exploring its extensive concessions, most of which have received only preliminary prospecting. In addition, a recent Scoping study indicates the mine's large tailings resource may be reprocessed economically.

In late 2005 Avino received exchange approval for purchase of up to remaining 51% of Mexican company which owns the Avino Mine. A recent study of the unexploited portion of the Avino mine and its surrounding mineral leases indicated significant potential for expansion of the mineral resource. These projects, along with examination of properties in North America, will remain the company's focus for the foreseeable future.

Avino Silver & Gold is debt free, un-hedged and its shares offer investors excellent leverage to silver price increases.

For more information please contact Investor Relations: ir@avino.com or go to the Company's web site www.avino.com.

Bear Creek Mining Corp.

Bear Creek Mining Corporation's focus is on the discovery of high quality economic gold and silver deposits in Peru. Our flagship project is the Corani deposit which represents an emerging exploration discovery of potentially bulk-mineable, silver-lead-zinc (+gold) mineralization. Based upon drilling results from June 2005 through January 2006, the first resource estimate contained 250M ounces silver, 2.5 billion pounds lead, and 1.25 billion pounds zinc; making Corani a world class silver discovery within a very small population of bulk-tonnage silver deposits worldwide. Drilling continues to expand mineralization and a scoping study is anticipated in the 2nd half, 2006.

The property portfolio also includes five additional prospects with high quality silver, gold or copper-gold targets, including Bear Creek's Santa Ana project; another potentially important grass-roots exploration, bulk-tonnage silver discovery. Bear Creek also maintains an active and aggressive exploration and property acquisition program.

Bear Creek's management share an unparalleled instinct for successful mineral projects. Our Chairman, Catherine McLeod-Seltzer, co-founded Arequipa Resources which was acquired by

Barrick in mid-1996. Numerous deposit discoveries are also attributed to Andrew Swarthout, President, and David Volkert, Vice-President of Exploration. Bear Creek's board is comprised of experienced mining executives who have had distinguished careers throughout the world with major mining companies.

Bear Creek Mining Corporation is committed to achieving a highly professional exploration and project development process that is sensitive to local economic and environmental concerns. Our extensive experience in Peru has allowed us to develop the strong relationships within communities which are crucial for successful exploration projects.

Commodities Now

Commodities Now is the quarterly magazine and associated website for the traded commodities markets globally. The primary sectors covered are base and precious metals, power and energy, and agricultural and soft markets. Our focus is on trends and developments within these sectors addressing issues including supply and demand, trading and risk management, and technology through to regulation. Read by professional commodity market participants around the world, Commodities Now has regular updates on the bullion and precious metals markets with contributions and special reports from leading metal market and mining specialists such as CPM Group, TheBullionDesk, Dow Jones Newswires and many more.

The associated website: www.commodities-now.com provides daily news and research of interest to players throughout the commodity complex with prices and charts from leading precious metals exchanges included [logon for a free trial].

Commodities Now also produces an annual LME Week Supplement [October] focusing on base and precious metals/mining.

For more information contact Charlotte James:
T: + 44 (0) 20 7402 9222 or E: char@commodities-now.com

Endeavour Silver Corp.

Endeavour Silver Corp. is a small-cap silver mining company focused on the growth of its silver production and resources in Durango, Mexico. After tripling production in 2005, the Company forecasts production to double once again in 2006 to 2.0-2.2 million oz. silver plus gold as a by-product. Given the capacity of the plant is up to 3.5 million oz. silver per year, the expansion plan now underway at its Guanacevi project should propel Endeavour into the ranks of the top 5 primary silver producers.

Through strategic alliances with large Mexican mining companies such as Industriales Penoles, Endeavour can now also grow through the acquisition of other attractive silver mines and districts in Mexico that may be too small for these large companies. Endeavour plans to more than double its silver output and resources over the next two years through acquisitions where the Company can quickly add value through its operating and exploration expertise and capital investments.

Endeavour stands out from other primary silver companies for its high silver grades (+15 oz. per ton), its high silver leverage (+90%) and the substantial exploration potential of the Guanacevi property (+30 million oz). The company generates positive cash flow, has US$15 million in cash, zero debt and production is not hedged. There are 32.5 million shares issued and 40.0 million shares fully diluted. The shares trade under the symbol EDR on the Toronto Stock Exchange, EJD on the Frankfurt Exchange and EDRGF on the pink sheets. For additional information, please visit our website www.edrsilver.com or call Hugh Clarke at 1 877 685 9775 (Toll-free USA & Canada).

Excellon Resources Inc.

Excellon Resources Inc. is test-mining and developing the high-grade silver-zinc-lead mineralization on its 14,692-hectare (36,000-acre) Platosa/Saltierra Properties in northeastern Durango State, Mexico. Platosa resembles several of the world-class Carbonate Replacement Deposits of Mexico. Mining operations commenced in September 2004, with the Company receiving its first production payment on July 25, 2005, and every two weeks thereafter.

The test-mining operation was based on an NI 43-101 compliant resource estimate prepared in September 2002 by Roscoe Postle Associates Inc., independent geological and mining consultants. The estimate consists of an indicated resource of 69,900 tons grading 79.9 oz/T Ag (silver) with 15% Pb (lead), and 11.9% Zn (zinc). (Readers are cautioned that mineral resources that are not classified as mineral reserves do not have demonstrated economic viability.)

The resources were contained in a series of six isolated flat-lying mantos. Development of the mine has now shown that there are vertical chimney connections linking these mantos as well as other significant mineralization in lateral extensions. Surface drilling since the start of test-mining has identified three more mantos; including the largest discovered to date, with grades similar to those in the resource estimate. Surface drilling is continuing with two drill rigs working and a third to commence shortly. As well, underground exploration is proceeding with one drill rig. An updated NI 43-101 resource study is expected to be completed by early May.

Excellon now has in excess of $4,000,000 cash and has established production and cash-flow from its test-mining program. The Company has 130,403,720 shares outstanding (157,688,765 fully diluted; exercise of the warrants and options would raise $8,001,766 of additional cash). The year's high is CDN $0.82 and low $0.16, and the shares are very liquid.

First Majestic Resource Corp.

First Majestic Resource Corp. is an emerging mid-tier Silver producer that is establishing a solid position for near and long-term growth. Expanding silver reserves and entering silver production has been the foundation for the Company since its formation. First Majestic is run by a committed, aggressive and experienced management team with an extremely successful history and knowledge in building large companies. The Company has been successful securing a host of advanced silver projects - all situated in the heart of several of Mexico's premier mining districts.

First Majestic is a pure silver company, in early production with a large upside in reserves. Our asset package has a low purchase price and low cap-x giving shareholders dramatic leverage as the Company develops its assets. The Company offers a very low market cap compared to its peers and a good share structure in early stage of market acceptance. In addition, exponential revenue growth is anticipated over the next few years.

Management is determined to build First Majestic into a mid-tier silver producer and to that end will continually add to its production profile and additionally pursue those acquisition opportunities that make fiscal sense and will bring continued value to the Company's shares and thus shareholders.

Great Panther Resources Ltd.

Great Panther is an emerging silver producer well-positioned to become one of the top five primary silver producers in the world. Great Panther's strength is a combination of highly-experienced international & local management teams with high-quality silver projects in Mexico. The Company is led by Bob Archer, C.E.O., a successful geologist with 15 years experience on projects for several mining majors including Newmont and Placer Dome. With its 100% acquisition of both the high-grade Topia Silver Mine in Durango State and the Santa Fe Silver-Gold Mines in Guanajuato, Great Panther is leveraged to become one of the leading silver exploration & development companies in Mexico.

Projects:

The Santa Fe Silver-Gold Mines, located in Guanajuato, one of the most historically prolific and best-known silver districts in the world, expects to be producing at an annualized rate of about 2.5 million ounces of silver equivalent.

The Topia Silver-Lead-Zinc Mine and Property has a 200-tonne per day mill, which at full capacity will produce approximately 1.5 million ounces of silver equivalent.

Great Panther is also exploring 2 grassroots projects known as Virimoa and San Antonio. These projects offer blue sky potential, while the Company generates positive cash flow from silver production.

Great Panther Resources Limited is a Tier 1 issuer on the TSX Venture Exchange (TSX-V:"GPR") and is currently making application to move to the main board of the Toronto Stock Exchange. The Company has filed its 20-F registration statement with the SEC and is Standard & Poor's listed.

www.greatpanther.com

Hecla Mining Company

Established in 1891 in northern Idaho's Silver Valley, Hecla Mining Company's rich history of mining has distinguished it as a respected precious metals producer. Now headquartered in Coeur d'Alene, Idaho, this international, publicly traded company is 115 years old.

Hecla is the lowest-cost primary silver producer in North America, producing 6 million ounces of silver at an average total cash cost of $2.96 per ounce in 2005. Hecla also produced 140,559 ounces of gold at an average total cash cost of $337 per ounce. The company has exploration properties and operating mines in five major world-class mining districts. Hecla's excellent exploration prospects, operating expertise, minimal debt and good cash position make this an excellent precious metals investment vehicle.

Hecla mines, processes and explores for silver and gold in the United States, Mexico and Venezuela. Hecla currently produces silver from two silver mines, Greens Creek and Lucky Friday, as well as mining gold at the La Camorra Unit in Venezuela. In 2005, the Greens Creek mine in Alaska contributed 2.9 million ounces of silver to Hecla's account, the Lucky Friday mine in northern Idaho produced 2.4 million ounces and the San Sebastian mine in Mexico produced approximately 0.8 million ounces of silver. The La Camorra Unit in Venezuela produced 101,474 ounces of gold in 2005.

Hecla has long been well known in the United States as a major primary silver producer and quality gold producer. The name "Hecla" is commonly associated with both precious metals by investors. Hecla's common stock has been traded on the New York Stock Exchange for over 40 years under the symbol "HL."

IMA Exploration Inc.

IMA Exploration Inc. (IMR-AMEX, IMR-TSX.V) is a publicly traded silver exploration company that is focused on the exploration and development of its 100% owned Navidad Silver Project in northern Patagonia, Argentina. IMA has internationally recognized Management and Exploration Teams with outstanding track records, and a large and diverse network of contacts that can quickly identify new opportunities for socially and environmentally responsible exploration and development.

To date (Feb 2006), IMA has defined an Indicated Resource of 306 million ounces of silver and 2.9 billion pounds of lead (93.4 million tonnes at 102 g/t silver and 1.41% lead using a 50 g/t silver equivalent cut-off), quickly making it one of the world's largest bulk tonnage silver deposits.

The Company's immediate objectives are to continue our highly successful drill programs and build on the overall silver resource at Navidad. Drilling has already defined a world-class deposit with many targets that have yet to be drill tested. Concurrent with exploration, the Company is moving towards the development of the project, bringing on the skill set required at this stage and moving towards scoping and pre-feasibility studies.

IMA Exploration Inc. is managed by The Grosso Group.
www.imaexploration.com

Kimber Resources Inc.

Kimber Resources Inc. (AMEX:KBX, TSX:KBR) is focused on silver-gold exploration and development in Mexico. The Company's wholly-owned 28,000 hectare Monterde property is located in southwestern Chihuahua state, in the heart of the Sierra Madre Occidental Range.

Since going public in 2002, the Company has been exploring and developing the Carmen gold-silver deposit, a former producing underground mine between 1937 and 1943. In 2005 the Company kicked off an exploration program that made two new discoveries, the Carotare and El Orito Norte. These discoveries and the Carmen now identify three kilometres of continuous alteration. The Company is advancing the Carmen towards feasibility and has undertaken an exploration drill program at Carotare and El Orito Norte.

Kimber's goal is to demonstrate at least three million gold equivalent resource ounces from the altered area and to advance the project towards production. The Company's C$15 million exploration budget for 2006 is aimed at increasing its resources from the current levels (March 2006) of 54 million ounces of silver (41 million ozs Measured & Indicated, 13 million ozs Inferred) and 980,000 ounces of gold (640,000 ozs Measured & Indicated, 340,000 ozs Inferred).

For more information on Kimber Resources Inc. please contact Darren Klinck (Investor Relations) at 604 669 2251 or info@kimberresources.com.

Macmin Silver Ltd.

Macmin Silver Ltd is an Australian listed (ASX-MMN), silver focused junior mining company. Mine construction is nearing completion at the Texas silver project in South East Queensland, Australia. Total resources at present are 56 million ounces of silver and the company expects initial annual production of between 2.5 and 4 million ounces of silver, commencing from mid 2006. The Company is completely unhedged, has minimal debt and the cash flow is highly leveraged to any increases in the silver price.

The company has extensive tenement holdings in the Texas district and is confident of increasing its resource base. The Company also has significant equity interests in New Guinea Gold Corporation (TSX-NGG), TasGold and Malachite Resources (both ASX listed companies). Macmin website is: [www.macmin.com.au]

Minera Andes Inc.

Minera Andes is approaching near-term silver/gold production and cash flow at its San Jose discovery in southern Argentina. The company focuses on silver, gold and copper exploration in Argentina where it controls about 500,000 acres of mineral rights.

Founded by exploration geologists with records of discovery in the western hemisphere, Minera Andes has traditionally emphasized its proven strengths in all phases of mineral exploration and exploration management. Following a discovery, Minera Andes adds value through systematic exploration then markets the discovery on a profit-sharing basis to a proven, well-capitalized mining company with expertise in development and mining operations. The goal: production and income generation to fund more exploration leading to new discoveries and further value enhancement.

At the San Jose project a positive bankable feasibility study has been completed and the environmental impact assessment has been approved. Silver and gold production is anticipated in 2007.

The initial discovery at San Jose and the related Frea discovery, are high-grade silver-rich veins. The San Jose project has an initial proven and probable reserve base of 15.3 million ounces of silver and 288,000 ounces of gold. Ore grades average 406 grams-per-ton silver (about 13 ounces) and 7.7 grams-per-ton gold. These reserves have been identified on less than 15 percent of the 32-kilometer length of four structural trends as currently known. Ten other targets within the 99,000-acre San Jose project area have also been identified, and four new silver-rich discoveries have been announced since the third quarter of 2005. Minera Andes is traded on the US OTC market (MNEAF) and in Canada, on the TSX-V (MAI).

Mines Management, Inc.

Mines Management, Inc. (Amex: MGN, TSX: MGT) is a junior mineral exploration and development company currently focused on the advancement of the Montanore Silver-Copper Project in northwestern Montana.

Originally discovered in the early 1980's, drilling on the Montanore outlined a deposit with more than 100 million tons of material containing 230 million ounces of silver plus 2 billion pounds of copper. The northern boundaries of the deposit were undefined, and so there remains significant scope for growth beyond the current resource. Currently in the permitting and engineering stage, the mine is designed to initially produce at a rate of 8 million ounces of silver and 60 million pounds of copper annually, ramping up in future years. At its initial production rate, the Montanore would rank as the 6th largest silver mine in the world if it were in production today.

Mines Management is committed to using innovative technologies toward responsible development and operation of the Montanore Project, to being an active participant and good neighbor in the local community, and has received strong pledges of support from both state and local government.

Having acquired its 100% ownership of the project in 2002, the company's management team and board of directors reflects the unique challenges of advancing such a large project toward development. With a truly world class team, Mines Management views the Montanore Project as an excellent foundation from which to build a new mid-tier, highly leveraged mining company.

Noah Financial Innovation (Pty) Ltd.

Noah Financial Innovation ("Noah") is a niche South African-based stockbroking firm with an enviable track record of providing innovative, tailored execution and independent research services to institutional investors. Noah's business model is specifically designed to cater for unbundled execution and research services in accordance with global market trends.

Orko Silver Corporation

Orko (OK: TSX-V) is a dynamic mineral exploration company focused on silver and gold properties in Mexico. The Company's principal project, La Preciosa, is a 100%-owned epithermal vein hosted silver-gold deposit located near the city of Durango in north-central Mexico.

An independently verified Initial Inferred Mineral Resource Estimate (news release January 19, 2006) concluded, based on work completed to date, that the property contains an Inferred Resource of 2.72 million tonnes grading 227.2 g/t silver and 0.463 g/t gold, for a silver-equivalent grade of 255.0 g/t. Contained metal is equivalent to approximately 19.9 million ounces of silver and 40,400 ounces of gold for a sliver-equivalent of 22.3 million ounces of silver.*

Less than 20% of the initial target area has been drilled along strike and only to a depth of 300 metres, and the deposit remains open to the North, South and at depth. A Phase 3 (10,000 metre) drill program is currently underway on the La Preciosa property to expand the known areas of mineralization. The most recent results have successfully proven that significant mineralization is found 200 metres south of the area used to calculate the Inferred Resource Estimate. Highlights from the most recent drill results of Phase 3 (March 21, 2006) include 8.55 metres at 521.6 g/t Ag (532 g/t Ag-Eq) including 1.2 metres at 2290 g/t Ag (2319.5 g/t Ag-Eq) from the Abundancia Vein in Hole BP05-28.

Goldcorp Inc. (G: TSX) is a significant shareholder and strategic partner of Orko.

**-Silver equivalent calculated by using a 60 to 1 silver/gold ratio with no provisions for relative anticipated recovery rates*

2610 - 1066 West Hastings Street
Vancouver, BC Canada V6C 3X2
Tel: (604) 684-4691
Fax: (604) 684-4601
info@orkogold.com
www.orkogold.com

Sabina Silver Corporation

Sabina Silver Corporation (SBB:TSX-V) is a Canadian public mineral exploration and development company with assets at the Hackett River silver-zinc project in the Canadian Arctic, the Del Norte project in the Stewart-Eskay Creek Mining District, and several projects in the Red Lake gold camp.

Sabina Silver Corporation is well financed with over C$30 million in working capital made up of over C$17 million in cash and approximately C$16 million in liquid investments (www.sabinasilver.com).

Sabina's principal development asset is a 100% interest in the polymetallic Hackett River Project, Nunavut that contains a recently delivered NI 43-101 compliant total mineral resource of 160 million ounces silver (and 660 million ounces silver equivalent), based on 46,000m of drilling at Hackett River. The magnitude of the silver resource alone at Hackett River ranks well-leveraged Sabina Silver Corporation among the top 12 silver-focused companies operating in the Western Hemisphere. Canada is one of the world's most stable, mining friendly jurisdictions.

Sabina's primary objective is to advance the Hackett River Project to production pre-feasibility in 2006 through additional drilling and engineering work worth C$9.6 million. The area has been transformed into a world class mining supply and service centre as a result of the construction of the nearby Ekati and Diavik diamond mines. With this new infrastructural platform in place and an apparent sea change taking place in precious and base metal demand going forward, the future for Hackett River in this well endowed commodity-rich area of the Canadian Shield is bright.

Scorpio Mining Corporation

Scorpio Mining Corp. is a silver-based company with a focus on Mexico. The Company's flagship asset is the Nuestra Senora silver property.

Over $20 million has been invested to date in surface and underground development, resource definition, and mill purchase at Nuestra Senora. Asarco was a previous owner and explorer of the property. The company is poised to commence production at the rate of 1,000 TPD in the near future. At the Nuestra Senora property, the former exploration company that mined the area developed the seventh through to the tenth levels, but didn't extract any resources from these levels before shutting the mine down. Scorpio controls a land position of over 16,000 hectares with no underlying royalties or payments. The company is now the largest employer in the village of Cosala with over 130 employees.

Scorpio Mining Corp. also has underground gold properties in Nova Scotia including the Caribou mine comprising of 16 contiguous mineral claims covering about 256 hectares. Historically, $13 million has been spent to perform all the underground work on the company's Caribou and Cochrane Hill mine sites in Nova Scotia. Scorpio's plan is to construct a central milling facility and feed it from both the Cochrane Hill and Caribou mines.

Over 70% of its shares are owned by major financial institutions and the company is in strong financial shape. Currently, there are approximately 44.8MM shares issued and outstanding and 55.2MM on a fully diluted basis.

Contact:
Peter Hawley 604-678-9639
phawley.scorpio@tlb.sympatico.ca

Silver Dragon Resources Inc.

Silver Dragon Resources Inc. (SDRG - Nasdaq OTC BB) is a mining and metal company focused on the exploration, acquisition, development and operation of silver mines in proven silver districts globally.

MEXICO - Silver Dragon's property Cerro las Minitas Silver Mine in Durango, Mexico consists of approximately 1,402 hectares. This large land package is located in a prolific silver district in Mexico and includes 4 mines. Production at the mines during the first 12 months of this year will continue at a rate of approximately 50-100 tons per day with an anticipated increase to 200 tons per day, and year 2, anticipated increases in production to 500 tons per day. Average ore grades being mined are presently 280 grams/tonne silver and approximately 4-6% lead and zinc values.

Silver Dragon's Joint Venture Agreement with Linear Gold Corp. whereby Silver Dragon has been granted the option to acquire 55% of Linear's interest in and rights to any revenues derived as a result of the exploration, evaluation and development of the Tierra Blanca Project located 250 kilometers WNW of the City of Durango and 21 kilometers south of Peñoles La Cienega gold mine assays 1,470 grams per Tonne/47.3 Ounces Silver.

CHINA - Silver Dragon Resources owns a 60% interest in Sanhe Sino-Top Resources and Technologies, Ltd. a Chinese company, which holds the exploration and mining rights to several properties and a mine located in the Erbaohuo Silver District in Northern China. Also Strategic relationships with Chinese authorities North China Geological Exploration Bureau (NCGEB) and with China International Trust and Investment Corporation (CITIC). This project has significant potential for major silver discoveries.

Marc Hazout (416) 661-4989 info@silverdragonresources.com

Silver Standard Resources Inc.

Silver Standard Resources Inc. (Nasdaq: SSRI, TSX: SSO) is a silver development and exploration company with projects in Argentina, Mexico, Peru, Australia, Chile, the United States and Canada. The company now controls the largest in-ground silver resources of any publicly traded silver company. Silver Standard's strategy is to acquire projects with defined resources in jurisdictions favorable to mining and to advance these projects with higher silver prices.

At March 31, 2006, the company controls measured and indicated silver resources totaling 562.7 million ounces plus inferred resources totaling 554.3 million ounces. The wholly-owned Pirquitas project in Argentina is at feasibility stage, and the recently discovered Pitarrilla silver project in Mexico continues to grow through focused drilling. Another priority exploration project is the San Luis property in Peru, a high-grade gold-silver discovery that is held by a joint venture with Esperanza Silver Corporation.

Silver Standard is well financed with cash, marketable securities and 1.95 million of physical silver valued at approximately CDN$141.7 million in March, 2006.

Silver Users Association

Founded in 1947, the Silver Users Association in Fairfax, VA (703-934-0219) represents the interests of corporations that make, sell and distribute products and services in which silver is an essential part. SUA membership includes representatives from the photographic, chemical, electronic, silverware, and jewelry industries, producers of semi-fabricated and industrial products; and, service providers for the industry.

The SUA is active in providing up to date research on the industry for its members. The SUA is actively engaged on the legislative and regulatory fronts in Washington on behalf of its members. And, the SUA offers two annual meetings where industry representatives can gather and network with one another and also hear from industry experts about issues affecting their businesses. The SUA is the premiere industry association and one every company in the industry should belong to.

The members, which account for the bulk of U.S. silver used, include the following:

Cookson Material Products Group; Gannon & Scott, Inc.; Ferro Corporation; Ames Goldsmith; Precision Engineered Products, Inc.; J.W. Harris Company, Inc.; DuPont; Fideli Trade Inc.; QML Metals & Logistics; Eastman Kodak Company; Lenox Brands Metals; Metalor Technologies USA Corporation; Bank of America Precious Metals; Engelhard Corporation; The Dow Chemical Company; Tiffany & Company; Heraeus Metal Processing, Inc.; James Avery Craftsman, Inc.; Ohio Precious Metals, Inc.; Technitrol, Inc.; Reed & Barton Corporation; Mitsui & Company (USA) Inc.; SIPI Metals Corporation; Prudential Financial Derivatives, LLC; and Karlan Services, Inc.

Silver Wheaton

Vancouver, BC
TSX - SLW, AMEX - SLW

Silver Wheaton Corp. is the only "pure silver" mining company with 100% of its revenue from silver production. In 2006, Silver Wheaton expects to sell approximately 15 million ounces growing to 20 million ounces of silver from 2009 onwards. All the silver is purchased at cash costs of $3.90 per ounce from the mines. Silver Wheaton is unhedged and plans to grow through acquisition.

Silver purchase agreements allow the Company rights to the silver production even though it is not the owner or operator of the mine. In the initial contract, the price for future production is set out ensuring costs are fixed. This allows Silver Wheaton to avoid variations in operational costs and overhead, long term liabilities and, most importantly, allows the Company to be 100% pure to silver.

These transactions position Silver Wheaton for strong earnings and cash flow generation and the company plans to enter into similar agreements with other companies that have silver production. Since approximately 70% of all silver production occurs as a by-product of base or precious metals production, there are numerous growth opportunities. More agreements to purchase silver will limit Silver Wheaton's exposure to any one project.

Silver Wheaton's management and board of directors have demonstrated a strong track record of creating shareholder value through acquisitions and Silver Wheaton plans to become the leading silver producer in the world.

Silvercorp Metals Inc.

Silvercorp Metals Inc. (TSX:SVM) is an emerging Canadian silver mining company engaged in acquisition, exploration, and mining of mineral properties in China.

Silvercorp's strategy is to become a significant silver producer by quickly developing the Ying Silver Project while expanding its concentrate grade resources.

The Ying project was acquired in April of 2004. On April 18 of 2005, an independent National Instrument 43-101 report was completed revealing 99.1 million oz of equivalent silver in the measured, indicated and inferred categories from the exploration work to date carried out on faction of five (5) vein sheets out of plus 40 vein sheets on the property.

The company achieved US $7 million revenue as an exploration and development company; and, completed 30,000m if tunnelling and 12,000m of drilling by March of 2006. Approximately 2,500 metres (m) of tunnels and 1,500m of underground drilling is completed each month.

On site there are twenty-eight professional geologist, engineers and surveyors, overseeing 400+ miners working on over 40 development and exploration tunnel faces, 6 underground drill rigs and 2 surface deep hole drill rigs on a day-to-day basis.

Silvercorp is well financed with sufficient working capital and short term profitability potential to carry out its exploration and development needs. Silvercorp also holds about 31% interest in New Pacific Metals Corp., a public company listed in the TSX Venture Exchange under the symbol NUX. New Pacific is exploring for Ni-Cu-PGM metals in China.

The Institute of Scrap Recycling Industries, Inc.

ISRI is a trade association whose 1,300 industry member companies process, broker, and consume scrap commodities, including metals, paper, plastics, glass, rubber, and textiles. There are 21 affiliated chapters. ISRI's primary publications are: Scrap Magazine and Scrap Specifications Circular: Guidelines for Ferrous Scrap, Nonferrous Scrap, Paper Stock, Plastic Scrap, Glass Scrap. The association also publishes a variety of print and electronic newsletters exclusively for members. ISRI sponsors an annual convention and exposition, seminars, commodities round tables, and workshops. Visit ISRI's website at www.isri.org.

The Prospector Exploration & Investment Newspaper

The Prospector newspaper is North America's leading source of in-depth information about news making junior mining companies. Published in Vancouver, the bimonthly journal includes company profiles, area play analysis, commodities studies, and investment advice from leading stock analysts. The Prospector also produces Internet Daily Mining News, the only daily source of mining news coverage of its kind.

UC Resources Ltd.

UC Resources Ltd. (TSX-V:UC) is a Canadian silver and gold exploration and development company focused in Mexico. UC Resource's recently bought out its JV partner (Oct. 2005) and now owns a 100% interest in the 192 sq. km Copalquin Mining District in NW Durango, Mexico. Copalquin is centrally located in Mexico's prolific Sierra Madre mining belt with significant exploration and development potential. This 19,269 hectare (192 sq km's) historically productive Gold and Silver district is reputed to have produced at least 250,000 ounces Gold and 11 million ounces Silver from just 336,000 tonnes of ore.

UC Resource's corporate objective of becoming an emerging Gold and Silver producer in 2006 will be achieved through acquisition of quality production opportunities by Richard J. Hamelin, President & CEO. Richard's first career was in the mines of Timmins, Ontario, allowing him to understand both international finance and mining. Richard J. Hamelin resides in Torreon, Mexico and heads up all new and existing operational activities in conjunction with our Canadian office.

Copalquin is UC Resource's flagship property and its location in the heart of Mexico's prolific Sierra Madre mining belt offers exceptional long-term value and a firm basis for the company's growth in Mexico. Copalquin has returned both high-grade Gold and Silver from the Phase 1 drilling exploration program in 2005. The company is actively searching for additional quality assets that will make UC Resources a producing Gold and Silver exploration and development company in Mexico in 2006.
www.ucresources.net

The CPM Silver Yearbook, 2006

Table of Contents

I. Review and Outlook

II. Supply

III. Fabrication Demand

IV. Investment Demand

V. Inventories

VI. Markets

VII. Prices

Review and Outlook

Review and Outlook

Silver prices began 2005 by declining, following through on a sell-off that began in early December. The decline in prices was short-lived, however, and silver was rising once more by early February. The silver price then showed remarkable strength throughout the remaining 11 months of 2005 and the first three months of 2006. To be fair, the decline in silver prices in January 2005 was from a high peak above $8.00 that had been reached in the first two trading days of December 2004, and saw prices find support around $6.45.

Prices remained below $6.90 until early February, at which point silver moved into a higher trading range of $6.90 to $7.55 for most of the period from February through August. After August silver prices began to rise strongly once more. At that point, following the devastation wrought by Hurricanes Katrina and Rita in the Gulf Coast of the United States, a wide range of commodities prices rose, in conjunction with rising oil and natural gas prices. Silver joined in. Silver prices rose to $7.50 by late September, and kept moving. They touched $7.90 by late October. Prices moved even higher in November and December, rising to $8.353 on 28 November and $9.095 on 9 December. Prices touched an intraday high of $9.345 on 12 December, before backing off. Silver held above $8.40 for the rest of December, setting the stage for higher prices later.

Weekly Average Silver Prices

Comex Nearby Active Settlement, Through 24 March 2006.

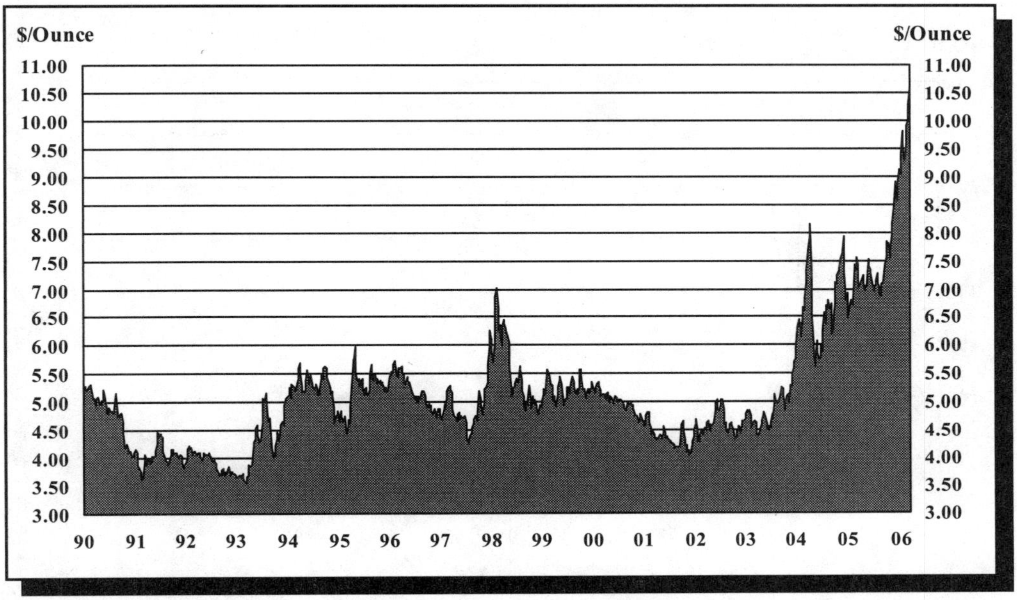

Silver prices averaged $7.35 per ounce in 2005. That was up 9.7% from $6.70 in 2004. It was the fourth year in a row of rising prices, and the highest annual average price since silver averaged $8.15 in 1984. The range of silver prices in 2005 was from a low of $6.45, on 7 January 2005, to a high of $9.10, on 9 December.

The increase in silver prices reflected strong investment interest in silver, primarily. Investors increased their activity in buying silver in physical form, in futures, forwards, and options. This push into silver, in conjunction with a broader move into commodities and precious metals in general on the part of investors around the world, was the single most important factor pushing silver prices higher.

While many investors, from individuals in India and the Middle East to institutional fund managers in Europe and North America, were buying silver, other investors were taking advantage of the higher prices to sell silver.

The silver market has been in a current account deficit since 1990. That is, since 1990 fabricators have been using more silver each year than is estimated to enter the market from mine production, secondary recovery from scrap, and government stockpile disposals. At the start of this period it is estimated that worldwide bullion inventories were in

The Price of Silver

Monthly Average Comex, Through February 2006.

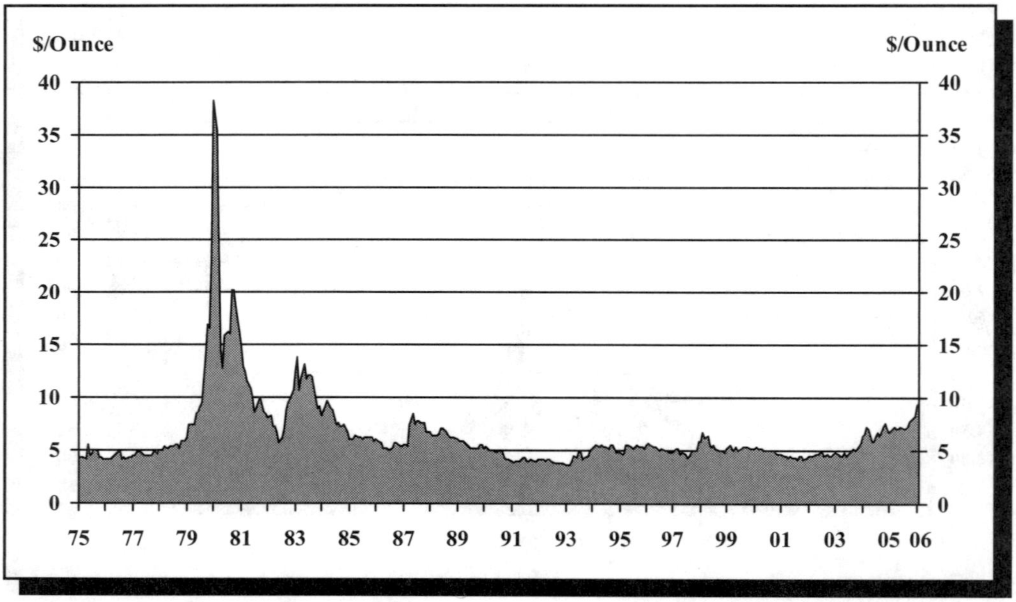

excess of 2.1 billion ounces. In the ensuing 16 years these stocks have been drawn down sharply. No one knows exactly how much silver remains in bullion form, but reasonable estimates are between 300 and 500 million ounces.

These persistent shortfalls of newly refined metal, and government sales, relative to fabrication demand have been compensated for by the sale of silver from these stockpiles. Many of the inventories held in 1990, and sold off over the past 16 years, were held by investors. In many cases there were investors who bought silver in the 1960s, 1970s, and 1980s. Bullion banks and dealers also had several hundred million ounces of silver bullion stocks at the start of the 1990s. The sales of these stocks kept the silver market supplied throughout this period of deficits of new supply relative to fabrication demand.

By 2005 the remaining levels of inventories were getting low. More important, the people holding much of the remaining silver bullion stocks had raised their price expectations. In some instances investors that had bought silver years ago had sold silver to new investors, who may have had higher price targets. In other cases, investors who had suffered through the long period of what they felt were low silver prices may have seen prices begin to rise in 2003 and 2004 and begun to feel that their long-held visions of higher silver prices were on the threshold of being realized.

Supply and Demand Balance

Projected Through 2006.

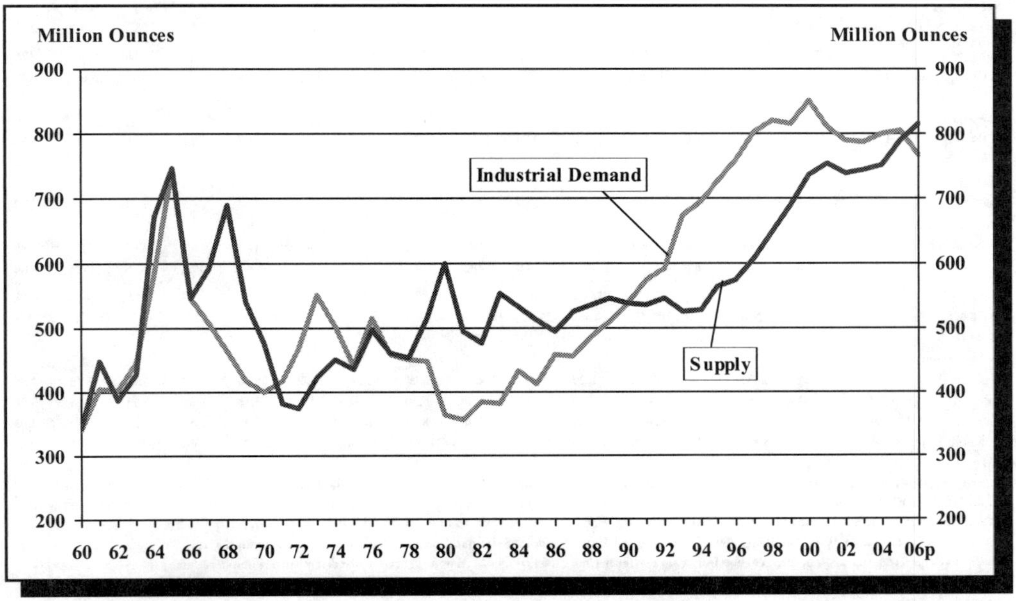

Silver Statistical Position
Million Troy Ounces

	1977	1978	1979	1980	1981	1982	1983	1984	1985	1986	1987	1988	1989	1990	1991
Mine Production															
Mexico	47.0	50.8	49.4	47.3	53.2	49.8	55.0	63.9	69.2	69.4	69.8	70.0	70.0	67.9	62.7
United States	38.2	39.4	37.9	32.3	40.7	40.2	43.4	44.6	39.4	34.2	39.8	53.4	60.8	66.5	61.0
Peru	39.1	37.0	41.9	44.8	42.6	54.4	55.6	53.3	54.9	59.9	63.6	47.7	56.8	55.6	56.9
Canada	42.2	40.7	36.9	34.4	36.3	42.2	38.7	42.0	38.5	35.0	38.1	44.1	41.3	44.4	40.6
Australia	27.5	26.1	26.7	25.0	23.9	29.2	33.2	31.3	34.9	32.9	35.9	35.8	37.3	37.8	38.0
Other	93.2	98.0	104.7	110.1	109.7	105.9	112.1	116.0	122.4	119.7	121.4	132.6	132.0	128.9	133.3
Total	287.2	292.0	297.6	293.9	306.4	321.7	338.0	351.0	359.3	351.1	368.6	383.6	398.2	401.1	392.5
% Change Year Ago	—	1.7%	1.9%	-1.2%	4.3%	5.0%	5.1%	3.9%	2.4%	-2.3%	5.0%	4.1%	3.8%	0.7%	-2.1%
Secondary Supply															
Old Scrap	93.0	82.0	130.0	164.0	125.0	111.0	133.4	123.5	101.5	103.4	113.3	121.9	125.0	120.0	117.6
Coin Melt	33.0	21.0	45.0	94.0	18.0	7.0	20.1	20.1	18.4	9.9	10.1	8.8	6.4	6.0	4.0
Indian Scrap	43.0	49.0	41.0	44.0	41.0	37.0	44.0	22.0	21.0	16.0	14.5	13.2	4.8	—	9.6
Total	169.0	152.0	216.0	302.0	184.0	155.0	197.5	165.6	140.9	129.3	137.9	143.9	136.2	126.0	131.2
% Change Year Ago	—	-10.1%	42.1%	39.8%	-39.1%	-15.8%	27.4%	-16.2%	-14.9%	-8.2%	6.6%	4.4%	-5.3%	-7.5%	4.2%
Other Supply															
Government Disposals	5	9	3	5	4	1	19	16	13	14	20	8.3	10.7	11	11.5
Net Exports from Transitional Economies	—	—	—	—	—	—	—	—	—	—	—	—	—	—	—
	5	9	3	5	4	1	19	16	13	14	20	8.3	10.7	11	11.5
% Change Year Ago	—	80.0%	-66.7%	66.7%	-20.0%	-75.0%	NM	-15.8%	-18.8%	7.7%	42.9%	-58.5%	28.9%	2.8%	4.5%
Total Supply	461.2	453.0	516.6	600.9	494.4	477.7	554.5	532.6	513.2	494.4	526.5	535.8	545.1	538.1	535.2
% Change Year Ago	—	-1.8%	14.0%	16.3%	-17.7%	-3.4%	16.1%	-3.9%	-3.6%	-3.7%	6.5%	1.8%	1.7%	-1.3%	-0.5%
Industrial Demand															
Photography	129.6	142.9	146.1	123.8	128.1	136.5	140.3	147.3	152.7	157.8	172.1	185.1	189.2	196.5	196.2
Jewelry & Silverware	91.0	91.9	82.8	52.3	47.8	56.4	47.6	47.4	55.5	75.3	87.2	91.2	114.1	128.3	155.3
Electronics and Batteries	78.7	79.3	80.4	71.2	62.2	62.6	60.9	63.1	67.8	69.4	69.4	74.6	80.3	84.3	83.7
Other Uses	87.5	84.0	86.2	71.0	66.1	62.6	61.9	69.3	68.0	66.2	78.5	77.8	94.2	102.0	109.7
Other Countries	73.1	54.3	52.8	46.1	51.3	43.4	45.8	49.6	37.2	41.3	23.5	24.7	0.2	3.2	3.4
Net Imports into the Transitional Economies	15.9	18.2	11.5	14.5	15.3	23.8	25.4	56.6	30.4	49.2	24.9	32.9	32.6	25.0	27.2
Total	475.8	470.6	459.7	378.8	370.7	385.2	381.8	433.3	411.6	459.2	455.5	486.2	510.6	539.1	575.6
% Change Year Ago	—	-1.1%	-2.3%	-17.6%	-2.1%	3.9%	-0.9%	13.5%	-5.0%	11.6%	-0.8%	6.7%	5.0%	5.6%	6.8%
Net Surplus or Deficit in the Bullion Market	-14.6	-17.6	56.9	222.2	123.8	92.6	172.7	99.4	101.6	35.2	71.0	49.6	34.6	-1.0	-40.4
Addenda															
Coinage	34.5	39.5	31.0	15.0	9.5	12.0	10.2	13.7	13.4	26.8	30.4	25.3	26.3	29.8	27.7
Changes in Inventories															
Unreported	-60.9	-39.6	32.7	190.5	143.6	66.5	114.3	86.2	45.6	50.9	41.3	6.9	-49.2	-61.3	-79.5
Reported	11.8	-17.5	-6.8	16.7	-29.3	14.0	48.2	-0.5	42.6	-42.5	-0.6	17.4	57.5	30.5	11.4
Total	-49.1	-57.1	25.9	207.2	114.3	80.5	162.5	85.7	88.2	8.4	40.7	24.3	8.3	-30.8	-68.1
% Change Year Ago	—	NM	NM	701.3%	-44.8%	-29.5%	101.7%	-47.3%	2.9%	-90.4%	382.3%	-40.2%	NM	-473.6%	120.8%
Price Per Ounce															
High	$4.98	$6.32	$34.45	$48.70	$16.29	$11.21	$14.72	$10.06	$6.84	$6.29	$9.66	$7.83	$6.19	$5.33	$4.55
Low	4.31	4.81	5.92	10.80	7.99	4.98	8.40	6.30	5.53	4.85	5.38	6.00	5.03	3.94	3.51
Average	4.63	5.34	11.20	20.65	10.53	7.93	11.46	8.15	6.15	5.47	6.99	6.53	5.50	4.82	4.03
% Change Year Ago	—	15.3%	109.7%	84.4%	-49.0%	-24.7%	44.5%	-28.9%	-24.5%	-11.1%	27.8%	-6.6%	-15.8%	-12.3%	-19.6%

Notes: Totals may not equal the sum of categories due to rounding. Mine production in Poland, Bulgaria, Romania, Hungary, the Czech Republic, and Slovakia is included in "other" mine production. Photography, jewelry and silverware, electronics, and 'other' industrial use reflects demand in Europe, the United States, and Japan. These sectors include Canada from 1979, Mexico from 1982, Hong Kong from 1985, Thailand from 1986, India from 1987, Australia, Brazil, Peru, Colombia, Argentina, Chile, Korea, Pakistan, and Bangladesh from 1989, and Taiwan from 1990. Demand excludes the transitional economies, except for imports. The price is the Comex nearby active settlement, percent change from year earlier period. 2006 through 24 March. There may be discrepancies due to rounding. p - projections. NM - Not meaningful.
Source: CPM Group.
March 27, 2006

	1992	1993	1994	1995	1996	1997	1998	1999	2000	2001	2002	2003	2004	2005	2006p
Mine Production															
Mexico	65.0	61.0	65.0	67.3	75.0	81.0	85.9	83.0	88.3	97.4	101.0	94.7	99.5	103.3	106.0
United States	61.0	55.7	54.0	49.5	50.0	59.0	62.4	65.3	65.6	55.9	43.4	39.9	40.2	39.2	40.4
Peru	48.0	47.0	48.0	51.0	55.0	63.0	61.4	67.1	78.4	83.0	92.3	93.9	98.4	102.7	105.7
Canada	36.3	28.3	23.6	41.3	42.0	39.4	37.9	39.6	39.0	42.4	45.3	42.1	43.0	36.1	36.9
Australia	40.1	39.1	36.8	32.0	35.0	38.7	50.8	57.7	68.4	63.3	66.6	60.1	71.0	75.8	80.0
Other	146.7	141.3	137.9	145.9	146.5	147.3	158.1	160.1	160.5	167.7	162.6	165.4	168.8	172.4	176.0
Total	397.2	372.3	365.2	387.0	403.6	428.4	456.5	472.8	500.2	509.8	511.1	496.1	520.9	529.6	545.0
% Change Year Ago	1.2%	-6.3%	-1.9%	6.0%	4.3%	6.1%	6.6%	3.6%	5.8%	1.9%	0.2%	-2.9%	5.0%	1.7%	2.9%
Secondary Supply															
Old Scrap	130.5	137.1	138.4	148.1	155.5	163.3	171.5	176.5	187.1	192.0	190.0	196.0	202.0	205.0	208.1
Coin Melt	3.0	2.0	1.3	1.5	1.7	1.7	2.5	18.5	6.0	2.0	3.0	5.0	5.0	5.0	7.0
Indian Scrap	7.2	3.8	6.5	9.6	6.4	10.0	13.5	12.9	6.4	9.6	4.8	16.1	9.7	16.1	22.0
Total	140.7	142.9	146.2	159.2	163.6	175.0	187.5	207.9	199.5	203.6	197.8	217.1	216.7	226.1	237.1
% Change Year Ago	7.2%	1.5%	2.3%	8.9%	2.7%	7.0%	7.1%	10.9%	-4.0%	2.0%	-2.8%	9.8%	-0.2%	4.4%	4.9%
Other Supply															
Government Disposals	8.1	11.2	15.8	19	8.1	5.3	6	10	20	25	15	15	10	35	32
Net Exports from Transitional Economies	—	—	—	—	—	—	—	—	15	15	15	15	5	—	—
	8.1	11.2	15.8	19	8.1	5.3	6	10	35	40	30	30	15	35	32
% Change Year Ago	-29.6%	38.3%	41.1%	20.3%	-57.4%	-34.6%	13.2%	66.7%	250.0%	14.3%	-25.0%	0.0%	-50.0%	133.3%	-8.6%
Total Supply	546.0	526.4	527.2	565.3	575.3	608.7	650.0	690.7	734.7	753.4	738.9	743.2	752.5	790.7	814.1
% Change Year Ago	2.0%	-3.6%	0.2%	7.2%	1.8%	5.8%	6.8%	6.3%	6.4%	2.5%	-1.9%	0.6%	1.2%	5.1%	3.0%
Industrial Demand															
Photography	198.6	201.0	215.5	221.2	230.9	242.2	257.1	267.2	261.7	256.7	255.5	249.2	242.7	208.2	182.5
Jewelry & Silverware	172.0	234.5	234.5	245.2	262.2	283.1	293.5	291.7	285.5	287.6	270.9	264.9	242.8	288.8	271.6
Electronics and Batteries	81.3	83.6	83.2	88.6	88.7	96.9	96.2	99.1	115.3	102.4	106.0	104.4	106.6	101.8	104.3
Other Uses	112.5	120.1	129.2	137.0	142.5	145.2	137.3	139.8	183.4	157.6	151.3	162.7	201.3	193.6	193.4
Other Countries	0.4	5.1	3.9	3.4	6.0	6.5	6.4	6.9	6.4	6.2	7.0	7.2	7.5	3.9	3.9
Net Imports into the Transitional Economies	27.5	30.0	28.0	29.3	27.9	29.6	31.2	11.0	—	—	—	—	—	10.0	10.0
Total	591.5	674.3	694.3	724.7	758.2	803.6	821.7	815.8	852.3	810.5	790.7	788.4	800.9	806.4	765.7
% Change Year Ago	2.8%	14.0%	3.0%	4.4%	4.6%	6.0%	2.3%	-0.7%	4.5%	-4.9%	-2.4%	-0.3%	1.6%	0.7%	-5.0%
Net Surplus or Deficit in the Bullion Market	-45.5	-147.9	-167.1	-159.5	-182.9	-194.9	-171.7	-125.1	-117.6	-57.1	-51.9	-45.2	-48.4	-15.7	48.4
Addenda															
Coinage	29.4	38.0	33.5	22.0	18.1	18.9	25.0	29.5	25.2	17.6	20.5	17.7	18.2	16.5	16.8
Changes in Inventories															
Unreported	-146.4	-189.6	-170.6	-60.3	-174.7	-107.7	-159.7	-165.2	-163.0	-80.5	-67.9	-60.1	-40.9	-43.9	—
Reported	70.7	5.6	-29.9	-121.2	-26.3	-106.0	-37.0	10.6	20.5	6.4	-4.0	4.9	-17.9	16.2	—
Total	-75.7	-184.0	-200.6	-181.5	-201.0	-213.7	-196.7	-154.6	-142.6	-74.1	-71.9	-62.8	-66.6	-32.2	31.6
% Change Year Ago	11.2%	143.0%	9.0%	-9.5%	10.8%	6.3%	-8.0%	-21.4%	-7.7%	-48.1%	-3.0%	-23.2%	20.7%	-51.7%	NM
Price Per Ounce															YTD
High	$4.32	$5.44	$5.78	$6.16	$5.84	$6.38	$7.28	$5.77	$5.57	$4.83	$5.13	$5.99	$8.22	$9.10	$10.74
Low	3.64	3.52	4.61	4.42	4.71	4.19	4.62	4.86	4.62	4.03	4.22	4.35	5.52	6.45	8.87
Average	3.93	4.30	5.28	5.20	5.21	4.91	5.53	5.23	5.00	4.38	4.60	4.90	6.70	7.35	9.65
% Change Year Ago	-2.5%	9.4%	22.8%	-1.4%	0.1%	-5.8%	12.7%	-5.3%	-4.5%	-12.4%	5.2%	6.3%	36.8%	9.7%	37.7%

Apparent private investment demand from new supply is total supply for a given year less fabrication demand and coinage. Apparent bullion demand from market stocks reflects the change in market inventories; a negative figure here indicates that investors were net sellers of metal that entered market stocks, while a positive figure indicates that market stocks fell to meet demand from investors, and fabricators of industrial products and coins. Changes in market inventories are year-end; 1999 through end-December. Reported inventories between 1992 and 1996 are adjusted to reflect Wilmington Trust silver stocks that would have been eligible for Comex delivery. Wilmington Trust became a licensed Comex depository on January 1, 1997.

A 2006 Surplus

Past editions of these reports have made the point that one of the key factors in the rise in silver prices in 1979 and 1980 was not so much the arrival of new investors buying silver, as it was the increased reluctance of existing holders of silver inventories to sell their silver at near-market prices. As silver prices began to rise in 1979, many investors who had been selling silver off, for much of the previous decade, began to pull back from such sales. They had been willing sellers at market prices during much of the 1970s because they felt these were good prices. When they saw prices break out of their previous range, around $4 - $5 per ounce, they decided to wait to see how high prices would rise before selling. When prices rose above $35, in January and February 1980, they sold. There were long lines of people selling silver at coin shops, refineries, and other outlets at that time. Prior to that, however, one of the key factors that had driven silver prices from $6.25 on average in January 1979 to $38.28 on average in January 1980 had been an increasing hesitance to sell silver at lower prices on the part of investors who already held silver.

A similar trend appeared to emerge in the silver market in 2005. Investors who already held silver became more reluctant to sell their metal at near-market prices, waiting to see how high prices

Silver Market Surplus/Deficit

Projected Through 2006.

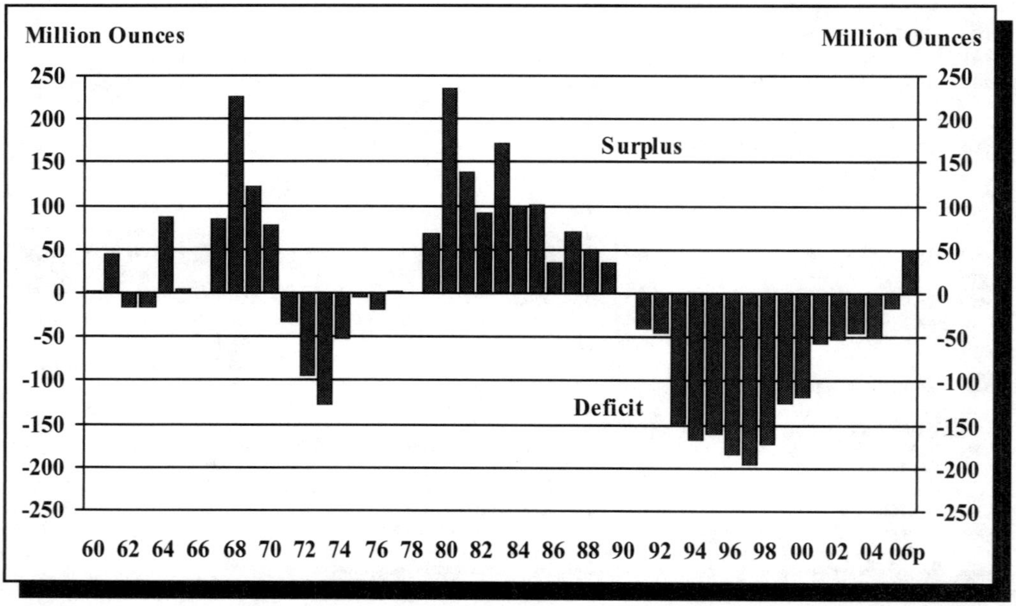

would go. As a result, the net sales from inventories into the market to make up for the supply shortfall dropped sharply in 2005, from around 48.4 million ounces in 2004 to perhaps only 15.7 million ounces. It took rising prices to induce this.

This trend is continuing in 2006. In fact, investors probably will be net buyers of silver in 2006, forcing the silver market back into a surplus of newly refined silver relative to fabrication demand. This surplus may be around 48.4 million ounces in 2006. This figure would represent the net purchases by investors and others for non-fabrication purposes. That is, for addition to bullion inventories. This will be the first year since 1989 in which investors will be net buyers of silver as a group.

The concepts surrounding the net surpluses and deficits in the silver market confuse and confound many observers. Partly this is because many people view these surpluses and deficits as a mathematical result of subtracting fabrication demand from total supply. Additionally, some observers make the mistake of including investment demand along with fabrication demand, further obscuring the market mechanics that these numbers are meant to convey. The fact that so much of silver's supply, fabrication demand, investment demand, inventories, and market flows are secretive does not help illuminate how the market works.

The analytical work that develops these supply and demand estimates treats the surpluses and deficits as de facto stock building or stock sales. These are dynamic parts of the model, and not residuals. The concept that the silver market is moving from a 16-year deficit to a surplus in 2006 is very much a result of the conclusion that investors are increasing their demand for physical silver, bidding the price of silver higher to the point where it elicits increased supply from mines and scrap recovery efforts, and discourages silver use in jewelry and silverware, the two most price-sensitive fabrication uses for silver. That is what has been happening in the silver market in 2005.

The Silver ETF Proposal Arrives

The price increases of 2005 continued into 2006, and in fact gained momentum.

Silver traded between \$8.85 and \$9.35 for much of January. Then, on 23 January 2006 the U.S. Securities and Exchange Commission posted a notice in the Federal Register that it was considering a proposal by the American Stock Exchange, on behalf of Barclays Global Investors, to authorize creation of a silver exchange traded fund. These commodities ETFs are designed to trade close to the price of the underlying commodity. Their sole asset is physical metal, held on an allocated basis. Several gold ETFs were launched between 2003 and early 2005, and have met with strong investor demand and shown initial successes as a new way for investors to build exposure directly to gold. Following the interest seen in the gold ETFs, which now hold around 16 million ounces collectively worldwide, Barclays Global Investors had moved to propose a silver ETF.

The announcement in the Federal Register on 23 January, opening the period for public comments on the proposal, led to a round of speculative and investor buying of silver. The consensus seemed to be that the proposal would be accepted, and that a silver ETF soon would be launched. Additionally, there seemed to be a view that such an ETF could command a large amount of silver for addition to allocated inventories, which would not be available for lending into the market. While some market observers scoffed at the idea, many market participants seemed to hold the view that the remaining inventories of good delivery silver bullion was relatively low, and that even a modestly successful silver ETF could take up much of what was available in bullion form.

It is anyone's guess how much silver investors may want to buy via such a silver ETF. Guesses can be qualified, however, by putting some quantitative and qualitative thought and analysis to the subject. Investors, bullion banks, traders, and others have been running various calculations to develop ranges of potential demand since 23 January. For example, one set of calculations was that there were around 15.5 million ounces of gold in ETF holdings as of the end of 2005. The gold price at that point was $518, so that the value of the gold in the ETF holdings was around $8.0 billion. Investors trying to gauge the potential interest in a silver ETF assumed, for the sake of their calculations, that a silver ETF might be one-tenth as popular as the gold ETFs. If that were the case, the reasoning went, then investors might be willing to spend around $800 million on silver ETF shares, which, at $10 per ounce for silver would equate to around 80 million ounces of silver. This is more than all of the silver registered against Comex futures positions, which totaled 70.8 million ounces by the end of January 2006. It is more than many observers estimate is available in London and Zurich bank vaults. In other words, by this one admittedly crude calculation, it would seem that a silver ETF could demand a lot more silver bullion than is readily available, with potentially enormous consequences for silver prices.

That was just one of many such hypothetical calculations that silver market participants were running in late January and through February. The conclusion of many of these participants was that a silver ETF could push silver prices sharply higher, at least during the initial period of its being available.

Consequently, they bought silver. The investor and speculative buying that began with the 23 January announcement pushed silver prices from \$8.93 on the trading day before the announcement to \$10.90 on 27 March (\$11.03 on an intraday basis).

Fundamentals Beyond the ETF

The advent of the silver ETF has commanded a great deal of attention in the market. It is only a part of the larger story of what has been happening in the silver market, however. The fact is that even without the silver ETF being around, investors have been buying more silver, other investors have been selling less silver, the price of silver has been rising, fabrication demand in many product areas has been declining, and silver supplies from mines and scrap refining operations has been increasing. These are the trends that have moved silver prices higher over the past few years. The potential that a silver ETF may make it easier for some investors to buy physical silver in the future, and may attract new groups of investors to physical silver in the future, really is a footnote to this larger story.

As stated above, the silver market continued to see a current account deficit in newly refined silver relative to fabrication demand in 2005. The size of the shortfall contracted sharply, however, from 48.4 million ounces in 2004 to 15.7 million ounces in 2005. This reflected greater reluctance to sell silver on the part of some investors, increased demand for silver from other investors, increased supplies of silver, and weaker demand in most industries that use silver.

The silver market is projected to shift into a surplus in 2006. The surplus could be as large as 48.4 million ounces. This will reflect further increases in investor demand for physical silver, partly boosted by the imminent launch of the silver ETF. It also will reflect increases in mine production and secondary recovery, and lower fabrication demand.

In addition to these fundamentals, silver supplies have been increased in 2005 by sales from long-held government stocks in India. The Indian government began 2005 by announcing that it wished to sell much of the 86.6 million ounces of silver it held. Of this, 67.5 million ounces are held by the Reserve Bank of India. Another 19.1 million ounces are held in other accounts, having been confiscated from smugglers in the 1980s. The Indian government indicated that it would sell the metal held by the central bank, and that it would funnel the metal into the domestic Indian market in a way that was intended to minimize any price weaknesses or market disruptions. In 2005 the Indian government sold around 35 million ounces of silver into the domestic Indian market. The Reserve Bank of India now has 32.5 million ounces remaining. This report assumes that that amount of metal will be sold during 2006, since it is less than the volume that the bank was able to sell in 2005, during a period of rising prices.

The Economy

	1994	1995	1996	1997	1998	1999	2000	2001	2002	2003	2004	2005	2006p
Real GDP (a)													
(Percent Change)													
United States	4.0	2.7	3.6	4.2	4.3	4.2	3.8	0.3	2.4	2.5	4.4	4.1	3.5
Japan	0.6	1.5	5.0	1.6	-2.5	0.3	1.7	0.7	-0.7	0.5	4.0	2.4	2.0
Germany	2.3	1.7	0.8	1.5	2.2	1.5	2.8	2.8	0.4	0.8	0.5	1.1	1.8
OECD Europe	2.9	2.4	1.6	2.6	2.8	2.1	3.5	2.8	0.9	1.5	1.8	2.1	2.2
Total OECD	2.9	2.2	2.6	3.1	2.3	2.8	3.7	2.4	1.0	1.7	3.6	2.7	2.9
Consumer Price Inflation (a)													
(Percent Change)													
United States	2.6	2.8	2.9	2.3	1.6	2.2	3.4	2.8	1.6	2.2	2.0	2.7	2.5
Japan	0.7	-0.1	0.1	1.7	0.6	-0.3	-1.7	-0.7	-0.9	-0.7	-2.3	-1.1	-0.1
Germany	2.7	1.7	1.2	1.5	0.6	0.7	1.2	2.4	1.3	1.5	1.8	2.0	1.7
OECD Europe	3.0	3.0	2.4	1.8	1.8	1.3	1.2	4.4	2.2	2.4	1.9	1.8	1.7
Total OECD	2.4	2.5	2.3	1.7	1.3	2.6	1.4	2.8	2.0	1.7	1.8	2.1	1.9
Industrial Output (a)													
(Percent Change)													
United States	5.3	3.3	3.2	5.0	4.9	3.5	5.6	-3.7	1.5	1.8	2.2	2.2	
Japan	0.8	3.5	2.6	4.4	0.1	1.7	6.3	-13.5	1.3	1.3	1.5	1.5	
Germany	3.6	2.0	0.1	3.7	4.0	3.4	5.4	0.8	1.0	1.0	1.1	1.1	
Total OECD	3.9	3.0	2.8	4.3	3.5	2.1	5.7	-3.6	2.5	1.3	1.6	1.6	
Interest Rates													
(Percent)													
United States	4.3	5.5	5.0	5.1	4.8	4.6	5.8	3.4	1.6	1.1	1.5	2.8	
Japan	3.7	2.5	2.2	1.7	1.1	1.8	1.7	1.3	1.4	0.0	0.0	0.0	
Germany	5.3	4.5	3.3	3.3	3.4	2.9	4.3	3.7	3.1	2.0	2.1	2.4	
United Kingdom	5.2	6.3	5.8	6.5	6.8	5.0	5.8	4.8	3.9	4.3	4.8	5.0	

Notes: (a) Seasonally adjusted annual rates of change from previous period. Projections are based on those of the OECD, modified by CPM Group. (b) U.S. interest rates are annual average rates on three-month Treasury bills. Japanese interest rates are annual average rates on government bonds. German and U.K. interest rates are average rates on treasury bills. Interest rate is through September 2005. (c) Europe is OECD Europe through 2001; Eurozone from 2002. Projections are CPM Group's, based on OECD's. p -- projections. e -- estimates.
Sources: OECD, IMF, U.S. Dept. of Commerce, CPM Group.
March 10, 2006

Total supply rose 5.1% in 2005, from 752.5 million ounces in 2004 to a record 790.7 million ounces. The increases came from rising mine production in several countries, higher scrap recovery rates, and the Indian government stockpile sales. There were no other government sales during the year.

Total supply is projected to rise another 3.0% this year, to 814.1 million ounces. The increase will reflect higher mine production and scrap recovery rates.

Mine production totaled 529.6 million ounces in 2005. That was 1.7% higher than the 520.9 million ounces produced in 2004. Mine production rose in Mexico, the largest producing nation: Peru, Australia, Poland, Bolivia, Chile, and several other countries. Silver mine production fell in Canada and the United States in 2005.

World mine output is projected to rise another 2.9% to 545.0 million ounces in 2006. Production is set to expand in most major producing countries. As discussed in the Supply chapter of this report, even larger increases should be anticipated for 2007, when several major new mines come onstream.

Secondary recovery of silver from scrap rose 4.4% from 216.7 million ounces in 2004 to 226.1 million ounces in 2005. Further increases, to 237.1 million ounces, are projected for this year. The largest increase in this source of supply was the increase in Indian silver scrap refining, mostly old jewelry and decorative objects. Indian silver scrap recovery rose from 9.7 million ounces in 2004 to 16.1 million ounces in 2005, the result of higher silver prices. Scrap recovery outside of India meanwhile rose a more modest three million ounces last year, from 202.0 million ounces to 205.0 million ounces. Much of the silver recovered outside of India is from photographic waste. As the photographic industry uses less silver each year, due to the shift to digital imaging, the flow of silver from this source of scrap is beginning to decline. This decline is being offset at present by higher recovery rates from electronic scrap and old jewelry, reflecting both higher silver prices and tighter environmental controls on the disposition of electronic equipment. Another 5.0 million ounces of silver is estimated to be recovered from old silver coins each year.

On the demand side of the market, silver use in fabricated products is estimated to have totaled 806.4 million ounces in 2005. That would have been 0.7% higher than the 800.9 million ounces used in a wide range of fabricated products in 2004. This total masks the fact that silver use decreased in most applications last year. There was a very large, 40.2 million ounce, increase in the amount of silver used in electroplated items in India in 2005. Most of this was said to be electroplated silver jewelry and gift items, reflecting the fact that Indians were shifting away from silver jewelry and silver gifts to cheaper electroplated jewelry and gifts due to the higher price of silver. Had this use not emerged as a very large absorber of silver in 2005, total silver use for the year would have declined.

For 2006 silver use is projected to decline, 5.0% to 765.7 million ounces. This is with the new Indian electroplated use remaining high.

Silver use in photography continues to contract. Silver use is estimated to have declined 14.2% in 2005 to 208.2 million ounces. Another 12.3% decline to 182.5 million ounces is projected for this year. The pace of decline is not as great as some market observers estimate, given that some photographic applications still use silver. Silver is suffering the greatest market loss in films used by professionals and amateurs. The sales of silver-bearing films are declining 20% - 28% per annum worldwide now. Silver-bearing paper, used to print high quality prints, including pictures taken with digital cameras, is holding up much better, meanwhile. In fact, some of the strength in silver-bearing paper sales is due to increased printing of pictures from digital imaging. Silver use also is strong in some graphic arts applications of photo-imaging, and in movie films.

Silver use in jewelry and silverware rose 19.0% to 288.8 million ounces in 2005, on the strength of the electroplated jewelry and silver objects in India. A 6.0% decline to 271.6 million ounces is projected for 2006. While Indian market sources expect the use of silver in electroplated objects to remain strong in 2006, silver use in jewelry is expected to decline in the United States, Europe, and other markets.

Electronic components and batteries used 4.4% less silver in 2005 than in 2004. Demand for silver in these products dropped from 106.6 million ounces in 2004 to 101.8 million ounces in 2005. This was seen as reflecting cyclical weakness in some of these applications, including some batteries, rather than representing the start of a major decline in silver use in electronics and batteries. The rising price of silver may have had a marginal effect on limiting demand. It seems that a more important factor related to cyclical weakness in demand for some of these components. Silver use consequently is projected to recover 2.4% to 104.3 million ounces in 2006.

Silver use in other applications declined 3.9% to 193.6 million ounces in 2005, from 201.3 million ounces. Again, a large part of this weakness was said by industry executives to represent cyclical patterns in some of these industries. For example, silver use in ethylene oxide catalysts had risen sharply in 2004, as several plants required recharged catalysts. It declined somewhat in 2005. For perspective, it needs to be noted that silver use in these various applications totaled 162.7 million ounces in 2003, so that even with the 7.7 million ounce drop last year silver use remained strong. Demand is projected to be

Deficits' Effects on Prices Depend On Inventories

Annual Surpluses and Deficits

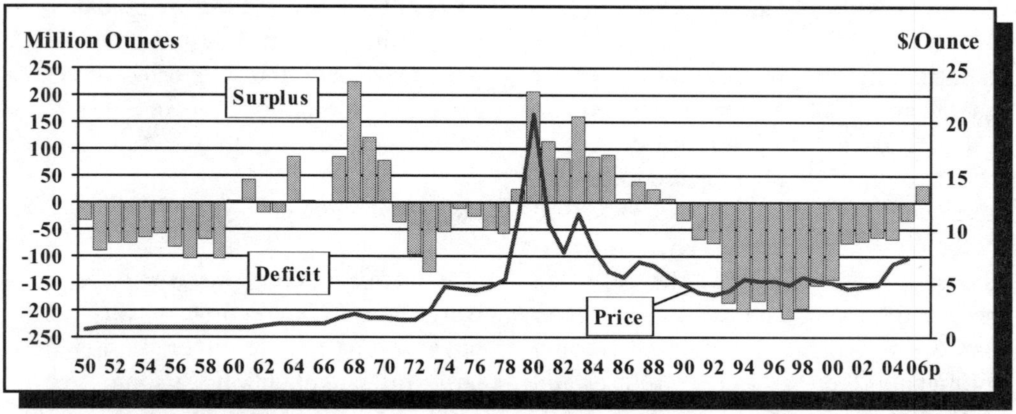

Estimated Total Silver Bullion Inventories, Year-End

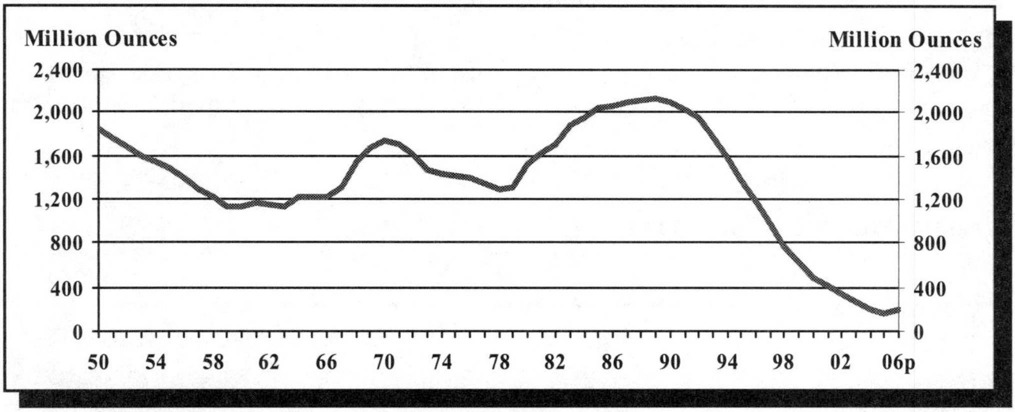

Silver Bullion Inventories as Months of Demand, Year-End

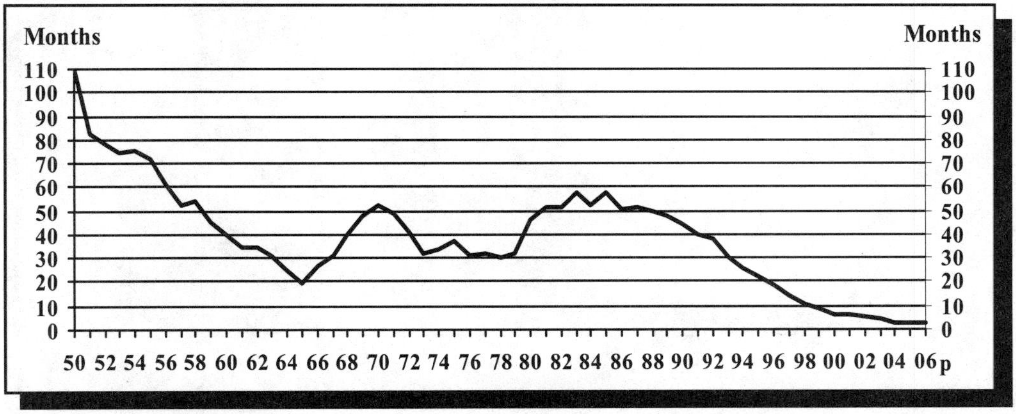

roughly flat around 193.4 million ounces in 2006.

Reported market inventories of silver rose from 123.2 million ounces at the end of 2004 to 139.3 million ounces at the end of 2005. This reflected increased silver held in the four depositories used by the New York Comex. These increases in stocks in these vaults reflected increased trading activity in the silver market, in the futures market. Trading volumes on the major silver futures and options markets rose 8.2% to 34.4 billion ounces last year. The amount of silver that cleared through the London interbank market meanwhile rose 5.7% to 27.9 billion ounces in 2005. Volumes of silver trading through these markets generally have risen since 2001 - 2002. The futures volumes growth has outpaced the rise in interbank volumes, which reflects the increased investor activity in futures over the past five years.

2006 and Beyond

The silver market appears to be at a watershed. Past reports in this series have compared the silver market to a large oil tanker, taking a long time to turn. The silver market since at least the 1950s has been characterized by long periods of building up inventories, followed by long periods of time in which the markets lived off of those inventories. Today the silver market appears to

Precious Metals Bullion Stocks

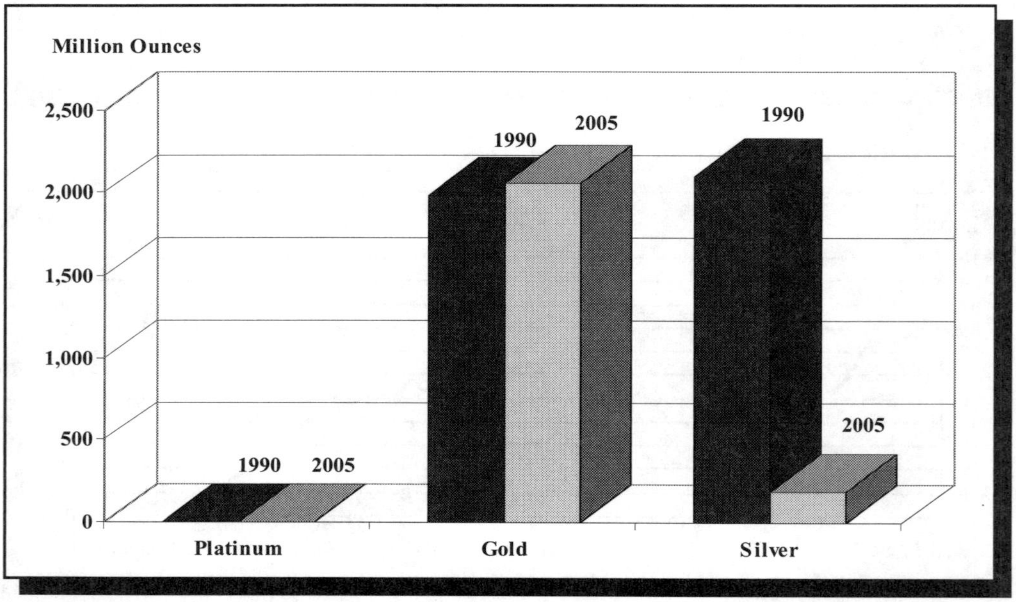

be ending a 16-year run of living off of inventories and beginning a new era in which investors start building up inventories once again. If they are to do that, the price of silver will have to remain high enough to accommodate their new found interest in physical silver. This will mean higher mine production and lower jewelry and silverware use of silver. Secondary supply may help some, especially if prices rise far enough to stimulate individuals to sell their old silver jewelry and silverware objects to refiners. That may not happen, however. Meanwhile, silver scrap recovery may decline, as less silver is used in photographic products, which account for the bulk of the source of silver for scrap refiners.

For most of the period of drawing down inventories the price of silver languished between $3.50 and $5.50 - from 1990 through 2003. These deficits were compensated for by the sale of silver from bullion and coin inventories. At the start of the period of deficits, in 1990, there were more than 2.1 billion ounces of silver in bullion form lying around the world. Most of this was held by investors, although banks and dealers that serve as market makers were estimated to have held several hundred million ounces of silver at that time.

The research that informs these reports had suggested that at some point these inventories would reach low enough levels that the price of silver would have to rise sharply enough to restore a balance between newly refined supply and fabrication demand. It was suggested that prices needed to rise into a range of $6.50 - $10.00 on a sustained basis to stimulate sufficient new mine production and to discourage the price-sensitive use of silver in jewelry and fabrication demand sufficiently to balance supply and demand.

It will be interesting to see if prices stabilize at higher levels, and if so, whether prices will be high enough to stimulate new mine production and discourage some fabrication demand. The contraction in silver use in photography may aid in the move toward a more balanced market. The rise of investor interest, perhaps accentuated by the arrival of the silver ETF, meanwhile may make the adjustment more volatile, boosting investor demand for silver from investors at a critical time.

The final chart in this chapter is a new illustration for the silver market. This research group has maintained a similar chart on gold since 1970. We have had the data for silver, but have never graphically portrayed it in this fashion. This chart shows estimates of the cumulative world production of silver since 1500, along with estimates of its potential broad distribution. The margin of error in these figures is enormous. Some suggest that the margin of error on historical silver production is plus or minus two billion ounces. That seems reasonable. That said, the estimates are that around 42.6 billion ounces of silver have been mined since time immemorial. Of this, perhaps half of it has been lost to mankind. Around 400 million ounces may remain in bullion form, with another 541 million ounces or so in silver coins. Another 20 billion ounces may be held in jewelry, decorative, and religious objects around the world. A study in the early 1990s estimated that such objects held more than 15 billion ounces of silver. Since then another 3.8 billion ounces of silver have been used in such products.

Estimated Silver Inventories in London and Zurich

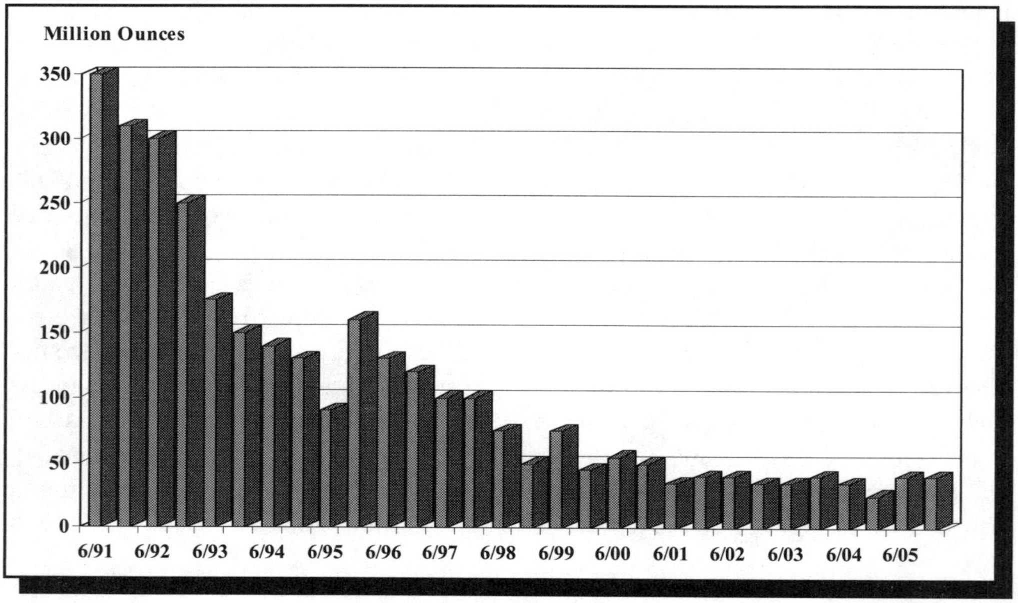

The Silver Market

2006 Annualized Through February.

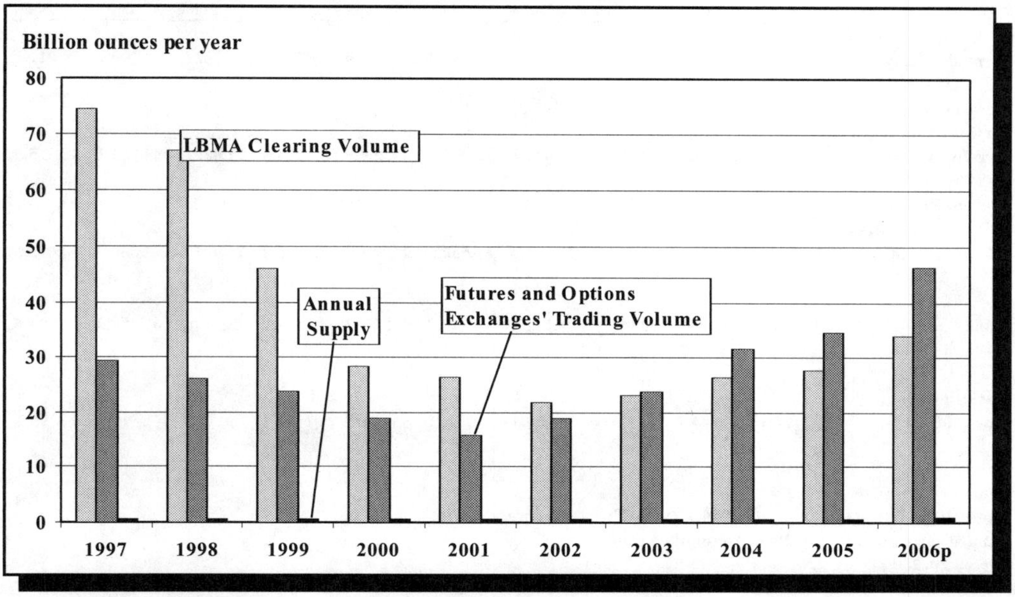

The Silver Market 1997 - 2006p

Million Ounces

	1997	1998	1999	2000	2001	2002	2003	2004	2005	2006p
Annual Supply	608.7	650.0	690.7	734.7	753.4	738.9	743.2	752.5	790.7	814.1
Futures and Options Exchanges Trading Volume	29,478.1	26,218.9	23,885.3	19,032.3	15,911.0	19,259.9	23,974.5	31,829.7	34,723.8	46,375.3
London Bullion Market Association Clearing Volume	74,573.9	67,059.3	46,111.9	28,475.4	26,552.5	21,888.9	23,460.0	26,402.5	27,886.4	34,035.0
Total	104,660.7	93,928.2	70,687.9	48,242.4	43,216.9	41,887.7	48,177.7	58,984.7	63,400.9	81,224.4
Ratio: Trading: Annual Supply	171:1	144:1	101:1	65:1	56:1	56:1	64:1	77:1	79:1	99:1

Source: CPM Group
Notes: Tocom through February 2006, Comex Through February 2006.
LBMA Through February 2006. Annualized Data.
March 20, 2006

Cumulative World Silver Production and Distribution

Estimated data as of end 2005

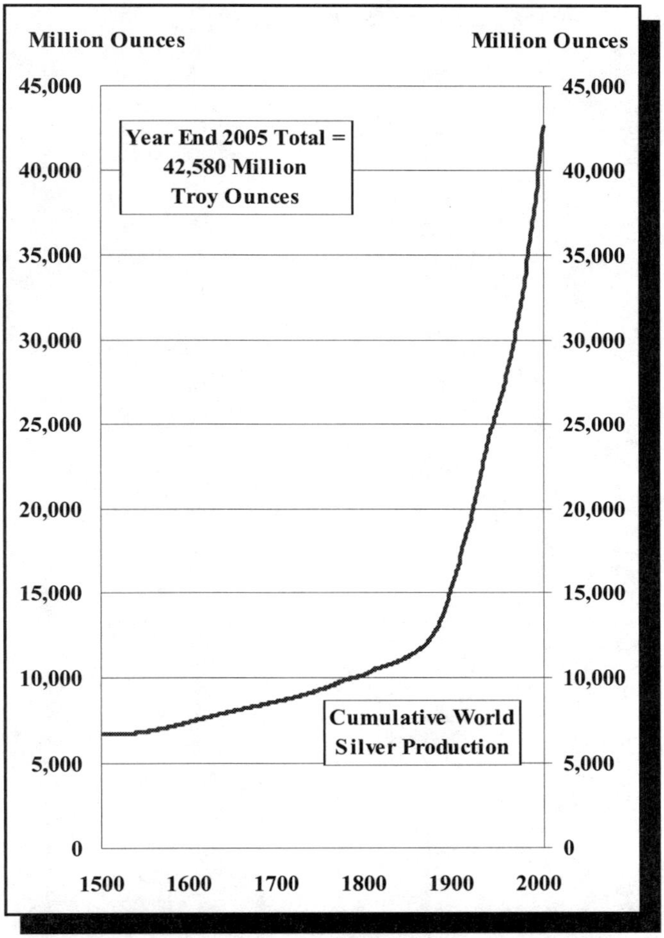

Estimated Disposition
(Million Troy Ounces)

Silver Bullion and Coins	
Bullion:	**400**
Coins:	**541**
Subtotal:	**941**
Jewelry, Decorative, and Religious Objects:	**20,111**
Industrial Use, Undetermined or Lost:	**21,528**
Total:	**42,580**

Notes: Total disposition may not equal cumulative production due to rounding and other discrepancies in the historical data. The distribution of 6,681 million ounces of pre-1493 production is not able to be discerned. Silver in product form includes jewelry, art, sterlingware, religious objects, museum pieces, and other silver-bearing objects. Historical information on the production and consumption of silver over the past five millennia necessarily has a high degree of potential error. Some estimates of cumulative production vary by a couple of billion ounces from the sources used here. Sources: Australian Minerals Economics Pty. Ltd., Schmitz, Metschaft, United Nations, Handy and Harman, Ministry of Natural Resources Ontario, Dr. Adolph Soetbeer 1493-1850, USGS, and CPM Group since 1850

World Silver Supply and Fabrication Demand

Million Troy Ounces

	Supply				Demand			
Year	Mine Output	Secondary	Other	Total	Industrial	Coinage	Imports into the Transitional Economies	Total
1950	169.5	NA	NA	169.5	157.4	44.1	—	201.5
1951	165.5	NA	NA	165.5	164.6	90.5	—	255.1
1952	180.6	NA	NA	180.6	142.1	114.3	—	256.4
1953	184.7	NA	NA	184.7	168.3	90.8	—	259.1
1954	178.6	NA	NA	178.6	160.8	83.4	—	244.2
1955	187.7	NA	10.3	198.0	192.8	52.6	—	245.4
1956	189.8	30.5	3.7	224.0	215.9	56.6	—	272.5
1957	194.6	25.0	3.8	223.4	212.6	84.2	—	296.8
1958	202.3	17.0	1.3	220.6	190.5	79.5	—	270.0
1959	195.6	33.4	42.0	271.0	212.9	86.4	—	299.3
1960	201.8	52.0	90.0	343.8	237.8	103.9	—	341.7
1961	203.9	65.0	181.0	449.9	269.6	136.0	—	405.6
1962	210.8	69.0	107.0	386.8	275.5	127.6	—	403.1
1963	214.0	68.0	147.0	429.0	278.9	166.4	—	445.3
1964	211.5	86.0	374.0	671.5	318.2	267.1	—	585.3
1965	218.4	103.0	426.0	747.4	358.5	385.1	—	743.6
1966	225.2	105.0	217.0	547.2	417.1	129.5	—	546.6
1967	214.7	126.0	252.0	592.7	401.9	105.3	—	507.2
1968	230.2	227.0	232.0	689.2	373.9	89.3	—	463.2
1969	248.7	174.0	119.0	541.7	386.3	32.7	—	419.0
1970	260.6	127.0	88.9	476.5	376.0	23.4	—	399.4
1971	249.7	127.0	7.0	383.7	389.5	27.8	2.4	419.7
1972	255.1	112.0	12.0	379.1	431.4	38.1	6.2	475.7
1973	261.8	122.0	46.0	429.8	522.5	28.5	7.8	558.8
1974	245.7	192.0	21.0	458.7	470.0	31.6	9.1	510.7
1975	249.9	177.0	15.0	441.9	407.7	33.4	10.9	452.0
1976	264.1	235.0	11.0	510.1	484.7	30.0	21.1	535.8
1977	287.2	169.0	5.0	461.2	459.9	34.5	15.9	510.3
1978	292.0	152.0	9.0	453.0	452.4	39.5	18.2	510.1
1979	297.6	216.0	3.0	516.6	448.2	31.0	11.5	490.7
1980	293.9	302.0	5.0	600.9	364.3	15.0	14.5	393.8
1981	306.4	184.0	4.0	494.4	355.4	9.5	15.3	380.2
1982	321.7	155.0	1.0	477.7	361.4	12.0	23.8	397.2
1983	338.0	197.5	19.0	554.5	356.4	10.2	25.4	392.0
1984	351.0	165.6	16.0	532.6	376.7	13.7	56.6	447.0
1985	359.3	140.9	13.0	513.2	381.2	13.4	30.4	425.0
1986	351.1	129.3	14.0	494.4	410.0	26.8	49.2	486.0
1987	368.6	137.9	20.0	526.5	430.6	30.4	24.9	485.8
1988	383.6	143.9	8.3	535.8	453.3	25.3	32.9	511.5
1989	398.2	136.2	10.7	545.1	478.0	26.3	32.6	536.8
1990	401.1	126.0	11.0	538.1	514.2	29.8	25.0	569.0
1991	392.5	131.2	11.5	535.2	548.4	27.7	27.2	603.3
1992	397.2	140.7	8.1	546.0	564.8	29.4	27.5	621.7
1993	372.3	142.9	11.2	526.4	642.4	38.0	30.0	710.4
1994	365.2	146.2	15.8	527.2	666.3	33.5	28.0	727.8
1995	387.0	159.2	19.0	565.3	695.5	22.0	29.3	746.8
1996	403.6	163.6	8.1	575.3	730.3	18.1	27.9	776.3
1997	428.4	175.0	5.3	608.7	773.9	18.9	29.6	822.4
1998	456.5	187.5	6.0	650.0	790.5	25.0	31.2	846.7
1999	472.8	207.9	10.0	690.7	804.7	29.5	11.0	845.2
2000	500.2	199.5	35.0	734.7	852.3	25.2	0.0	877.5
2001	509.8	203.6	40.0	753.4	810.5	17.6	0.0	828.1
2002	511.1	197.8	30.0	738.9	790.7	20.5	0.0	811.2
2003	496.1	217.1	30.0	743.2	788.4	17.7	0.0	806.1
2004	520.9	216.7	15.0	752.5	800.9	18.2	0.0	819.1
2005	529.6	226.1	35.0	790.7	796.4	16.5	10.0	822.9
2006p	545.0	237.1	32.0	814.1	755.7	16.8	10.0	782.5

Note: p - projections. na - not available.
Sources: CPM Group, industry sources.
March 14, 2006

Real and Nominal Silver Prices

Million Troy Ounces

Prices, Base=2005

Year	Real	% Change	Nominal	% Change	US CPI % Change
1950	$6.42	--	$0.74	--	--
1955	$6.98	4.9%	$0.89	4.5%	-0.4%
1960	$6.46	-1.5%	$0.91	0.2%	1.7%
1965	$8.62	-1.6%	$1.29	0.0%	1.6%
1970	$9.45	-7.0%	$1.76	-1.1%	5.8%
1975	$18.36	-12.3%	$4.54	-3.2%	9.1%
1976	$16.62	-9.5%	$4.37	-3.7%	5.7%
1977	$16.52	-0.6%	$4.63	5.9%	6.5%
1978	$17.80	7.7%	$5.34	15.3%	7.6%
1979	$35.32	98.5%	$11.20	109.7%	11.3%
1980	$60.34	70.8%	$20.65	84.4%	13.5%
1981	$24.53	-59.3%	$10.53	-49.0%	10.3%
1982	$16.97	-30.8%	$7.93	-24.7%	6.1%
1983	$23.98	41.3%	$11.46	44.5%	3.2%
1984	$16.02	-33.2%	$8.15	-28.9%	4.3%
1985	$11.52	-28.1%	$6.15	-24.5%	3.5%
1986	$10.03	-13.0%	$5.47	-11.1%	1.9%
1987	$12.45	24.1%	$6.99	27.8%	3.7%
1988	$11.12	-10.7%	$6.53	-6.6%	4.1%
1989	$8.83	-20.6%	$5.50	-15.8%	4.8%
1990	$7.26	-17.8%	$4.82	-12.4%	5.4%
1991	$5.77	-20.6%	$4.03	-16.4%	4.2%
1992	$5.45	-5.5%	$3.93	-2.5%	3.0%
1993	$5.85	7.5%	$4.34	10.4%	3.0%
1994	$6.97	19.1%	$5.28	21.7%	2.6%
1995	$6.67	-4.3%	$5.20	-1.5%	2.8%
1996	$6.49	-2.7%	$5.21	0.2%	2.9%
1997	$5.96	-8.1%	$4.91	-5.8%	2.3%
1998	$6.62	11.1%	$5.53	12.7%	1.6%
1999	$6.12	-7.5%	$5.23	-5.3%	2.2%
2000	$5.64	-7.9%	$5.00	-4.5%	3.4%
2001	$4.78	-15.2%	$4.38	-12.4%	2.8%
2002	$4.95	3.6%	$4.60	5.2%	1.6%
2003	$5.15	4.0%	$4.90	6.3%	2.3%
2004	$6.91	34.1%	$6.70	36.8%	2.7%
2005	$7.35	6.3%	$7.35	9.7%	3.4%
Annual Averages					
1950 - 2005	$10.97		$4.21		
1960 - 2005	$11.89		$4.93		
1977 - 2005	$12.53		$6.62		
1990 - 2005	$6.12		$5.09		

Source: CPM Group.
March 14, 2006

Supply

Supply

The supply of silver to the market totaled 790.7 million ounces in 2005. That was up 5.1% from 752.5 million ounces in 2004 and represented a record high level for silver supplies. The bulk of the 38.2 million ounce increase in supplies represented sales of silver by the Indian government, which began 2005 by announcing that it would sell off roughly two-thirds of the 86.6 million ounces of silver it held at the time. For the full year the Reserve Bank of India sold around 35 million ounces. Secondary recovery of silver from scrap also rose, an estimated 9.4 million ounces, largely reflecting increased sales of silver jewelry and decorative objects for their metal content in India. Mine production rose 8.7 million ounces, with output increasing in Mexico, Peru, Australia, and a host of other emerging silver producing nations.

The effects of higher silver prices clearly are being seen in the silver supply sector. Mine production is increasing, as is exploration and development. Secondary recovery of silver from silver objects with low mark-ups relative to their silver content is increasing. It may be said that the Indian move to dispose of long-held inventories has little to do with the fact that silver prices are rising, and reflects more a broader move on the part of the Indian government to liberalize and reorganize its financial management.

These price-inspired increases should be expected to continue in 2006. Total sup-

Annual Total Supply

Projected Through 2006.

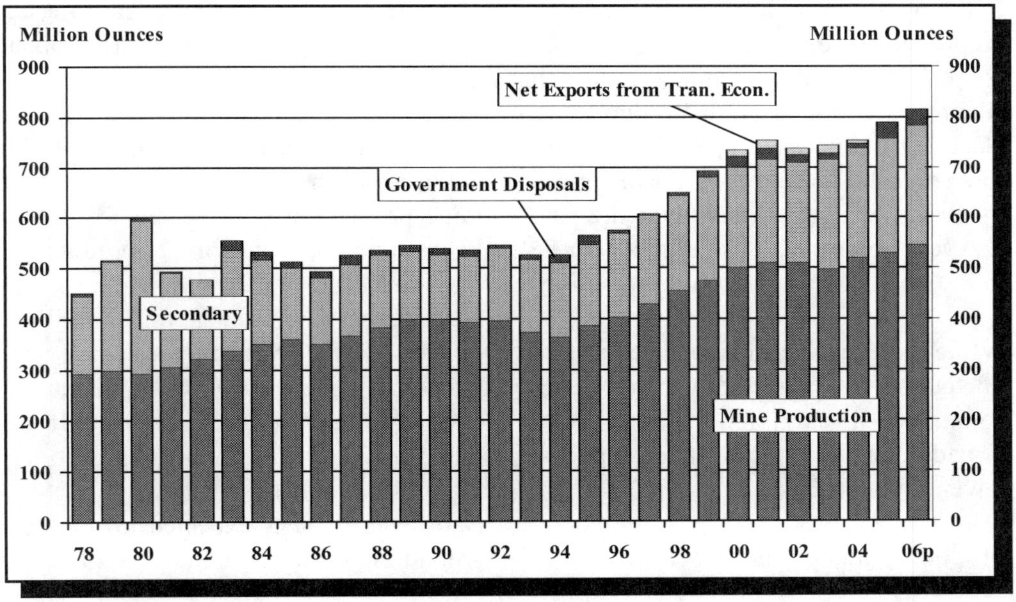

ply is projected here to rise 23.4 million ounces, due to increases in both mine production and secondary recovery from scrap. Indeed, the increase could be even greater than that, with total supply possibly rising 30 million ounces in 2006.

Mine Production

Mine production of silver in the market economies increased for the third consecutive year in 2005. Mine production in total rose 8.7 million ounces, or 1.7%, to 529.6 million ounces, from 520.9 million ounces in 2004. The increase reflected strong increases in Mexico, Peru, and Australia, as well as rising output in other countries.

Mine production in 2006 could rise to 545.0 million ounces, up 2.9% or 15.4 million ounces. These increases reflect the effects of both higher silver prices and higher gold and base metals prices. In the period from 2002 and 2003 silver output declined, in part because gold, copper, lead, and zinc mines at which silver was an important byproduct were closed or cut back on operations due to low prices for these metals. As the prices of these metals has risen over the past two years, along with that of silver, these mines, and silver mines, are re-opening.

While mine production increased in five of the seven largest silver-producing countries last year, it fell in two of them. Canada and the United States reported lower silver production.

In 2006 mine output is expected to increase in all seven of the largest silver-producing nations. These seven nations - Mexico, Peru, Australia, Chile, the United States, Poland, and Canada - together produced 444.0 million ounces of silver in 2005, a 1.8% increase from 435.9 million ounces the previous year. In 2006, mine production in these nations could increase to 457.1 million ounces, up 3.0% or 13.1 million ounces from 2005. These nations accounted for 83.7% of total mine production in 2004, 83.8% in 2005, and are expected to account for 83.9% in 2006.

Silver mine production is set to expand. Production is expanding at existing mines around the world. Older mines are being reopened. New mines are being developed. A wide range of companies are exploring for silver deposits that can be economically mined. With prices above $6.00 and even $7.00, many deposits that formerly were subeconomic are being re-examined. Other projects, newer discoveries, are being developed as well.

While production will continue to rise in 2006, an even larger increase in world mine production is projected for 2007. In just one country, Bolivia, production may rise from 15.0 million ounces in 2005 to as much as 25 to 30 million ounces in 2007. Apex Silver Mines' San Cristobal mine in Bolivia is slated to come onstream in the second half of 2007. It will have an annual capacity of 22 million ounces per year. The San Bartoleme mine is expected to produce around eight million ounces of silver in

2007, when it comes onstream in Bolivia, while the San Vicente mine could produce around 2.1 million ounces. These three mines alone may well more than double the silver output of Bolivia in 2007.

The largest producing country remains Mexico, although Peru has come up to virtually the same production level. Mexico produced 103.3 million ounces in 2005, up 3.8% from 99.5 million ounces in 2004. A further 2.6% increase to around 106.0 million ounces is projected for this year. The Alamo Dorado mine is coming onstream this year. It is expected to produce around 1.2 million ounces in 2006, ramping up to 5.0 million ounces in 2007. The Guanacevi silver mine meanwhile may boost production from 948,000 ounces in 2005 to 2.5 million ounces in 2006.

Peruvian output has risen sharply since the late 1990s. Production totaled 67.1 million ounces in 1999, for example. By 2004 Peruvian output had risen to 98.4 million ounces. Output rose another 4.3 million ounces, or 4.4% to 102.7 million ounces in 2006. A further increase, to 105.7 million ounces, is projected for this year. In Peru several existing mines are expanding their production in response to rising metals prices.

Australia now is the third largest silver mining country. Virtually all of Australia's output is byproduct of base metals and gold, although there is a silver deposit under development there

Mine Output in Major Silver Producing Countries, 1990-2006p

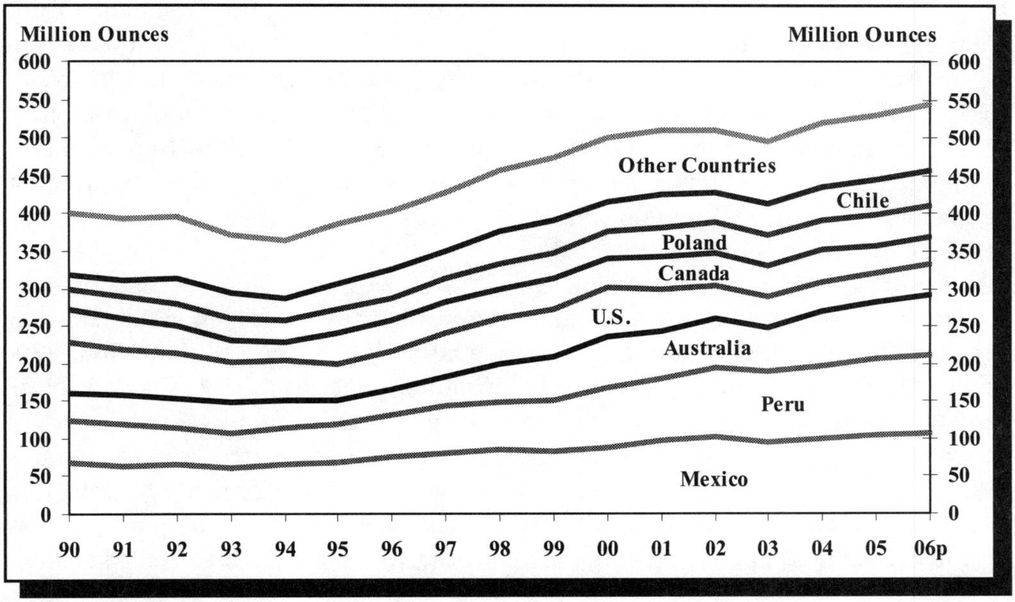

slated to start production in the middle of 2006. Australian production totaled 75.8 million ounces in 2005, up 6.8% from 71.0 million ounces the year before. BHP Billiton's Cannington lead and zinc mine increased its output from 41.3 million ounces to 43.9 million ounces, while Xstrata's Mount Isa Mines boosted production from 10.6 million ounces to 11.4 million ounces. These two properties, both base metals operations, accounted for 70.8% of the increase in Australian production last year.

Production in Australia is projected to increase to 80.0 million ounces this year, as these mines continue to expand production and other projects come onstream. MacMin Silver's Texas property is scheduled to start production in the middle of this year, and to produce somewhere between 2.5 million and 4.0 million ounces per year initially.

Canadian mine production declined 16.0% from 43.0 million ounces in 2004 to 36.1 million ounces in 2005. Several older mines are nearing the end of their planned lives, reducing output. Production fell from 15.4 million ounces in 2004 to 11.0 million ounces at the Eskay Creek gold mine, for example. Production is expected to remain under pressure. Some byproduct silver, especially at gold mines, may boost output modestly, to around 36.9 million ounces in 2006.

Production also fell in the United States in 2005. Output dropped from 40.2 million ounces in 2004 to 39.2 million ounces in 2005. Production is expected to recover to around 40.4 million ounces in 2006.

KGHM is one of the world's largest copper producers, based in Poland. It also is one of the world's largest silver producers, due to its byproduct silver. In 2005 KGHM produced 41.8 million ounces of silver, up from 40.2 million ounces in 2004. Production is expected to be maintained at that level in 2006.

Chilean silver production is rising meanwhile. Chile produced 43.7 million ounces of silver in 2004. Production rose to 45.0 million ounces last year, and could rise to 46.3 million ounces this year.

As mentioned above, Bolivia is set to rapidly increase its production in the next few years. Production totaled 15.0 million ounces in 2005, up slightly from 14.5 million ounces in 2004. Production may reach 17.0 million ounces this year, but in 2007, when several major new mines come onstream in Bolivia, silver output could rise to 25 to 30 million ounces.

Data for Chinese silver production suggests that silver production there rose to 90.0 million ounces in 2005, from 78.8 million ounces in 2004. It is not clear whether these figures include silver refined from imported ore concentrates or scrapped manufactured products. It is clear, however, that mine production is rising in China. Several companies are

Mine Production of Silver

Million Troy Ounces

Year	Australia	Canada	Mexico	Peru	United States	Other Market Economies	Total Market Economies	C.I.S.	Other Transitional Economies	Total	Year
1960	15.2	34.0	44.5	30.8	30.8	46.5	201.8	25.0	8.5	235.3	1960
1961	13.1	31.4	40.3	34.2	34.8	50.1	203.9	25.0	8.0	236.9	1961
1962	17.6	30.7	41.2	33.1	36.8	51.4	210.8	27.0	8.0	245.8	1962
1963	19.6	29.8	42.8	35.2	35.2	51.4	214.0	28.0	8.0	250.0	1963
1964	18.4	29.9	41.7	34.4	36.3	50.8	211.5	29.0	8.0	248.5	1964
1965	17.3	32.3	40.3	36.5	39.8	52.2	218.4	31.0	8.0	257.4	1965
1966	18.9	32.8	42.0	32.8	43.7	55.0	225.2	33.0	8.5	266.7	1966
1967	19.8	37.2	38.3	32.1	32.3	55.0	214.7	35.0	8.5	258.2	1967
1968	21.3	45.0	40.0	36.4	32.7	54.8	230.2	35.0	9.5	274.7	1968
1969	24.5	43.5	42.9	35.9	41.9	60.0	248.7	37.0	10.0	295.7	1969
1970	26.0	44.3	42.8	39.8	45.0	62.7	260.6	41.8	10.0	312.4	1970
1971	21.8	46.0	36.7	38.4	41.6	65.2	249.7	43.3	10.7	303.7	1971
1972	21.9	44.8	37.5	40.2	37.2	73.5	255.1	44.8	10.1	310.0	1972
1973	22.7	47.5	38.8	42.0	37.8	73.0	261.8	46.4	9.4	317.6	1973
1974	21.5	42.8	37.5	34.9	33.8	75.2	245.7	48.0	10.0	303.7	1974
1975	23.3	39.7	38.0	37.5	34.9	76.5	249.9	49.8	10.2	309.9	1975
1976	25.0	41.2	42.6	35.6	34.3	85.4	264.1	49.8	4.1	318.0	1976
1977	27.5	42.2	47.0	39.1	38.2	93.2	287.2	49.8	4.1	341.1	1977
1978	26.1	40.7	50.8	37.0	39.4	98.0	292.0	49.8	6.2	348.0	1978
1979	26.7	36.9	49.4	41.9	37.9	104.7	297.6	49.8	5.0	352.4	1979
1980	25.0	34.4	47.3	44.8	32.3	110.1	293.9	49.8	4.9	348.6	1980
1981	23.9	36.3	53.2	42.6	40.7	109.8	306.4	50.5	4.8	361.8	1981
1982	29.2	42.2	49.8	54.4	40.2	105.8	321.7	52.0	4.7	378.4	1982
1983	33.2	38.7	55.0	55.6	43.4	112.1	338.0	55.0	4.8	397.9	1983
1984	31.3	42.0	63.9	53.3	44.6	116.0	351.0	57.0	5.5	413.5	1984
1985	34.9	38.5	69.2	54.9	39.4	122.5	359.3	63.0	5.7	428.0	1985
1986	32.9	35.0	69.4	59.9	34.2	119.7	351.1	64.0	6.1	421.2	1986
1987	35.9	38.1	69.8	63.6	39.8	121.4	368.6	64.4	6.1	439.1	1987
1988	35.8	44.1	70.0	47.7	53.4	132.6	383.6	64.5	6.4	454.5	1988
1989	37.3	41.3	70.0	56.8	60.8	132.0	398.2	64.7	6.9	469.9	1989
1990	37.8	44.4	67.9	55.5	66.5	129.0	401.1	64.4	7.1	472.5	1990
1991	38.0	40.6	62.7	56.9	61.0	133.4	392.5	64.5	7.6	464.6	1991
1992	40.1	36.3	65.0	48.0	61.0	146.8	397.2	65.4	8.0	470.6	1992
1993	39.1	28.3	61.0	47.0	55.7	141.3	372.3	65.0	8.1	445.3	1993
1994	36.8	23.6	65.0	48.0	54.0	137.9	365.2	62.6	8.2	436.0	1994
1995	32.0	41.3	67.3	51.0	49.5	145.9	387.0	63.9	8.3	459.2	1995
1996	35.0	42.0	75.0	55.0	50.0	146.5	403.6	64.5	8.6	476.7	1996
1997	38.7	39.4	81.0	63.0	59.0	147.3	428.4	57.0	8.8	494.2	1997
1998	50.8	37.9	85.9	61.4	62.4	158.1	456.5	50.6	9.0	516.1	1998
1999	57.7	39.6	83.0	67.1	65.3	160.1	472.8	58.1	9.0	539.9	1999
2000	68.4	39.0	88.3	78.4	65.6	160.5	500.2	58.7	10.6	569.5	2000
2001	63.3	42.4	97.4	83.0	55.9	167.7	509.8	50.0	50.5	610.3	2001
2002	66.6	45.3	101.0	92.3	43.4	162.6	511.1	54.5	82.0	647.6	2002
2003	60.1	42.1	94.7	93.9	39.9	165.4	496.1	54.5	82.0	632.6	2003
2004	71.0	43.0	99.5	98.4	40.2	168.8	520.9	55.9	80.4	657.1	2004
2005	75.8	36.1	103.3	102.7	39.2	172.4	529.6	-	-	529.6	2005
2006p	80.0	36.9	106.0	105.7	40.4	176.0	545.0	-	-	545.0	2006p

Notes: Totals may not equal the sums of countries due to rounding. 'Other Market Economies' figure includes Poland, Hungary, Romania, Czech Republic, and Slovakia from 1970, and Bulgaria from 1973. NA -- not available.
Sources: U.S. Bureau of Mines, American Bureau of Metals Statistics, Statistics Canada, Silver Institute, Andean Report, Consejo de Recursos Minerales Mexico, Australian Bureau of Mineral Resources, government agencies, trade sources, CPM Group.
March 21, 2006

developing silver-intense mines or are exploring silver deposits in China at present, and increased production is expected in the years ahead.

Secondary Supply

Secondary recovery of silver totaled an estimated 226.1 million ounces in 2005. That was up 4.4% from 216.7 million ounces in 2004. The increase reflected the effects of higher prices on the willingness of holders of silver jewelry, silverware, and old coins to sell these items for their silver content. Secondary recovery of silver from these items is expected to rise another 4.9% to 237.1 million ounces in 2006, as higher silver prices continue to stimulate the sale of some of these materials.

Silver recovery from secondary sources is divided into three source categories: old scrapped fabricated products, coins, and Indian scrap. This division reflects differing characteristics in the flows of metals from these sources.

Old scrap is manufactured goods. Much of the silver recovered in this sector is from photographic solutions, papers, and films. As the use of silver in photography has been declining, there has been some reduction in the recovery of silver from these materials. This has been offset by the recovery of silver from other fabricated products. Silver use in electronics and recyclable batteries has increased in recent years, while the system for reclaiming and recycling these products has improved in many countries. This has helped boost silver recovery from these products. Silver also is being recovered from the manufacturing process scrap at companies that are using silver-treated cotton in t-shirts, underwear, and socks. The scrap from these manufacturing operations is collected, incinerated, and the silver then is recovered. Silver is recovered from a number of other industrial products as well.

In addition to these products, after photography perhaps the largest source of old silver scrap is old jewelry, sterlingware, and silverware. These items tend to have a high silver value relative to their overall product value. The silver value tends to be low in electronic household objects, mirrors, or air conditioning systems with silver brazed connections. The silver value is higher, and far more obvious, in silver jewelry and decorative objects. As a result, these products tend to get recycled. In this area there tends to be a steady flow of relatively low volumes of metal annually being recycled. In 1979 - 1981, when silver prices rose sharply, a large wave of such products was sold for its silver content. It took prices substantially above $20 before this wave of silver-bearing scrap became prominent.

Silver recovery from old scrap rose from 202.0 million ounces in 2004 to 205.0 million ounces in 2005. A further three million ounce increase, to around 208.1 million ounces, is projected for 2006.

Silver melted from old coins, and bullion coins, is estimated to have totaled around 5.0 million ounces per year since 2003, continuing into 2005. There may be some increase, perhaps to around 7.0 million ounces, in 2006, reflecting rising silver prices.

The third category of secondary recovery is silver recovered from scrap in India. Most of this is silver from silver household objects, statues, and jewelry. While this is secondary recovery, refining metal from scrapped jewelry and decorative objects, the Indian market is distinct from the majority of secondary recovery which occurs around the world. Silver recovery in India is much more oriented toward jewelry and silverware held by individuals, as opposed to the spent photographic materials that compose the bulk of secondary recovery elsewhere. As a result, it often is much more price sensitive than scrap recovery elsewhere, and bears being reviewed separately.

Silver recovered from scrap in India rose from 9.7 million ounces in 2004 to 16.1 million ounces in 2005. This reflected higher silver prices stimulating individuals to sell their silver objects for the metal content. This is carrying over into 2006, when Indian scrap recovery is projected to increase further, to 22.0 million ounces.

Annual Secondary Supply

Projected Through 2006

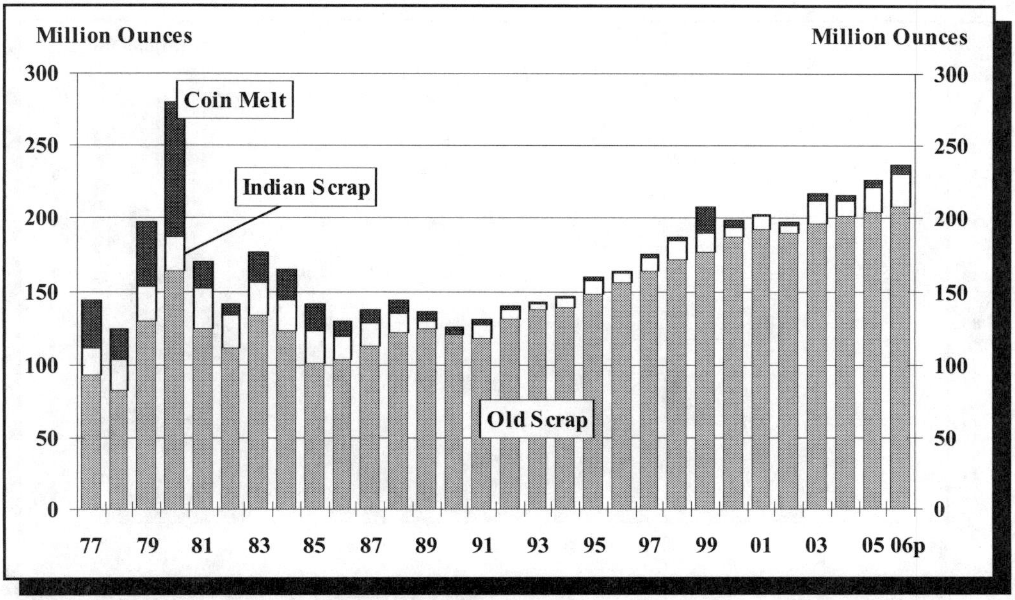

Government Sales

The only government to sell silver, except as a national market maker handling metal for domestic producers or refiners, in 2005 was India. The Indian government has held 86.6 million ounces of silver in inventories since the late 1980s. Most of this, 67.5 million ounces, were held by the Reserve Bank of India, the central bank. Another 19.1 million ounces of silver were held in a separate account, having been confiscated from smugglers in the 1980s. The Indian government announced in early January 2005 that it wished to sell much of this metal. It appeared that the government sought to dispose of the 67.5 million ounces in the Reserve Bank's inventories.

The sales initially got off to a slow start. In early 2005 the price of silver was somewhat weak. Additionally, silver exports from India remain illegal, so that silver brought into the market from abroad, or sold by domestic holders, can threaten to glut the domestic Indian bullion market even as the international market may see rising prices. In this environment, there was a great amount of resistance to purchasing the government silver. The sales program was further hampered by the fact that much of the silver was of low purity, with some of it having lead and other toxic metals alloyed to the silver. This made it more dangerous for small artisans and others to take this metal and use it, as they were not sure what the content was. Some of the metal sold early in the year was said by dealers to have silver purity far less

Indian Silver Market

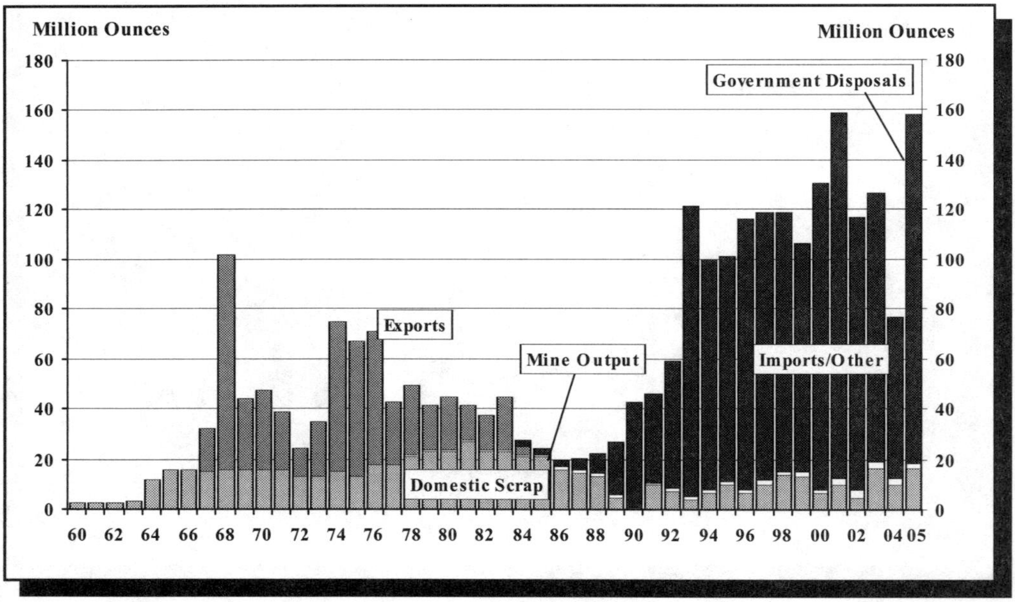

than the government had indicated.

As a result of these conditions, the sales program was relatively slow during the first half of 2005. As prices rose sharply after August, however, demand picked up in the Mumbai dealer market and dealer resistance to purchasing the government silver declined. Sales rose sharply, and for the full year totaled an estimated 35 million ounces of silver.

The government has said that it would pace its sales so as to not negatively affect the domestic market price. It has not been specific in how much metal it wishes to sell in any given period of time, other than to say that it wished to sell the 67.5 million ounces of RBI silver ultimately.

This report places 2006 sales by the Indian government at 32 million ounces, suggesting that if the Reserve Bank of India could sell 35 million ounces in 2005, it probably can complete the disposal program this year.

Other central banks have not been selling silver in 2005, and are not expected to sell silver going forward. As discussed in the Inventories chapter of this report, non-Indian central bank silver reserves are very low now. The U.S. government has sold all but 19.9 million ounces of silver held by the U.S. Treasury. The People's Bank of China, which formerly held silver, sold off the silver it held during the period 2000 through 2004. Other central banks hold around 16.7 million ounces of silver, and have not shown any propensity to sell this metal.

Other Supply

Projected Through 2006

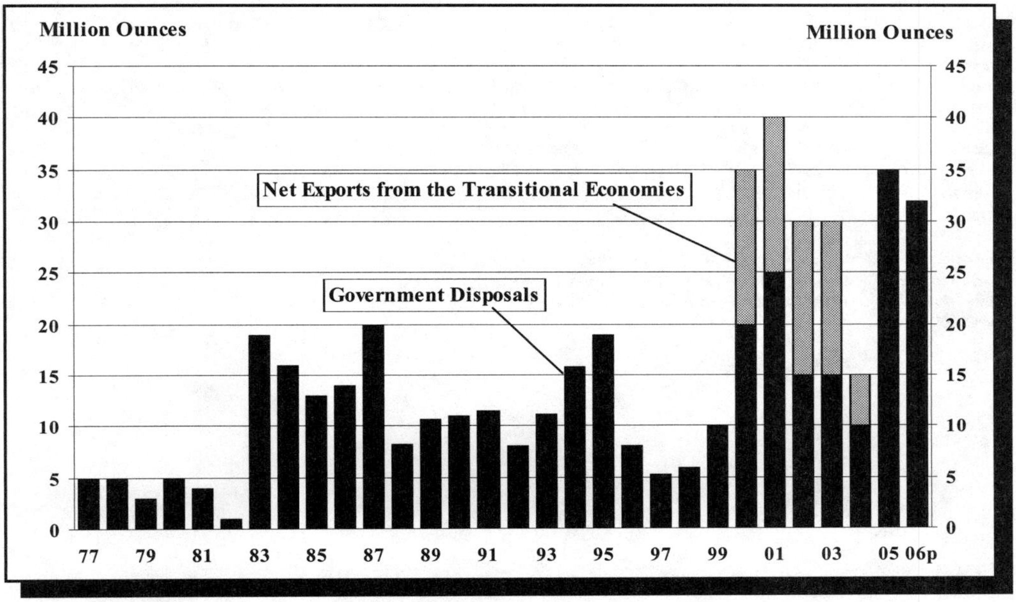

Mine Production By Country

Thousand Troy Ounces

	1979	1980	1981	1982	1983	1984	1985	1986	1987	1988	1989	1990	1991	1992
Africa														
Algeria	100	100	110	110	120	120	120	120	120	120	120	100	100	100
Ghana	20	18	17	17	14	14	14	20	25	25	25	25	50	50
Morocco	3,283	3,154	2,120	2,640	2,850	2,409	2,733	1,566	4,300	7,273	8,300	12,100	12,000	7,500
Namibia	3,617	3,365	3,456	3,150	3,532	3,255	3,400	3,981	3,331	3,472	4,437	2,958	2,926	2,900
South Africa	3,238	7,458	7,569	6,943	6,485	6,980	6,700	7,144	6,691	6,424	5,781	5,176	5,517	5,874
Tunisia	231	233	85	117	90	85	26	30	30	30	30	30	25	25
Zaire	3,420	2,535	2,575	1,905	1,288	1,499	1,520	1,499	1,400	1,400	1,499	2,700	1,890	950
Zambia	914	764	715	887	933	794	625	842	962	942	890	633	547	465
Zimbabwe	978	948	858	919	938	892	800	843	817	895	774	682	623	561
Total	15,801	18,575	17,505	16,688	16,250	16,048	15,938	16,045	17,676	20,581	21,856	24,404	23,678	18,425
Asia														
India	370	366	556	466	508	933	822	1,135	1,221	1,318	1,286	868	900	1,109
Indonesia	793	700	828	1,032	1,047	1,122	1,175	1,371	1,531	1,986	2,012	1,700	2,000	2,300
Iran	—	—	—	—	—	—	—	—	—	—	—	—	—	1,608
Japan	8,932	8,195	9,279	9,042	9,877	10,403	10,914	11,307	9,032	8,102	5,008	4,819	5,488	5,733
Malaysia	433	437	473	522	481	470	522	452	497	641	641	410	500	550
Mongolia	—	—	—	—	—	—	—	—	—	—	—	—	—	—
Myanmar	340	430	450	526	558	575	569	443	400	378	321	230	230	250
Philippines	1,838	1,951	2,021	1,983	1,823	1,574	1,743	1,689	1,638	1,759	1,852	1,528	1,235	926
Saudi Arabia	—	—	—	—	—	—	—	—	—	—	—	—	—	926
South Korea	2,823	2,293	3,147	3,523	3,366	3,759	3,990	2,584	2,823	1,571	2,762	1,700	2,250	2,250
Taiwan	84	96	216	505	344	364	366	405	373	268	268	210	250	260
Turkey	250	200	200	220	219	219	224	286	283	513	513	640	600	2,100
Total	15,863	14,668	17,170	17,819	18,223	19,419	20,325	19,672	17,798	16,536	14,663	12,105	13,453	18,012
Europe														
Bulgaria	805	773	741	805	805	837	837	2,315	2,476	2,733	3,054	3,215	3,054	3,054
Czech Republic/Slovakia	1,126	1,126	1,126	1,062	964	1,029	1,030	1,062	1,100	1,126	1,100	600	580	550
Finland	1,028	1,430	1,215	1,190	980	1,123	1,566	1,193	1,415	997	997	932	964	874
France	2,409	2,374	1,706	986	688	769	866	825	831	678	627	710	739	750
Germany	1,042	1,213	1,263	1,286	1,167	1,225	1,102	884	994	642	700	260	129	65
Greece	1,752	1,671	1,945	1,581	1,797	1,799	1,630	1,726	1,668	1,977	1,668	1,700	1,700	1,700
Greenland	763	771	720	758	607	335	425	385	402	458	470	300	300	0
Hungary	34	34	31	30	30	25	25	25	25	25	25	25	24	24
Ireland	1,058	773	595	352	318	280	277	262	232	177	231	282	338	289
Italy	1,065	1,365	1,779	1,791	2,362	1,560	513	577	449	513	510	360	200	150
Macedonia	—	—	—	—	—	—	—	—	—	—	—	—	—	320
Poland	22,569	24,628	20,577	21,058	21,800	23,900	26,717	26,652	26,717	34,176	34,000	26,750	28,903	28,936
Portugal	35	29	23	23	32	29	108	175	120	120	120	620	650	700
Romania	965	901	805	805	805	773	805	741	642	691	671	386	450	500
Spain	3,168	5,711	6,186	3,789	5,938	5,000	6,405	5,562	6,880	7,298	7,088	7,400	7,500	7,500
Sweden	5,650	5,337	5,171	5,396	5,491	7,677	8,038	7,554	8,520	7,201	6,099	7,000	6,500	7,694
Yugoslavia	5,214	4,789	4,422	3,342	3,987	4,051	5,017	5,702	4,859	4,468	4,276	3,376	2,894	2,600
Total	48,683	52,925	48,305	44,254	47,771	50,412	55,361	55,640	57,330	63,280	61,636	53,916	54,925	55,706

Sources: U.S. Bureau of Mines; American Bureau of Metals Statistics; Statistics Canada; Chamber of Mines of South Africa ; Silver Institute; Central Intelligence Agency; other government and industry sources; CPM Group.
March 20, 2006

1993	1994	1995	1996	1997	1998	1999	2000	2001	2001	2002	2003	2004	2005	
														Africa
100	100	100	100	100	100	100	100	48	48	48	55	55	55	Algeria
60	60	60	60	60	65	67	121	96	96	193	772	772	772	Ghana
6,500	6,500	6,500	6,000	7,100	7,800	8,295	8,295	8,978	8,978	8,906	8,000	7,500	7,500	Morocco
2,300	2,100	2,000	1,875	1,400	1,050	448	518	1,383	1,383	772	1,280	1,300	1,300	Namibia
6,186	6,295	6,400	6,400	6,025	5,171	4,886	5,421	3,524	3,524	3,633	3,215	3,215	3,000	South Africa
32	30	20	20	20	20	25	32	113	113	96	96	100	100	Tunisia
570	520	490	440	100	100	100	100	32	32	50	1,150	2,250	1,500	Zaire
400	400	380	380	390	360	360	360	193	193	225	225	225	300	Zambia
550	540	354	354	212	200	200	100	57	57	64	24	50	25	Zimbabwe
16,698	16,545	16,304	15,629	15,408	14,865	14,481	15,046	14,424	14,424	13,987	14,817	15,467	14,552	Total
														Asia
1,250	1,150	1,617	1,145	1,616	1,640	2,198	1,640	2,926	2,926	2,926	2,950	2,926	2,251	India
2,200	2,200	5,800	7,684	9,370	10,560	9,768	10,648	10,931	10,931	11,253	8,500	7,500	8,500	Indonesia
1,929	1,929	2,315	2,083	1,994	1,894	1,966	1,988	1,929	1,929	1,929	1,929	1,929	1,929	Iran
4,401	4,299	3,525	2,600	2,742	2,660	2,633	2,912	2,588	2,588	2,604	2,600	3,000	3,000	Japan
600	600	640	365	389	389	212	164	164	164	164	164	164	100	Malaysia
—	—	—	621	627	633	640	640	643	643	868	868	868	900	Mongolia
100	100	120	184	253	329	332	332	332	332	332	332	332	300	Myanmar
900	940	1,000	804	745	659	622	746	547	547	289	305	500	500	Philippines
579	547	539	514	543	445	442	422	322	322	450	450	450	450	Saudi Arabia
2,200	2,200	2,200	2,100	1,800	1,800	1,962	1,962	1,962	1,962	1,922	1,922	1,922	1,922	South Korea
260	260	240	225	220	220	220	220	220	220	0	0	0	0	Taiwan
2,000	2,000	2,100	2,000	3,076	3,170	3,233	3,188	3,750	3,750	4,050	3,950	4,180	4,180	Turkey
16,419	16,225	20,096	20,325	23,375	24,400	24,228	24,861	26,314	26,314	26,788	23,971	23,771	24,032	Total
														Europe
1,500	1,200	1,000	1,125	1,020	989	1,009	1,009	804	804	804	1,200	1,600	1,600	Bulgaria
600	630	660	300	250	263	268	268	268	268	268	268	268	268	Czech Republic/Slovakia
830	803	868	900	1,035	955	1,013	1,013	739	739	965	965	965	1,000	Finland
430	430	400	64	0	0	0	0	32	32	32	32	32	32	France
50	50	50	0	0	0	0	0	0	0	0	0	0	0	Germany
1,700	1,700	1,700	965	900	972	991	1,400	2,005	2,005	2,411	2,411	2,500	2,540	Greece
0	0	0	0	0	0	0	0	0	0	0	0	0	0	Greenland
24	24	24	0	0	0	0	0	0	0	0	0	0	0	Hungary
420	390	450	514	466	461	492	537	643	643	161	450	643	643	Ireland
300	300	400	386	393	440	486	490	129	129	129	129	130	130	Italy
320	320	320	320	320	320	320	320	320	320	322	322	321	321	Macedonia
29,800	29,418	31,500	30,543	33,070	35,293	35,129	36,000	38,300	38,300	39,500	39,750	40,200	41,800	Poland
700	700	1,000	1,286	1,330	1,520	1,389	1,245	643	643	611	700	800	800	Portugal
650	700	700	700	700	700	700	700	579	579	579	625	600	650	Romania
5,000	5,300	3,125	3,070	1,812	1,376	1,175	2,265	2,411	2,411	1,608	1,608	1,600	1,600	Spain
8,600	7,877	8,616	9,000	8,836	8,604	8,839	8,983	9,645	9,645	9,613	9,800	10,000	10,000	Sweden
2,100	2,100	1,300	1,930	1,255	1,192	1,216	1,216	1,216	1,216	0	0	0	0	Yugoslavia
53,024	51,942	52,113	51,104	51,386	53,084	53,027	55,445	57,734	57,734	57,001	58,258	59,659	61,384	Total

Mine Production By Country – Continued

Thousand Troy Ounces

	1979	1980	1981	1982	1983	1984	1985	1986	1987	1988	1989	1990	1991	1992
North & Central America														
Canada	36,874	34,390	36,311	42,234	38,692	42,001	38,485	34,980	38,118	44,100	41,310	44,374	40,554	36,277
Costa Rica	2	2	2	2	2	2	2	2	2	2	2	2	2	2
Dominican Republic	2,268	1,642	2,062	2,112	1,270	1,222	1,609	1,318	1,149	1,400	700	700	700	750
El Salvador	152	146	137	86	23	22	20	17	17	17	17	17	17	17
Guatemala	10	10	8	8	3	0	0	0	0	0	0	0	0	0
Honduras	2,186	1,721	1,665	2,050	2,587	2,698	2,765	1,747	741	796	796	1,000	1,000	1,200
Mexico	49,408	47,344	53,204	49,841	55,000	63,900	69,200	69,400	69,800	70,000	70,000	67,900	62,700	65,000
Nicaragua	388	163	82	76	63	50	52	26	29	23	23	40	50	55
United States	37,896	32,329	40,683	40,248	43,431	44,592	39,357	34,221	39,790	53,402	60,797	66,488	60,984	60,957
Total	129,184	117,747	134,154	136,657	141,071	154,487	151,490	141,711	149,646	169,740	173,645	180,521	166,007	164,258
Oceania														
Australia	26,749	24,981	23,920	29,161	33,212	31,250	34,916	32,890	35,912	35,815	37,295	37,800	38,000	40,123
Fiji	9	9	9	19	12	13	15	15	0	0	34	25	16	20
New Zealand	2	1	1	1	0	0	41	41	0	59	156	275	355	400
Papua New Guinea	1,434	1,187	1,365	1,394	1,531	1,426	1,487	1,802	2,004	2,100	1,966	2,600	3,215	3,530
Total	28,194	26,178	25,295	30,575	34,755	32,689	36,459	34,748	37,916	37,974	39,451	40,700	41,586	44,073
South America														
Argentina	2,209	2,357	2,518	2,684	2,502	1,983	2,170	2,135	1,899	1,608	1,547	2,200	2,200	1,500
Bolivia	5,742	6,099	6,394	5,472	6,024	4,559	3,614	3,057	4,565	7,451	8,586	9,984	10,835	9,077
Brazil	1,065	737	765	748	750	2,275	2,301	1,913	1,966	2,252	2,056	1,100	1,000	5,000
Chile	8,740	9,596	11,608	12,288	14,955	15,776	16,642	16,080	16,068	16,301	17,701	20,416	21,733	33,115
Colombia	99	146	134	137	134	128	155	187	167	211	220	210	200	267
Ecuador	70	70	32	9	3	3	2	2	2	2	2	0	0	130
Peru	41,900	44,815	42,553	54,379	55,565	53,257	54,854	59,924	63,576	47,657	56,830	55,548	56,882	48,000
Total	59,825	63,820	64,004	75,717	79,933	77,981	79,738	83,298	88,243	75,482	86,942	89,458	92,850	97,089
Subtotal	297,550	293,913	306,433	321,710	338,003	351,036	359,311	351,114	368,608	383,593	398,193	401,104	392,499	397,562
Transitional Economies														
China	1,928	1,928	2,091	2,252	2,300	2,600	2,800	3,214	3,214	3,500	4,000	5,500	6,000	6,400
East Germany	1,543	1,511	1,447	1,447	1,382	1,286	1,318	1,318	1,318	1,286	1,298	—	—	—
North Korea	1,543	1,447	1,286	965	1,100	1,600	1,600	1,600	1,600	1,600	1,600	1,600	1,600	1,600
Russia	—	—	—	—	—	—	—	—	—	—	—	—	—	27,328
Kazakhstan	—	—	—	—	—	—	—	—	—	—	—	—	—	32,151
Tajikistan	—	—	—	—	—	—	—	—	—	—	—	—	—	2,251
Uzbekistan	—	—	—	—	—	—	—	—	—	—	—	—	—	2,894
Armenia	—	—	—	—	—	—	—	—	—	—	—	—	—	482
Kyrgyzstan	—	—	—	—	—	—	—	—	—	—	—	—	—	—
Other C.I.S.	—	—	—	—	—	—	—	—	—	—	—	—	—	322
Soviet Union	49,834	49,834	50,500	52,000	55,000	57,000	63,000	64,000	64,400	64,500	64,700	64,400	64,500	—
Total	54,848	54,720	55,324	56,664	59,782	62,486	68,718	70,132	70,532	70,886	71,598	71,500	72,100	73,427
WORLD TOTAL	352,398	348,633	361,757	378,374	397,785	413,522	428,029	421,246	439,141	454,479	469,791	472,604	464,599	470,989

1993	1994	1995	1996	1997	1998	1999	2000	2001	2001	2002	2003	2004	2005	
														North & Central America
28,255	23,613	41,306	42,041	39,351	37,892	39,587	38,979	42,440	42,440	45,254	42,122	43,001	36,134	Canada
2	2	2	2	2	25	17	9	16	16	16	16	16	16	Costa Rica
200	600	677	650	520	364	100	100	2	2	2	2	2	2	Dominican Republic
20	20	25	25	25	25	25	26	26	26	26	26	26	26	El Salvador
0	0	0	0	0	0	0	0	0	0	0	0	0	0	Guatemala
777	888	971	1,170	1,379	1,381	1,496	1,697	1,506	1,506	1,704	1,750	1,750	1,800	Honduras
61,000	65,000	67,300	75,000	81,000	85,860	83,000	88,300	97,400	97,400	101,000	94,700	99,450	103,315	Mexico
55	55	50	77	180	161	177	177	133	133	96	100	100	100	Nicaragua
55,655	54,001	49,500	50,000	59,000	62,422	65,293	65,620	55,942	55,942	43,404	39,867	40,189	39,224	United States
145,964	144,179	159,831	168,965	181,457	188,130	189,695	194,907	197,465	197,465	191,502	178,583	184,533	180,618	Total
														Oceania
39,100	36,750	32,000	35,000	38,700	50,810	57,700	68,449	63,337	63,337	66,550	60,100	71,000	75,833	Australia
20	20	67	63	83	73	88	80	68	68	68	50	50	40	Fiji
460	887	900	960	1,021	736	775	804	804	804	1,029	1,030	1,000	1,000	New Zealand
3,700	2,112	2,095	1,898	1,553	1,854	2,109	2,623	2,315	2,315	2,411	2,410	2,000	2,400	Papua New Guinea
43,280	39,769	35,062	37,921	41,357	53,474	60,672	71,956	66,524	66,524	70,058	63,590	74,050	79,273	Total
														South America
900	900	800	900	900	1,440	1,615	1,615	4,913	4,913	4,051	4,305	4,823	5,000	Argentina
10,700	11,317	13,664	12,668	12,800	12,925	13,632	14,104	14,146	14,146	14,468	14,490	14,468	15,000	Bolivia
5,000	4,900	4,200	3,800	3,360	3,394	3,523	3,523	1,318	1,318	1,479	1,480	1,480	1,500	Brazil
32,900	31,000	33,500	36,800	35,000	43,000	44,400	40,000	43,500	43,500	39,000	42,200	43,700	45,000	Chile
240	255	230	230	127	129	132	132	257	257	225	300	300	300	Colombia
170	200	220	240	228	233	235	235	235	235	235	235	235	250	Ecuador
47,000	48,000	51,000	55,000	63,000	61,425	67,138	78,370	83,000	83,000	92,260	93,910	98,375	102,662	Peru
96,910	96,572	103,614	109,638	115,415	122,545	130,673	137,978	147,369	147,369	151,718	156,920	163,381	169,712	Total
372,295	365,232	387,020	403,582	428,398	456,497	472,777	500,193	509,830	509,830	511,053	496,139	520,861	529,571	Subtotal
														Transitional Economies
6,450	6,550	6,700	6,970	7,200	7,430	7,430	8,991	8,991	48,869	80,377	80,377	78,769	90,022	China
—	—	—	—	—	—	—	—	—	—	—	—	—	—	East Germany
1,600	1,600	1,600	1,600	1,600	1,600	1,600	1,600	1,600	1,608	1,608	1,608	1,608	NA	North Korea
26,900	25,300	25,933	24,636	20,900	17,723	18,989	18,742	18,742	19,933	19,933	19,933	20,000	NA	Russia
32,100	31,500	32,130	33,737	30,370	27,333	33,439	34,275	34,275	24,113	28,678	28,678	30,000	NA	Kazakhstan
2,300	2,200	2,200	2,222	2,222	2,222	2,222	2,222	2,222	2,222	2,222	2,222	2,222	NA	Tajikistan
2,900	2,800	2,800	2,828	2,400	2,208	2,366	2,366	2,366	2,572	2,572	2,572	2,572	NA	Uzbekistan
500	500	500	500	500	500	500	500	500	500	500	500	500	NA	Armenia
—	—	—	300	300	300	300	300	300	300	300	300	300	NA	Kyrgyzstan
300	300	300	310	310	310	310	310	310	310	310	310	310	NA	Other C.I.S.
—	—	—	—	—	—	—	—	—	—	—	—	—	—	Soviet Union
73,050	70,750	72,163	73,102	65,802	59,627	67,157	69,306	69,306	100,427	136,500	136,500	136,281	90,022	Total
445,345	435,982	459,182	476,684	494,200	516,124	539,933	569,499	579,136	610,257	647,553	632,640	657,142	619,593	WORLD TOTAL

Secondary and Other Supplies

Million Troy Ounces

Year	Old Scrap	Demon-etized Coin	Secondary Indian Scrap used Domestically	South Asian Exports	Government Disposals	Net Exports from T.E.	Total Secondary and Other	U.S. Treasury Sales	U.S. Treasury Coinage	Total	Year
1960	40.0	10.0	2.0	—	12.0	10.0	74.0	22.0	46.0	142.0	1960
1961	43.0	20.0	2.0	—	7.0	55.0	127.0	63.0	56.0	246.0	1961
1962	47.0	20.0	2.0	—	4.0	25.0	98.0	1.0	77.0	176.0	1962
1963	50.0	15.0	3.0	—	10.0	—	78.0	25.0	112.0	215.0	1963
1964	54.0	20.0	12.0	—	20.0	—	106.0	151.0	203.0	460.0	1964
1965	57.0	30.0	16.0	—	17.0	9.0	129.0	80.0	320.0	529.0	1965
1966	61.0	28.0	16.0	—	10.0	10.0	125.0	143.0	54.0	322.0	1966
1967	59.0	35.0	15.0	17.0	5.0	8.0	139.0	195.0	44.0	378.0	1967
1968	75.0	50.0	16.0	86.0	15.0	—	242.0	180.0	37.0	459.0	1968
1969	80.0	50.0	16.0	28.0	—	11.0	185.0	89.0	19.0	293.0	1969
1970	55.0	25.0	16.0	31.0	10.0	10.9	147.9	67.0	1.0	215.9	1970
1971	68.0	20.0	16.0	23.0	7.0	—	134.0	—	—	134.0	1971
1972	73.0	15.0	13.0	11.0	12.0	—	124.0	—	—	124.0	1972
1973	72.0	15.0	13.0	22.0	46.0	—	168.0	—	—	168.0	1973
1974	82.0	35.0	15.0	60.0	21.0	—	213.0	—	—	213.0	1974
1975	90.0	20.0	13.0	54.0	15.0	—	192.0	—	—	192.0	1975
1976	92.0	72.0	18.0	53.0	11.0	—	246.0	—	—	246.0	1976
1977	93.0	33.0	18.0	25.0	5.0	—	174.0	—	—	174.0	1977
1978	82.0	21.0	21.0	28.0	9.0	—	161.0	—	—	161.0	1978
1979	130.0	45.0	23.0	18.0	3.0	—	219.0	—	—	219.0	1979
1980	164.0	94.0	23.0	21.0	5.0	—	307.0	—	—	307.0	1980
1981	125.0	18.0	27.0	14.0	4.0	—	188.0	—	—	188.0	1981
1982	111.0	7.0	23.0	14.0	1.0	—	156.0	—	—	156.0	1982
1983	133.4	20.1	23.0	21.0	19.0	—	216.5	—	—	216.5	1983
1984	123.5	20.1	21.0	1.0	16.0	—	181.6	—	—	181.6	1984
1985	101.5	18.4	21.0	—	13.0	—	153.9	—	—	153.9	1985
1986	103.4	9.9	16.0	—	14.0	—	143.3	—	—	143.3	1986
1987	113.3	10.1	14.5	—	20.0	—	157.9	—	—	157.9	1987
1988	121.9	8.8	13.2	—	8.3	—	152.2	—		152.2	1988
1989	125.0	6.4	4.8	—	10.7	—	146.9	—	—	146.9	1989
1990	120.0	6.0	0.0	—	11.0	—	137.0	—	—	137.0	1990
1991	117.6	4.0	9.6	—	11.5	—	142.7	—	—	142.7	1991
1992	130.5	3.0	7.2	—	8.1	—	148.8	—	—	148.8	1992
1993	137.1	2.0	3.8	—	11.2	—	154.1	—	—	154.1	1993
1994	138.4	1.3	6.5	—	15.8	—	162.0	—	—	162.0	1994
						—					
1995	148.1	1.5	9.6	—	19.0	—	178.2	—	—	178.2	1995
1996	155.5	1.7	6.4	—	8.1	—	171.7	—	—	171.7	1996
1997	163.3	1.7	10.0	—	5.3	—	180.3	—	—	180.3	1997
1998	171.5	2.5	13.5	—	6.0	—	193.5	—	—	193.5	1998
1999	176.5	18.5	12.9	—	10.0	—	217.9	—	—	217.9	1999
2000	187.1	6.0	6.4	—	20.0	15.0	234.5	—	—	234.5	2000
2001	192.0	2.0	9.6	—	25.0	15.0	243.6	—	—	243.6	2001
2002	190.0	3.0	4.8	—	15.0	15.0	227.8	—	—	227.8	2002
2003	196.0	5.0	16.1	—	15.0	15.0	247.1	—	—	247.1	2003
2004	202.0	5.0	9.7	—	10.0	5.0	231.7	—	—	231.7	2004
2005	205.0	5.0	16.1	—	35.0	—	261.1	—	—	261.1	2005
2006p	208.1	7.0	22.0	—	32.0	—	269.1	—	—	269.1	2006p

Note: "Government Disposals" includes silver used in coins from stocks and bullion sales from governments other than the United States for the years through 1970. The U.S. Treasury bullion sales and the use of silver from the U.S. Treasury Stocks in coins during the 1960s are separated. After 1970, U.S. government bullion sales and use of government stocks in coinage are included in the "Government Disposals" category.

T.E. -- Transitional Economies.

Sources: U.S. Bureau of Mines; Handy & Harman; Samuel Montagu; Silver Institute; trade sources; CPM Group

March 14, 2006

Indian Silver Supply

Troy Ounces

	1987	1988	1989	1990	1991
Mine Production	1,221,727	1,318,179	1,286,028	868,069	900,220
Secondary Supply	14,467,815	13,181,787	4,822,605	—	9,645,210
Imports	4,404,646	8,037,675	20,897,955	42,052,910	35,237,167
Total	20,094,188	22,537,641	27,006,588	42,920,979	45,782,597
% Change Year Ago	—	12.2%	19.8%	58.9%	6.7%

	1992	1993	1994	1995	1996
Mine Production	1,109,000	1,250,000	1,150,000	1,617,000	1,145,000
Secondary Supply	7,233,908	3,800,000	6,500,000	9,645,210	6,430,140
Imports	50,894,558	113,528,526	85,844,169	78,458,401	106,439,352
Other	—	3,210,116	7,295,890	11,206,577	2,305,610
Total	59,253,740	121,788,643	100,790,060	100,927,188	116,320,101
% Change Year Ago	29.4%	105.5%	-17.2%	0.1%	15.3%

	1997	1998	1999	2000	2001
Mine Production	1,616,000	1,640,000	2,198,000	1,639,686	2,925,714
Secondary Supply	9,966,717	13,503,336	12,860,280	6,430,140	9,645,210
Imports	106,258,875	102,776,845	90,455,994	122,976,428	146,665,937
Other	1,250,211	750,130	964,521	32,151	160,754
Total	119,091,803	118,670,310	106,478,795	131,078,405	159,397,615
% Change Year Ago	2.4%	-0.4%	-10.3%	23.1%	21.6%

	2002	2003	2004	2005
Mine Production	2,925,714	2,950,000	2,926,000	2,251,000
Secondary Supply	4,800,000	16,100,000	9,650,000	16,100,000
Imports	109,137,801	107,704,845	64,301,600	104,490,000
Other	—	—	—	—
Government	—	—	—	35,366,000
Total	116,863,515	126,754,845	76,877,600	158,207,000
% Change Year Ago	-26.7%	8.5%	-39.3%	105.8%

Note: Other includes unofficial imports.
Source: CPM Group, Indian trade sources.
March 21, 2006

South Asian Silver Trade

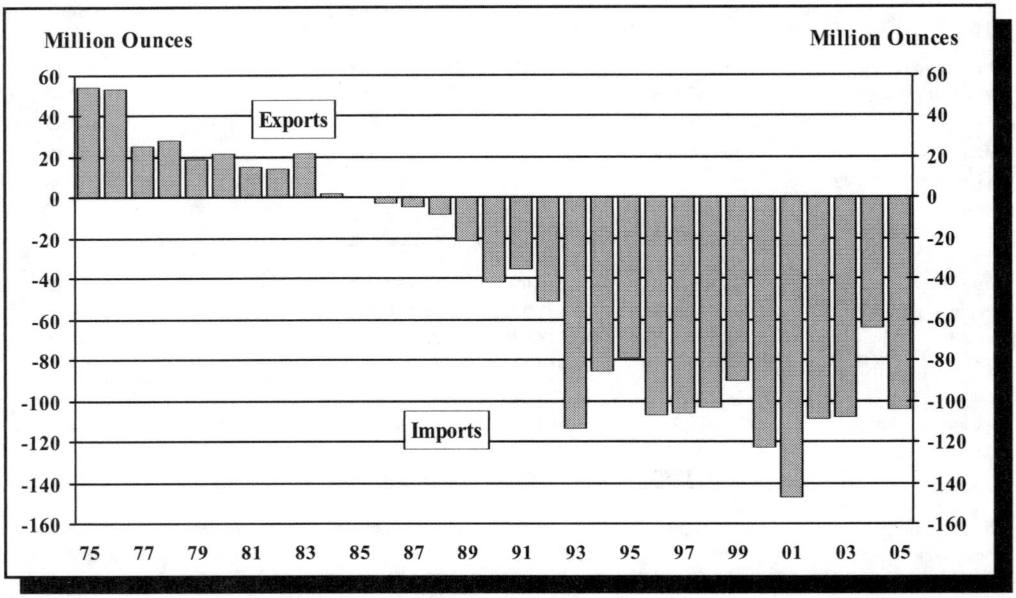

Fabrication Demand

Fabrication Demand

The total use of silver in fabricated products was roughly flat in 2005. Total silver use is estimated to have been 806.4 million ounces, up a slight 0.7% from 800.9 million ounces in 2004. This total masks a major shift. Indian market sources report an enormous increase in silver use in eletroplating in 2005. Much of this was for electroplated jewelry and gift items. India has a long tradition of using silver in large volumes in jewelry and silver decorative objects, statues, household items, and such. There was a shift reported in this area in 2005. Indian market participants estimate that the use of silver in such eletroplated objects, which also includes things like mirrors and electronic components, may have increased from 8.0 million ounces in 2004 to as much as 48.2 million ounces in 2005. Furthermore, they suggest that demand for these products - much of which is a substitute for more expensive solid silver gift items now that silver prices have risen sharply - may remain high in 2006.

This 40.2 million ounce increase in this category is solely responsible for the increase in silver demand last year. Demand declined in photography, other jewelry and silverware categories, and

Annual Total Demand

Projected Through 2006.

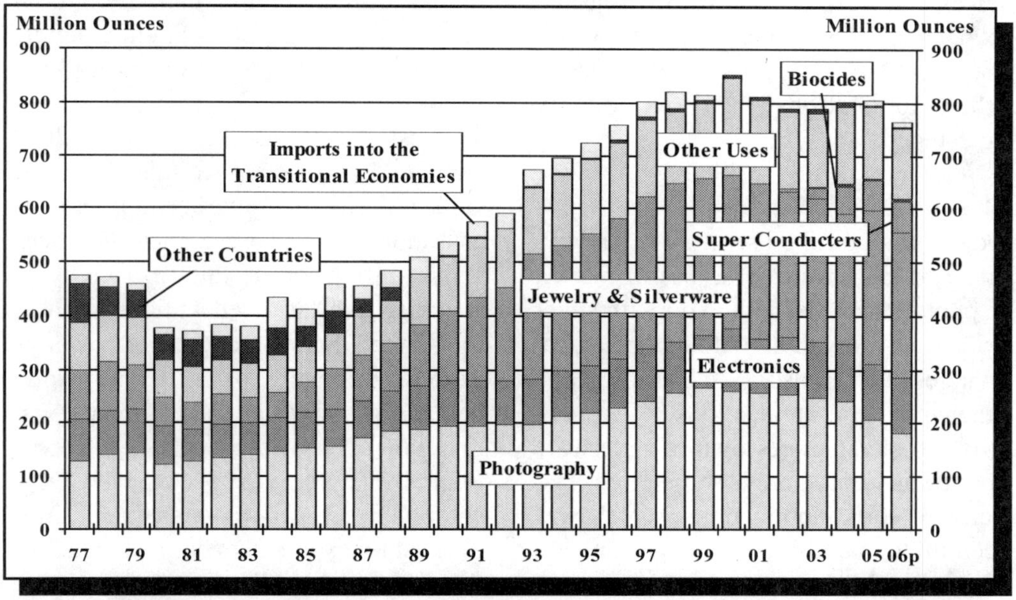

Note: Photography, jewelry and silverware, electronics, and "other" industrial uses includes Canada from 1979, Mexico from 1982, Hong Kong from 1985, Thailand from 1986, India from 1987, South Korea, Australia, Brazil, Chile, Argentina, Peru, Colombia, Pakistan, and Bangladesh from 1989, and Taiwan from 1990.

industrial applications such as bearings, solders and brazing alloys, and ethylene oxide catalysts. Demand rose modestly in electronics and electrical components. Excluding this increased Indian use in electroplated objects, silver use on a world total basis might have declined around 4.3% last year. However, this one sector's increased silver use to extremely high levels instead kept silver use on a world total basis relatively stable.

Silver use in fact is projected to decline this year, roughly 5.0% to around 765.7 million ounces, even as the use of silver in eletroplated objects in India remains strong. Silver use in photography is expected to continue to decline, as parts of this industry shifts to digital imaging. Jewelry and silverware use is projected to decline. Electronics and battery use may rise about 2.3%, while silver use in other applications may be roughly unchanged.

The price of silver clearly has had a major effect on the use of silver in jewelry and silverware. The loss of market in photography has less to do with silver prices and more to do with technological changes. Silver use in electronics and other industrial applications is less sensitive to silver prices than is silverware and jewelry, but there is some price elasticity in some applications, which was seen in 2005 and is likely to continue to be seen in 2006.

Photography

Silver use in photography is estimated to have totaled 208.2 million ounces in 2005. This would have been down 14.2% from 242.7 million ounces in 2004. Silver use in photography is estimated to have peaked at 267.2 million ounces in 1999, and to have declined each year since then. The declines in the early part of this period, from 2000 into 2003, were relatively modest, on the order of 0.5% - 2.5% per annum. During this time the weakness in demand did not reflect a shift to digital imaging so much as it did a glut of silver-bearing films and papers during a period of recessionary economic conditions and reduced travel for vacations. With wars and the SARS epidemic in Asia, starting in 2001 and continuing until 2006, travel was off sharply; photographic picture taking is related to vacation taking.

The loss of markets gained pace in 2004 and 2005, however. At this time, the shift to digital imaging began to emerge as a more potent factor. There had been some shift prior to this, especially in wealthy, industrialized nations such as the United States, Japan, and parts of Europe. In many parts of the world demand for silver-bearing film still was rising at double-digit rates, however. Digital imaging was too expensive and complicated for many consumers. Over the past two years, this has changed, and the shift to digital imaging for picture taking has gained pace around the world, including in emerging market economies.

This trend, primarily reflecting the loss of the conventional photographic film market to digital imaging, is expected to continue in 2006. Silver use in photography is projected to decline 12.3% to 182.5 million ounces in 2006.

The decline in silver use in photography has not been as dramatic as some market observers had expected. While silver-halide technology is rapidly losing market share to digital imaging in the taking of pictures, conventional silver-based films and papers are holding up better in other segments of the imaging market. Silver use in film has been declining roughly 20% - 28% per annum over the past few years.

Silver use in photographic paper meanwhile has held up far better. In fact, there has been an increase in the number of prints made from digital images, as this has become easier and less expensive, so that demand for silver-bearing paper actually has increased in some markets. Longer term silver bearing papers are facing the same threat as silver-bearing films. Papers may do better for a longer period of time, however, for several reasons. For one thing, prints made on non-silver photographic papers generally speaking are not as attractive and crisp of images. People who thought that photographs printed on these papers would look as good as photos printed on traditional silver-bearing papers have shown some consumer dissatisfaction.

Photographic Demand

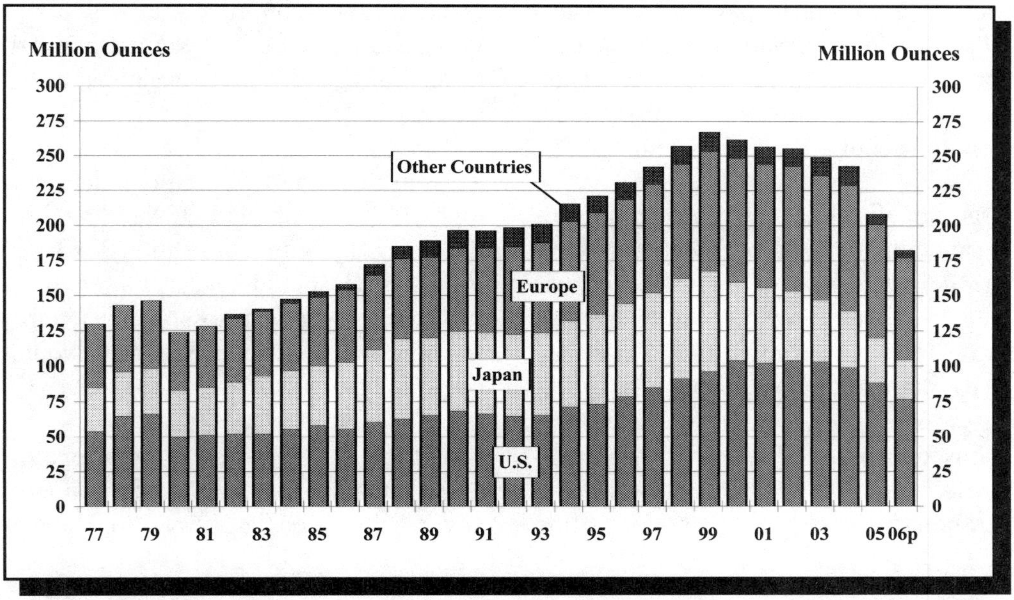

The pictures also have begun fading. Photo printer paper manufacturers have advertised enhanced quality papers and systems that are said to last much longer, but by dating the useful life of these images - generally saying they will last for a few decades - these manufacturers are focusing consumer attention on the fact that such images will not hold up as well as the old pictures they have of ancestors, in some cases more than a century old.

Aiding this process of keeping consumers interested in using traditional silver-bearing papers for the prints made of digital imaging has been some very effective marketing which has helped stimulate the use of traditional papers to print digital images. Many of the early introducers of digital cameras and imaging systems focused on technology-oriented consumers - shutterbugs and other early innovators, mostly males, who would be willing to pay large amounts of money for a myriad of electronic gear to use in capturing and processing images, and then make the effort to learn how to use all of the equipment.

Traditional photo imaging companies meanwhile focused on what they term the demographics of photographic use by consumers in positioning their products. They have known that while men may take many photos, generally speaking women order the prints. They have focused also on the desire of many consumers to have simple, easy, and straight-forward ways of generating these prints. Finally, they focused on the quality issues related to photos printed on silver-bearing paper versus print-outs from home computers. Accordingly, they positioned their products to allow people with digital images to easily and cheaply order prints, both on-line and through a range of other arrangements. They have developed kiosks at stores to facilitate this. Some have developed systems in which a consumer can take a picture, perhaps of a grandchild, in one city or country, and have it developed and delivered to a grandparent in another city or country, for pick-up at the local grocery store or drugstore. By keeping the methods of having prints made low cost and easy to accomplish, they have facilitated an increased number of prints being made, most often on conventional silver-bearing paper.

These developments have led to conditions in the photographic market in 2004 and 2005, and continuing, in which silver use in films, used to capture images, is declining, while silver use in papers is strong.

This bifurcation of the commercial photographic imaging market, wedding digital imaging with conventional silver-based prints, should not surprise anyone. It is exactly what many companies in the imaging industry have predicted would occur for the past 25 years.

Silver use also is strong in other photographic market segments. The amount of silver being used in X-rays, for dental, medical, and industrial applications, is rising. The use of silver in graphic arts, advertising, and print media such as magazines also rose in 2005. Silver use in movie film also is rising strongly, according to manufacturers.

Silver in Photography in 2005

Million ounces

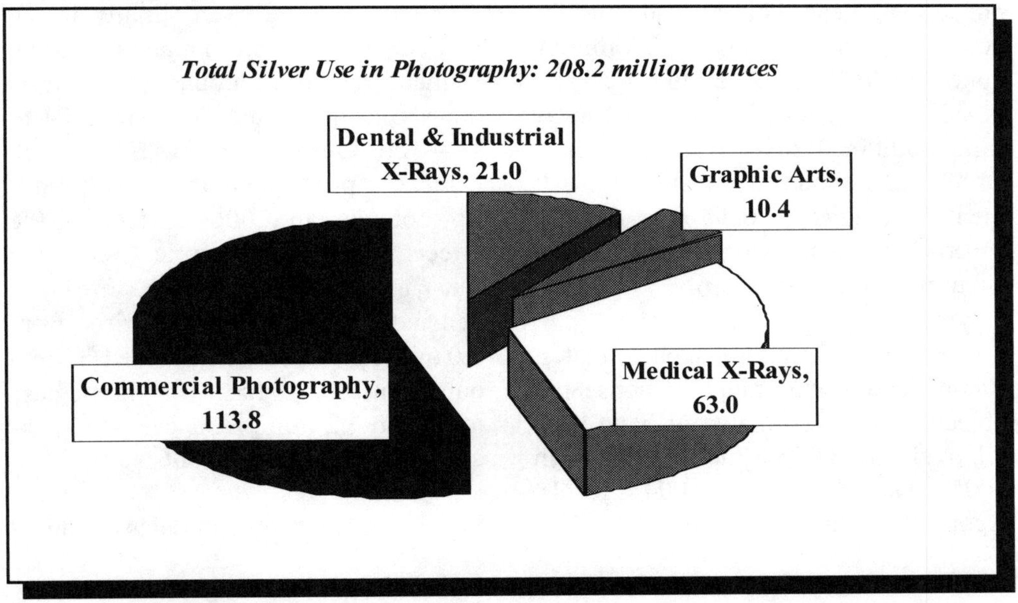

Jewelry and Silverware

Silver use in jewelry and silverware is estimated to have risen 19.0% to 288.8 million ounces in 2005, from 242.8 million ounces. The increase is entirely due to the rise in silver use in eletroplated objects and jewelry in India, which is estimated to have risen from around 8.0 million ounces in 2004 to 48.2 million ounces in 2005. Without that increase, demand for silver in jewelry and silverware would have declined approximately 0.9% to 240.6 million ounces last year.

Demand for silver for use in these products is projected to drop 6.0% in 2006, to 271.6 million ounces.

The big story in silver use in jewelry and silverware in 2005 was in India. Demand for silver in jewelry is estimated to have been flat at 19.3 million ounces last year. This was, it must be noted, down from a peak of 32.2 million ounces in 2002, and 22.5 million ounces in 2003. There has been a shift away from traditional silver jewelry, both as an adornment, and as a form of investment or savings, in India over the past several years. This already had reduced silver use in jewelry sharply.

Silver use in silverware, such as plates, statues, and a wide range of household objects, also is estimated to have been relatively flat at 25.6 million ounces in 2005, unchanged from 2004's levels. Again, this was down from 48.2 - 48.3 million ounces per year estimated to have been converted into these products from 2001 through 2003.

Silver use in eletroplated objects, including what many in the Indian market call imitation or fashion jewelry and gift items, reportedly saw enormous increases in 2005. Demand for silver in these products is estimated to have been around 8.0 million ounces in 2004. It is estimated to have risen fivefold to around 48.2 million ounces in 2005. It is expected to remain high in 2006. In addition to the effects of high prices for silver and a shift away from using such products as a form of investing in silver, the imposition of value added taxes on gold and silver jewelry and solid metal household objects is said to have contributed to this shift.

Silver use in jewelry and silverware, including silver electroplated objects, is estimated to have risen slightly in the United States and Japan in 2005. Demand rose from around 14.1 million ounces in the United States in 2004 to 14.4 million ounces in 2005. U.S. demand is projected to drop to 13.6 million ounces in 2006, reflecting the effects of rising silver prices since the final four months of 2005. In Japan demand is estimated to have risen from 3.0 million ounces in 2004 to 3.1 million ounces in 2005. A further slight increase to around 3.2 million ounces is projected for Japanese use in 2006.

Silver use in these products declined

from 72.7 million ounces in 2004 to 67.7 million ounces in Europe in 2005. A further decline to 64.3 million ounces is projected for this year. The largest user of silver in these applications in Europe is Italy, which saw silver use in sterlingware, its major use, declined from 42.8 million ounces in 2004 to 38.5 million ounces in 2005. A further decline, to around 36.5 million ounces, is projected for 2006. Silverplating was relatively flat, while jewelry use of silver declined from 6.5 million ounces in 2004 to 6.0 million ounces in 2005. The Italian sterlingware and jewelry industries are seeing lower consumer demand for their products coupled with a shift in the site of manufacturing to countries such as Turkey, India, Thailand, and China.

Silver use also declined in other European countries in these applications. Demand was off in Germany and the United Kingdom, but up modestly in France. The full effect of higher silver prices, including prices having strengthened in euro and pounds sterling terms, is expected to be seen in 2006, when demand may weaken further.

Jewelry and Silverware Demand for Silver

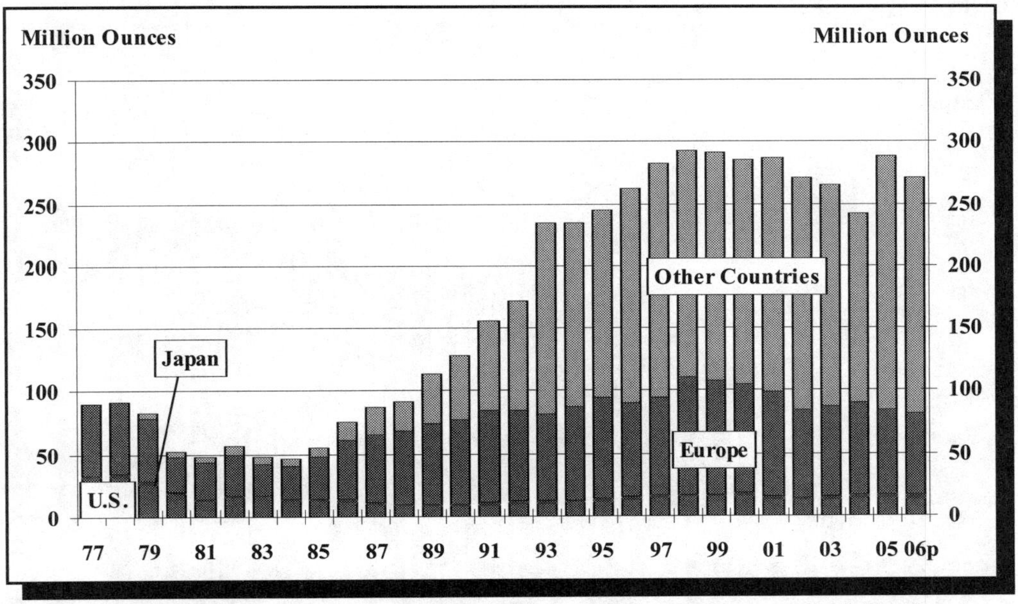

Note: Other Countries includes Mexico from 1982, Hong Kong from 1985, Thailand from 1986, India from 1987, Korea from 1989, and Taiwan from 1990.

Electronics and Batteries

Silver use in electronic and electrical components, and in batteries is estimated to have declined about 4.4% in 2005 to 101.8 million ounces. That was down from 106.6 million ounces in 2004. Silver use in these applications peaked in 2000 at the height of the high-tech boom. In that year silver use was around 115.3 million ounces. Demand fell a sharp 11.2% the following year, to 102.4 million ounces. It had been between 104.4 and 106.6 million ounces annually for three years from 2002 through 2004, prior to last year's decline. The decline in 2005 may have reflected cyclical weakness in some applications, and not the start of another downturn. Silver use in these applications may rise another 2.4% to 104.3 million ounces in 2006.

Demand is suffering slightly from the effects of higher silver prices, but for the most part these uses tend to be relatively price inelastic. Additionally, in some applications silver is being substituted for gold and palladium, which are much more expensive and also have seen their prices increase sharply in recent years. Thus, while silver price increases may be distasteful to companies in these, and other industries, they tend to be less distasteful than some alternatives.

Silver use in these applications increasingly is shifting to Asian nations. Some of the conversion of silver into plating

Electronics and Batteries

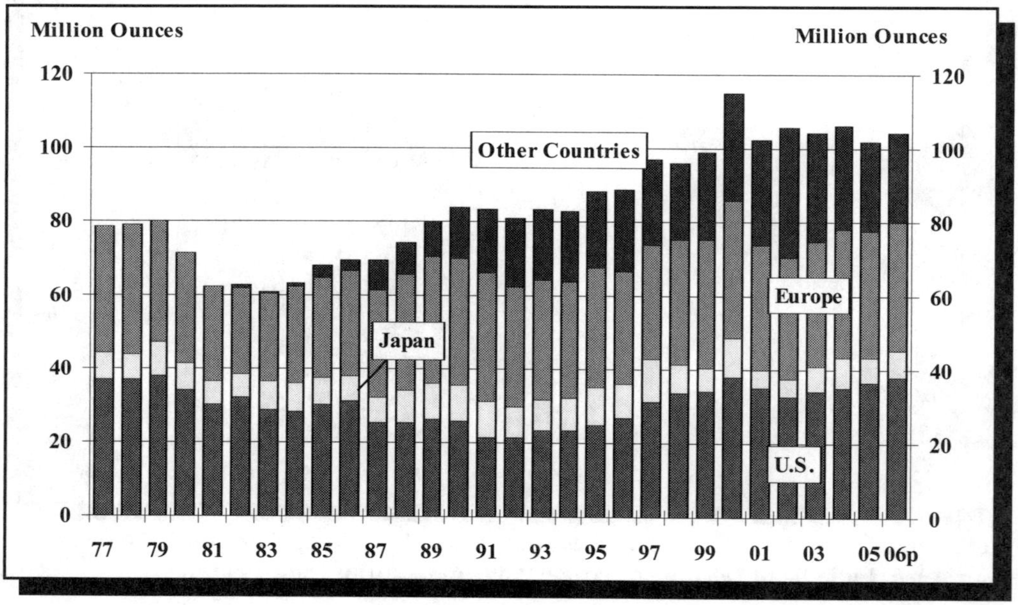

salts, solutions, sputtering targets, and other semi-fabricated forms for use in electronics component manufacturing occurs in Europe, the United States, and Japan. Increasingly, even the silver conversion is shifting to industrializing nations such as India, China, Taiwan, and other nations.

Silver use in batteries meanwhile faces a mixed future. In some applications silver-bearing battery technologies are facing stiff competition from newer battery types that do not use silver. In other applications silver-bearing batteries appear to be gathering market share. Overall, the use of silver in batteries is estimated to be rising modestly, a trend that should continue for the next several years.

Other Uses

Another 193.6 million ounces of silver were used in a wide range of manufactured products in 2005. This was down 3.8% from 201.3 million ounces. Demand is projected to be roughly flat in 2006, around 193.4 million ounces. The rise in silver prices is having a modest effect on many of these applications. Cyclical shifts in some of these industries also is reducing silver requirements on a temporary basis.

One of the most important segments of this use is as a catalyst in the manufacture of ethylene oxide, a basic feedstock for the manufacture of polyethylene. Silver also is used in brazing alloys and solders, mirrors, other chemical process

Other Uses

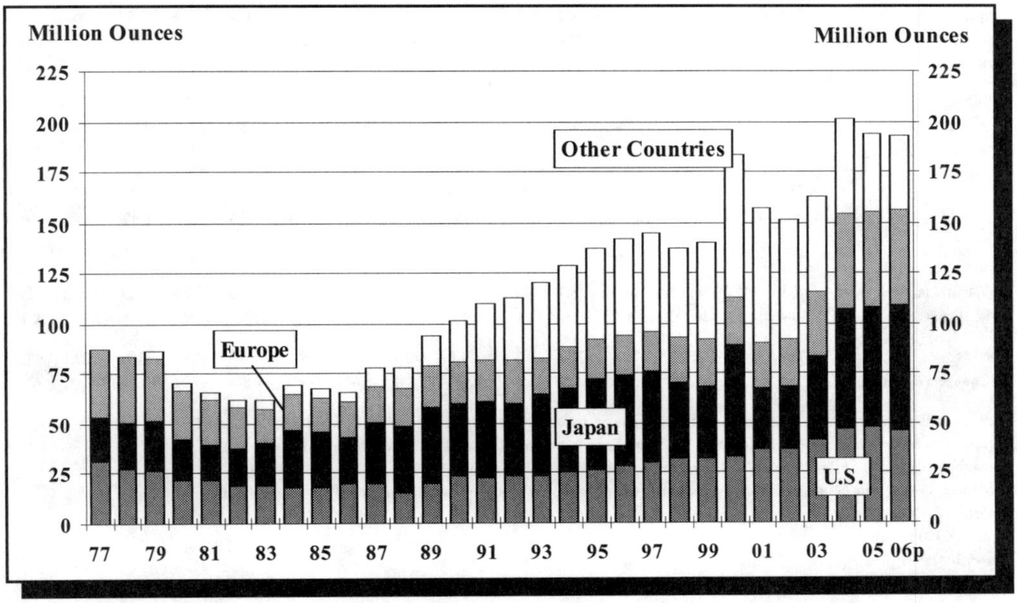

Annual Silver Use
Million Troy Ounces

	1977	1978	1979	1980	1981	1982	1983	1984	1985	1986	1987	1988	1989	1990	1991
Photography															
United States	53.7	64.3	66.0	49.8	51.0	51.8	51.8	55.3	57.9	55.4	60.2	62.5	65.2	68.0	66.0
Japan	31.2	31.4	32.2	32.6	33.9	36.6	40.9	41.3	42.2	47.0	51.3	56.8	54.8	56.5	57.8
Western Europe	44.7	47.2	47.9	41.4	43.2	44.9	45.6	47.6	48.1	51.1	52.6	57.0	57.1	59.0	60.0
Other Countries	-	-	-	-	-	3.2	2.0	3.1	4.5	4.3	8.0	8.8	12.1	13.0	12.4
Subtotal	129.6	142.9	146.1	123.8	128.1	136.5	140.3	147.3	152.7	157.8	172.1	185.1	189.2	196.5	196.2
% of Total	27.2%	30.4%	31.8%	32.7%	34.6%	35.4%	36.7%	34.0%	37.1%	34.4%	37.8%	38.1%	37.1%	36.4%	34.1%
% Change Year Ago	—	10.3%	2.2%	-15.3%	3.5%	6.6%	2.8%	5.0%	3.7%	3.4%	9.1%	7.5%	2.2%	3.8%	-0.1%
Jewelry and Silverware															
United States	31.6	32.0	26.6	19.4	13.7	16.2	17.1	13.0	13.0	12.3	10.5	9.0	8.5	8.3	8.3
Japan	2.2	2.5	2.2	1.0	1.1	1.3	1.1	1.0	1.4	1.7	1.4	1.6	1.7	1.4	3.5
Western Europe	57.2	57.4	50.3	27.5	28.7	32.7	23.9	27.3	33.1	47.3	53.3	57.3	63.8	68.3	73.1
Other Countries	-	-	3.7	4.4	4.3	6.2	5.5	6.1	8.0	14.0	22.0	23.3	40.1	50.3	70.4
Subtotal	91.0	91.9	82.8	52.3	47.8	56.4	47.6	47.4	55.5	75.3	87.2	91.2	114.1	128.3	155.3
% of Total	19.1%	19.5%	18.0%	13.8%	12.9%	14.6%	12.5%	10.9%	13.5%	16.4%	19.1%	18.7%	22.4%	23.8%	27.0%
% Change Year Ago	—	1.0%	-10.0%	-36.9%	-8.6%	18.0%	-15.6%	-0.4%	17.1%	35.7%	15.7%	4.6%	25.2%	12.4%	21.1%
Electronics and Batteries															
United States	37.1	36.8	38.1	33.8	30.2	31.9	28.9	28.3	30.0	31.1	25.2	25.5	26.3	25.8	21.4
Japan	6.9	7.0	8.9	7.6	6.4	6.6	7.7	7.8	7.5	6.8	7.0	8.4	9.5	9.7	9.7
Western Europe	34.7	35.5	33.4	29.8	25.6	23.2	23.8	26.2	27.2	28.5	28.9	31.5	34.8	34.7	34.8
Other Countries	-	-	-	-	-	0.9	0.5	0.8	3.1	3.0	8.3	9.2	9.7	14.1	17.8
Subtotal	78.7	79.3	80.4	71.2	62.2	62.6	60.9	63.1	67.8	69.4	69.4	74.6	80.3	84.3	83.7
% of Total	16.5%	16.9%	17.5%	18.8%	16.8%	16.2%	16.0%	14.6%	16.5%	15.1%	15.2%	15.3%	15.7%	15.6%	14.5%
% Change Year Ago	—	0.8%	1.4%	-11.4%	-12.6%	0.6%	-2.6%	3.6%	7.5%	2.4%	-0.1%	7.5%	7.7%	5.0%	-0.6%
Other Uses															
United States	31.2	27.1	26.6	21.8	21.8	19.1	18.5	18.3	17.7	20.1	19.4	15.0	20.0	23.2	23.0
Japan	22.9	24.0	25.5	20.3	18.2	18.7	22.4	28.7	28.3	23.1	31.8	33.8	38.2	36.9	37.9
Western Europe	33.4	32.9	30.4	24.5	21.8	20.3	16.5	17.8	17.3	18.0	17.7	18.5	20.9	20.7	21.3
Other Countries	-	-	3.7	4.4	4.3	4.5	4.5	4.5	4.7	5.0	9.7	10.4	15.1	21.2	27.5
Subtotal	87.5	84.0	86.2	71.0	66.1	62.6	61.9	69.3	68.0	66.2	78.5	77.8	94.2	102.0	109.7
% of Total	18.4%	17.9%	18.7%	18.7%	17.8%	16.3%	16.2%	16.0%	16.5%	14.4%	17.2%	16.0%	18.5%	18.9%	19.1%
% Change Year Ago	—	-4.0%	2.6%	-17.6%	-6.9%	-5.2%	-1.2%	12.0%	-1.9%	-2.7%	18.7%	-0.9%	21.1%	8.2%	7.6%
	73.1	54.3	52.8	46.1	51.3	43.4	45.8	49.6	37.2	41.3	23.5	24.7	0.2	3.2	3.4
% of Total	15.4%	11.5%	11.5%	12.2%	13.8%	11.3%	12.0%	11.4%	9.0%	9.0%	5.2%	5.1%	0.0%	0.6%	0.6%
Net Imports into the Transitional Economies	15.9	18.2	11.5	14.5	15.3	23.8	25.4	56.6	30.4	49.2	24.9	32.9	32.6	25.0	27.2
% Change Year Ago	—	14.2%	-36.7%	25.8%	5.7%	55.5%	6.9%	122.7%	-46.2%	61.8%	-49.5%	32.1%	-0.9%	-23.3%	8.9%
Total	475.8	470.6	459.7	378.8	370.7	385.2	381.8	433.3	411.6	459.2	455.5	486.2	510.6	539.1	575.6
% Change Year Ago	—	-1.1%	-2.3%	-17.6%	-2.1%	3.9%	-0.9%	13.5%	-5.0%	11.6%	-0.8%	6.7%	5.0%	5.6%	6.8%

Notes: Totals may not equal the sums of the categories due to rounding. The "Other Countries" categories for individual sectors include Mexico from 1982; India from 1987; Hong Kong from 1985; Thailand from 1986; Korea, Australia, Brazil, Colombia, Argentina, Chile, Pakistan, and Bangladesh from 1989; and Taiwan from 1990. In 2000, the transitional economies shifted from being net importers of silver to net exporters. See "silver statistical position" table for related statistics. Excludes coins.
Source: CPM Group
March 10, 2006

1992	1993	1994	1995	1996	1997	1998	1999	2000	2001	2002	2003	2004	2005	2006p	
															Photography
64.4	65.0	71.0	72.9	78.3	84.6	91.0	96.0	104.0	102.0	104.0	103.0	99.0	88.0	76.6	United States
58.0	58.5	61.1	63.6	65.7	67.3	71.0	71.5	55.5	53.5	49.2	43.9	40.0	31.8	28.0	Japan
62.2	63.9	70.6	72.6	74.4	77.5	81.8	85.6	88.6	88.3	89.3	88.8	89.8	81.0	72.2	Western Europe
14.0	13.6	12.8	12.1	12.5	12.8	13.3	14.1	13.6	12.9	13.0	13.5	13.9	7.4	5.7	Other Countries
198.6	201.0	215.5	221.2	230.9	242.2	257.1	267.2	261.7	256.7	255.5	249.2	242.7	208.2	182.5	Subtotal
33.6%	29.8%	31.0%	30.5%	30.4%	30.1%	31.3%	32.8%	30.7%	31.7%	32.3%	31.6%	30.3%	25.8%	23.8%	% of Total
1.2%	1.2%	7.2%	2.6%	4.4%	4.9%	6.2%	3.9%	-2.1%	-1.9%	-0.5%	-2.5%	-2.6%	-14.2%	-12.3%	% Change Year Ago
															Jewelry and Silverware
9.8	10.3	11.0	12.0	13.1	14.1	15.7	15.9	16.2	13.5	12.4	13.5	14.1	14.4	13.6	United States
2.8	2.9	2.7	2.4	2.7	2.7	2.3	2.0	3.0	2.8	2.6	2.9	3.0	3.1	3.2	Japan
71.8	68.7	74.3	80.9	74.0	78.0	92.4	90.4	86.5	82.4	69.0	71.2	72.7	67.7	64.3	Western Europe
87.6	152.6	146.5	149.9	172.4	188.3	183.1	183.4	179.8	188.9	186.9	177.4	153.0	203.6	190.5	Other Countries
172.0	234.5	234.5	245.2	262.2	283.1	293.5	291.7	285.5	287.6	270.9	264.9	242.8	288.8	271.6	Subtotal
29.1%	34.8%	33.8%	33.8%	34.6%	35.2%	35.7%	35.8%	33.5%	35.5%	34.3%	33.6%	30.3%	35.8%	35.5%	% of Total
10.8%	36.3%	0.0%	4.6%	6.9%	8.0%	3.7%	-0.6%	-2.1%	0.7%	-5.8%	-2.2%	-8.4%	19.0%	-6.0%	% Change Year Ago
															Electronics and Batteries
21.4	23.1	23.1	25.0	26.8	31.3	33.3	34.2	37.9	34.8	32.7	33.8	34.9	36.5	38.0	United States
8.4	8.7	8.9	10.1	9.3	11.3	7.9	6.0	10.8	4.8	4.9	7.0	8.3	6.6	7.0	Japan
32.4	32.1	31.5	32.2	30.6	31.3	34.0	35.1	37.1	34.4	33.1	34.0	34.9	34.6	35.1	Western Europe
19.1	19.7	19.7	21.3	22.0	23.0	21.0	23.8	29.5	28.4	35.4	29.6	28.5	24.1	24.2	Other Countries
81.3	83.6	83.2	88.6	88.7	96.9	96.2	99.1	115.3	102.4	106.0	104.4	106.6	101.8	104.3	Subtotal
13.7%	12.4%	12.0%	12.2%	11.7%	12.1%	11.7%	12.2%	13.5%	12.6%	13.4%	13.2%	13.3%	12.6%	13.6%	% of Total
-2.9%	2.9%	-0.5%	6.5%	0.1%	9.3%	-0.8%	3.1%	16.3%	-11.2%	3.6%	-1.6%	2.1%	-4.4%	2.4%	% Change Year Ago
															Other Uses
23.3	23.7	25.0	26.3	28.5	30.5	32.3	32.4	33.0	37.1	37.1	41.8	47.2	47.9	46.2	United States
37.4	41.6	42.8	46.4	45.8	45.4	38.4	36.7	56.1	30.9	31.2	42.2	60.3	60.7	63.1	Japan
21.2	17.1	20.8	20.0	19.7	20.2	22.1	23.1	23.8	22.2	23.7	31.9	47.1	46.8	47.0	Western Europe
30.6	37.7	40.6	44.4	48.5	49.2	44.5	47.7	70.5	67.4	59.3	46.8	46.7	38.2	37.1	Other Countries
112.5	120.1	129.2	137.0	142.5	145.2	137.3	139.8	183.4	157.6	151.3	162.7	201.3	193.6	193.4	Subtotal
19.0%	17.8%	18.6%	18.9%	18.8%	18.1%	16.7%	17.1%	21.5%	19.4%	19.1%	20.6%	25.1%	24.0%	25.3%	% of Total
2.6%	6.7%	7.6%	6.1%	4.0%	1.9%	-5.5%	1.8%	31.1%	-14.1%	-4.0%	7.5%	23.7%	-3.8%	-0.1%	% Change Year Ago
-0.4	5.1	3.9	3.4	6.0	6.5	6.4	6.9	6.4	6.2	7.0	7.2	7.5	3.9	3.9	Other Countries
-0.1%	0.8%	0.6%	0.5%	0.8%	0.8%	0.8%	0.8%	0.8%	0.8%	0.9%	0.9%	0.9%	0.5%	0.5%	% of Total
															Net Imports into the
27.5	30.0	28.0	29.3	27.9	29.6	31.2	11.0	-	-	-	-	-	10.0	10.0	**Transitional Economies**
0.9%	9.1%	-6.7%	4.7%	-4.8%	6.3%	5.3%	-64.7%	NA	NA	NA	NA	NA	NA	NA	% Change Year Ago
591.5	674.3	694.3	724.7	758.2	803.6	821.7	815.8	852.3	810.5	790.7	788.4	800.9	806.4	765.7	Total
2.8%	14.0%	3.0%	4.4%	4.6%	6.0%	2.3%	-0.7%	4.5%	-4.9%	-2.4%	-0.3%	1.6%	0.7%	-5.0%	% Change Year Ago

catalysts and materials, dental alloys, medical devices, rear-window defrosting systems for automobiles, and many other applications. In India silver also is used in foils used to wrap foods, in ayurvedic medicines, and in jari, a popular cloth for saris with gold or silver threads woven into it.

Silver also has some new uses emerging. These reports estimate that silver use in superconductors may be using as much as 50 million ounces per year. That is a very high number, but a variety of indications in the market suggest that silver use in these wires may be that high. The silver is used as a tube around the polymetallic ceramic superconductive wire. The silver helps insulate the wire, which is used at the temperature of liquid nitrogen and conducts electricity with far less resistance and loss of electricity due to drainage than conventional wires. High-temperature superconductive wires have been under development since their discovery in the late 1980s. In recent years several companies have moved toward commercialization, and have built commercial plants to manufacture these wires, for use in super-efficient motors and other wire applications. The companies involved in manufacturing these wires are extremely secretive about how much metal they are using, leading market observers to have a wide range of estimates as to how much silver actually is being used. Efforts to develop a greater degree of confidence in estimated silver use in this emerging sector continue. As stated above, there are various indications that the volume of silver being used in this application may have approached or exceeded 50 million ounces in 2005, and may be around that level, if not higher, again in 2006.

Another area in which silver use is growing is in a wide range of biocides used to kill bacteria. Water purification systems, for drinking water and swimming pools, have emerged over the past few years. Silver is being used to treat cotton under garments, including socks, shirts, and underpants, as a way of killing bacteria that cause bad odors. Silver is being used in a variety of surface applications, on everything from kitchen cutlery to the liners inside refrigerators, and industrial paints used on buildings near the ocean and on ships. Several million ounces of silver is estimated to be used per year now in biocides. There was talk about silver use in wood preservatives, to replace chromated copper arsenate, which was found to be harmful. These uses have not emerged. Instead, other copper-based chemicals have been registered with various health, safety, and environmental agencies around the world that are said to perform better as wood preservatives than silver-based chemicals at a fraction of the cost.

U.S. Fabrication Demand

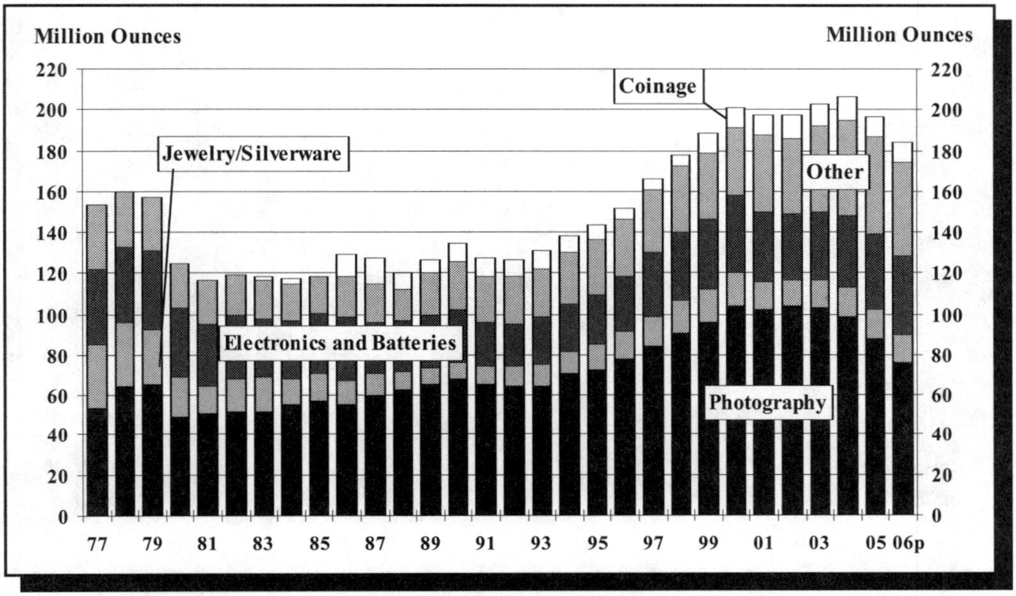

Indian Silver Fabrication Demand

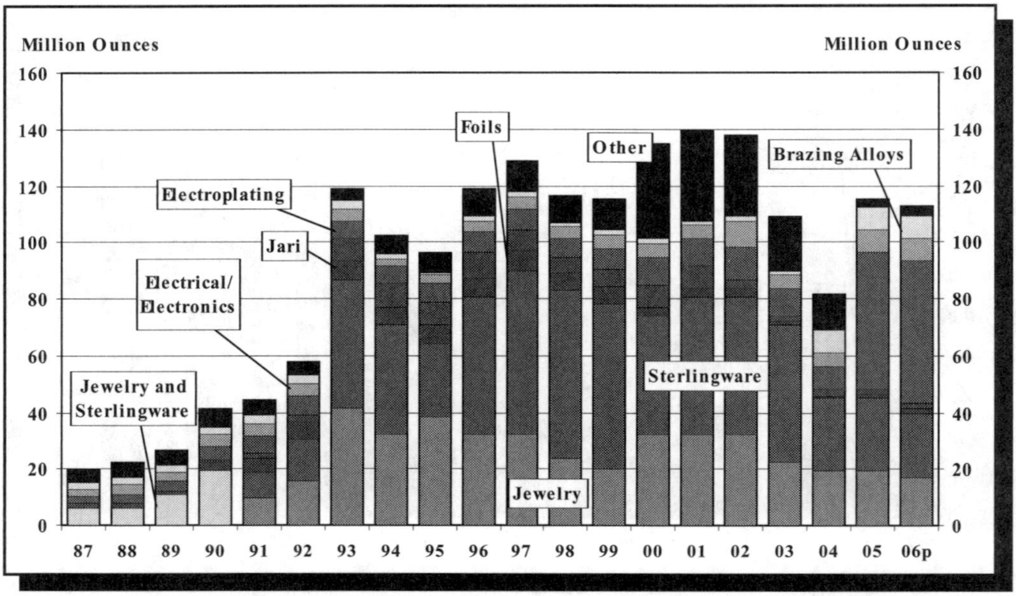

Italian Fabrication Demand

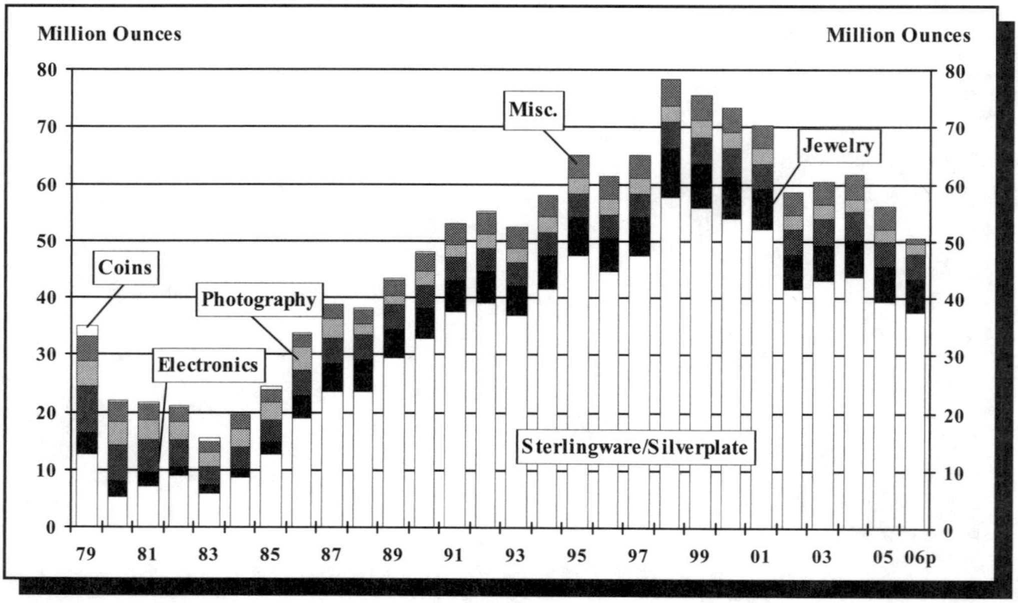

Japanese Fabrication Demand

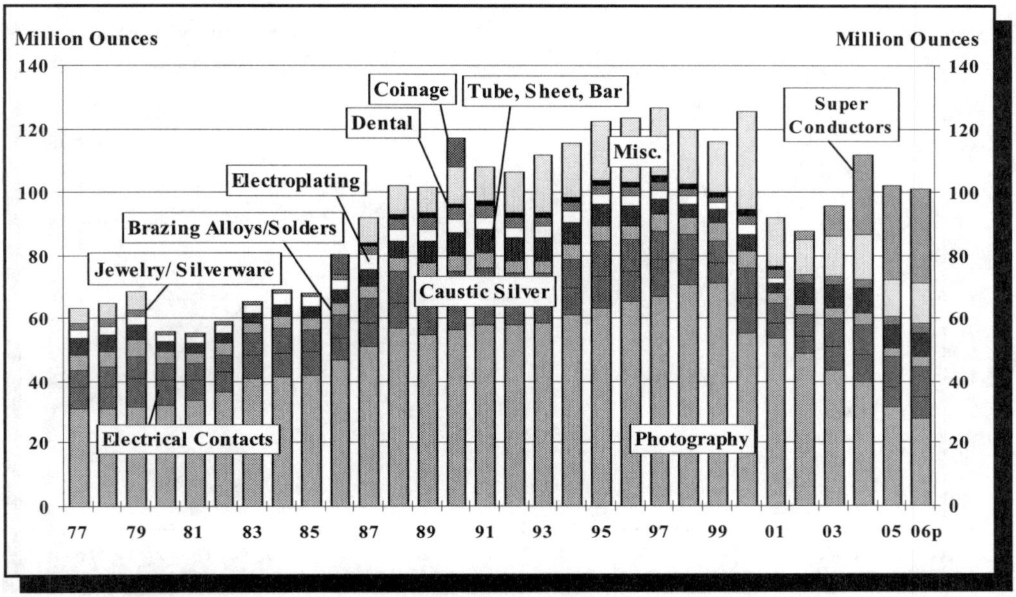

European Fabrication Demand

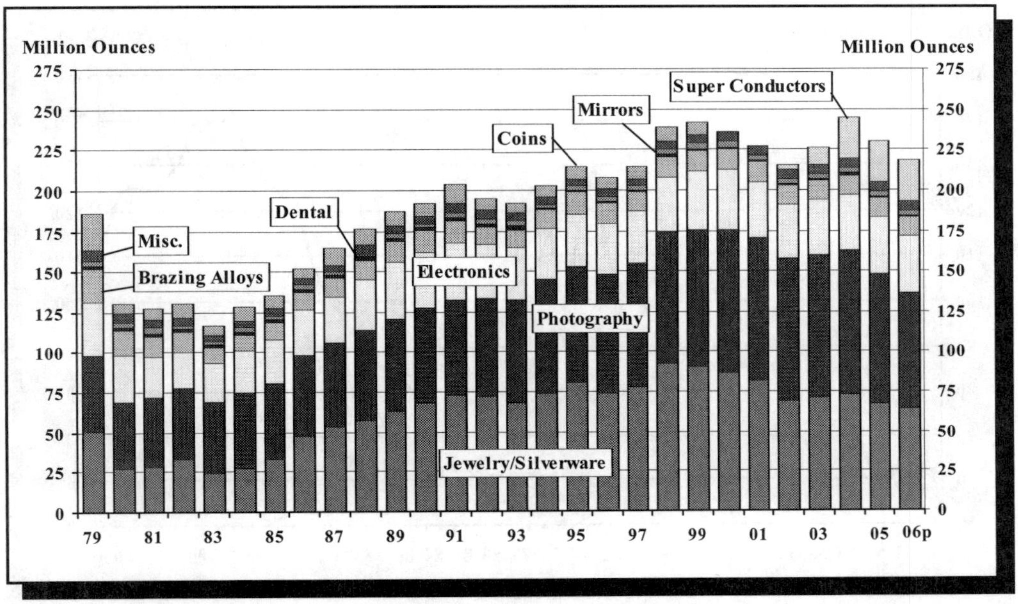

World Silver Use Per Unit of GDP

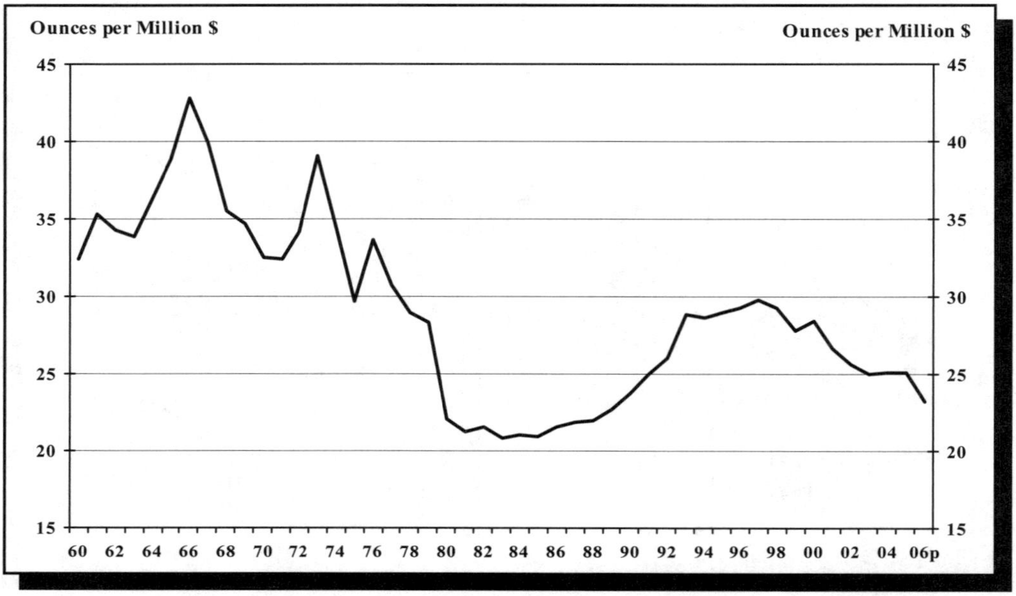

World Silver Use Per Capita

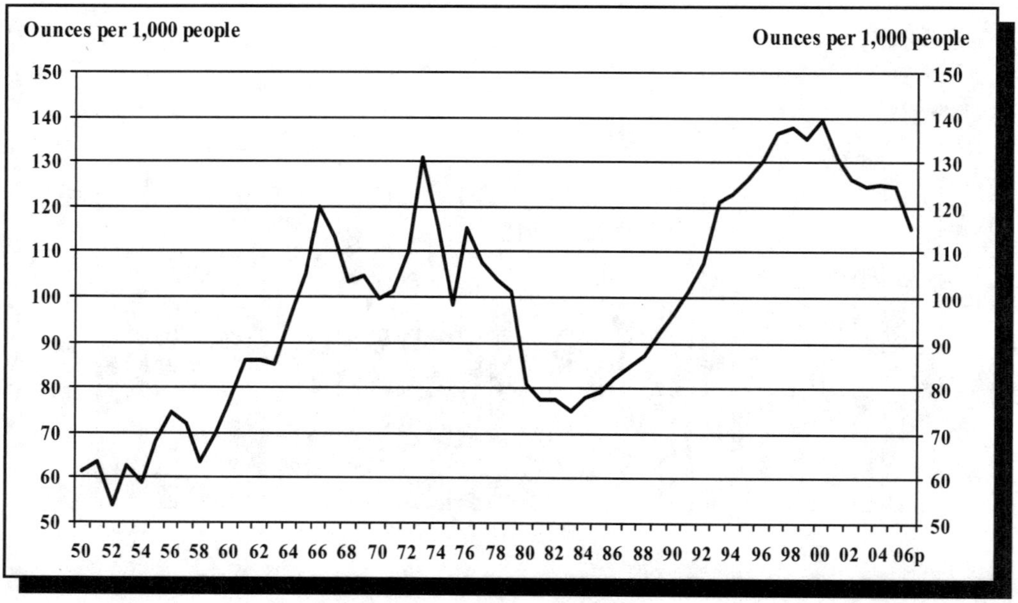

The Indexed Price of Silver in Dollars, Euros, and Rupees since 1999

Daily, Through 9 March 2006. 4 January 1999 = 100.

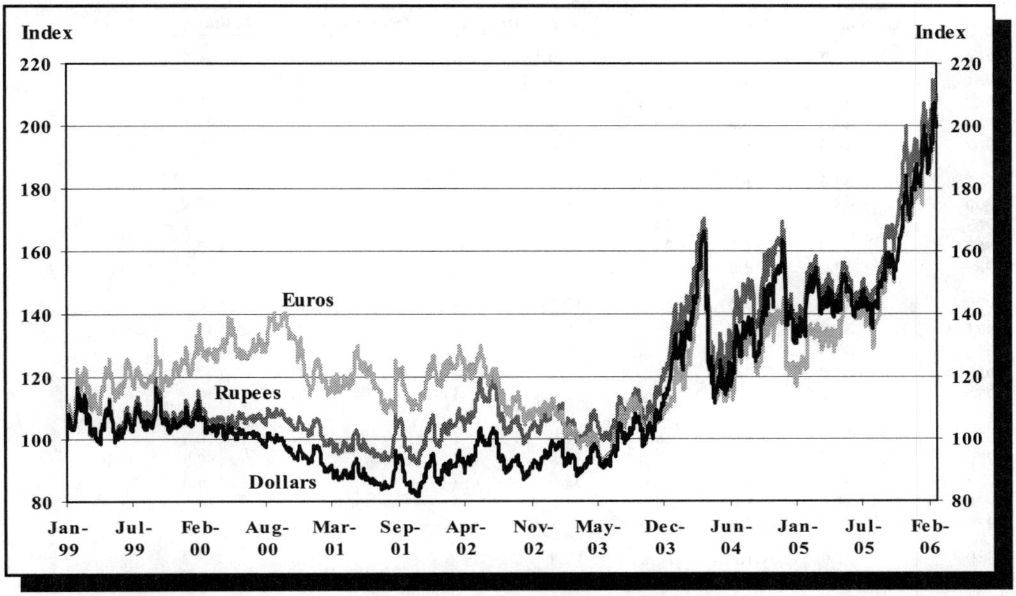

Fabrication Demand by Country, 1960-2006p
Million Troy Ounces

				Europe			
Year	**Germany**	**Italy**	**U.K.**	**France**	**Belgium**	**Other Europe**	**Subtotal**
1960	40.2	-i-	16.5	13.0	-i-	-i-	69.7
1961	43.5	20.0	20.0	14.0	-i-	-i-	97.5
1962	41.8	22.0	20.0	13.5	-i-	-i-	97.3
1963	40.5	25.0	20.0	13.9	-i-	-i-	99.4
1964	46.3	25.0	23.0	14.8	-i- -i-	-i-	109.1
1965	54.6	25.0	25.0	14.0	-i-	-i-	118.6
1966	48.2	30.0	25.0	14.7	-i-	-i-	117.9
1967	48.2	28.2	24.0	14.7	-i-	-i-	115.1
1968	50.0	22.5	23.0	18.0	-i-	-i-	113.5
1969	50.0	29.0	24.5	19.3	-i-	-i-	122.8
1970	48.2	32.0	25.0	15.5	-i-	-i-	120.7
1971	59.9	30.5	25.0	15.6	-i-	-i-	131.0
1972	60.0	32.0	27.0	16.5	-i-	-i-	135.5
1973	60.0	33.5	31.5	22.5	-i-	-i-	147.5
1974	55.0	30.0	33.0	21.0	-i-	-i-	139.0
1975	38.9	28.9	28.0	21.0	-i-	-i-	116.8
1976	52.9	38.5	27.6	31.8	-i-	-i-	150.8
1977	48.1	36.3	29.4	32.6	-i-	-i-	146.4
1978	42.0	31.0	29.0	24.6	-i-	-i-	126.6
1979	39.8	33.3	27.6	24.1	14.8	22.4	162.0
1980	31.9	21.8	19.5	19.8	14.6	15.6	123.2
1981	29.3	21.5	18.4	18.9	16.0	15.2	119.3
1982	32.7	20.8	18.1	17.1	17.0	15.4	121.1
1983	30.3	15.0	17.7	16.5	16.3	14.0	109.8
1984	32.2	19.4	19.2	17.1	16.8	14.2	118.9
1985	34.6	24.0	19.1	16.9	16.4	14.7	125.7
1986	36.3	33.5	19.1	17.0	17.6	21.4	144.9
1987	39.1	38.6	21.1	17.6	17.9	18.2	152.5
1988	44.1	43.0	22.7	21.3	19.2	14.0	164.3
1989	46.9	45.7	24.5	22.1	19.2	18.2	176.6
1990	48.4	47.9	24.4	22.4	19.4	20.2	182.7
1991	52.3	53.0	21.7	21.9	19.7	20.6	189.2
1992	49.1	54.9	21.7	21.7	20.4	19.8	187.6
1993	45.8	52.3	23.2	22.0	21.9	20.1	185.3
1994	45.8	58.0	24.4	23.3	24.5	21.2	197.2
1995	43.6	65.1	25.6	23.8	26.9	20.6	205.7
1996	41.1	61.5	27.5	22.4	28.5	17.6	198.7
1997	42.7	65.2	28.7	23.1	29.9	17.4	207.0
1998	47.5	78.4	31.2	23.7	31.8	17.7	230.3
1999	48.8	75.7	32.5	24.7	34.5	18.0	234.2
2000	47.0	73.5	34.8	27.2	37.0	16.5	236.0
2001	44.0	70.4	33.8	26.7	37.8	14.6	227.3
2002	44.6	58.7	33.4	25.4	39.5	13.5	215.1
2003	53.3	60.4	34.0	25.6	38.8	13.7	225.8
2004	69.0	61.8	34.3	26.1	39.2	14.1	244.5
2005	68.2	56.0	31.9	24.9	35.0	14.1	230.1
2006p	67.4	53.5	30.1	22.9	31.0	13.7	218.6

Notes: Excludes silver use in coinage. Totals may not equal the sums of countries due to rounding. "Other Europe" prior to 1979 is included in "Other." i -- included in Other. In 2000, the transitional economies shifted from being net importers of silver to net exporters.

U.S.	Japan	India	Thailand	Canada	Mexico	Other	Tran. Econ.	Total	Year
102.0	21.6	1.5	-i-	4.3	6.8	31.9	-	237.8	1960
105.5	19.1	1.5	-i-	3.4	5.3	37.3	-	269.6	1961
110.4	19.6	1.5	-i-	3.3	5.2	38.2	-	275.5	1962
110.0	20.0	2.5	-i-	3.2	5.0	38.8	-	278.9	1963
123.0	20.0	12.0	-i-	4.1	6.4	43.6	-	318.2	1964
137.0	25.8	16.0	-i-	5.7	7.4	48.0	-	358.5	1965
183.7	31.5	16.0	-i-	5.8	6.1	56.1	-	417.1	1966
171.0	33.2	15.0	-i-	5.8	7.9	53.9	-	401.9	1967
145.3	35.0	16.0	-i-	6.2	7.9	50.1	-	373.9	1968
141.5	41.5	16.0	-i-	5.7	6.9	51.9	-	386.3	1969
128.4	46.0	16.0	-i-	6.0	8.5	50.4	-	376.0	1970
129.1	46.5	16.0	-i-	6.8	8.0	54.5	2.4	391.9	1971
151.7	54.3	13.0	-i-	8.3	11.0	63.8	6.2	437.6	1972
196.4	69.0	13.0	-i-	10.4	16.5	77.5	7.8	530.3	1973
176.0	57.7	14.0	-i-	10.3	10.2	71.9	9.1	479.1	1974
157.7	46.4	13.0	-i-	10.3	8.8	65.6	10.9	418.6	1975
170.6	60.8	18.0	-i-	9.3	10.2	86.1	21.1	505.8	1976
153.6	63.2	17.6	-i-	9.1	8.6	77.3	15.9	475.8	1977
160.2	64.9	21.0	-i-	9.6	9.1	79.2	18.2	470.6	1978
157.3	68.8	22.5	-i-	7.3	8.6	33.2	11.5	459.7	1979
124.7	61.5	22.5	-i-	8.7	4.9	33.3	14.5	378.8	1980
116.7	59.6	26.5	-i-	8.5	5.0	35.1	15.3	370.7	1981
118.8	63.2	23.0	-i-	9.0	5.7	44.4	23.8	385.2	1982
116.3	72.1	22.5	-i-	8.9	3.5	48.8	25.4	381.8	1983
114.8	78.8	20.9	-i-	9.0	5.5	85.4	56.6	433.3	1984
118.6	72.6	21.0	-i-	9.1	8.0	56.7	30.4	411.6	1985
118.9	78.6	19.3	5.9	9.6	7.7	74.4	49.2	459.2	1986
115.3	92.3	20.1	7.4	10.4	6.9	50.6	24.9	455.5	1987
112.0	102.0	22.4	8.2	11.0	7.1	59.1	32.9	486.2	1988
120.0	102.5	27.0	11.2	12.0	7.1	54.2	32.6	510.6	1989
125.1	106.9	41.8	11.0	12.5	7.2	26.9	25.0	539.1	1990
118.7	108.9	44.5	30.4	13.1	11.7	31.9	27.2	575.6	1991
118.9	106.5	57.8	34.5	13.6	14.7	30.4	27.5	591.5	1992
121.1	111.7	119.0	41.4	15.2	14.7	36.0	30.0	674.3	1993
130.1	115.5	102.9	49.7	15.1	15.0	41.0	28.0	694.3	1994
136.2	122.5	96.5	52.0	16.9	15.0	50.7	29.3	724.7	1995
146.7	123.5	119.0	55.1	17.7	15.3	54.3	27.9	758.2	1996
160.5	126.7	128.6	56.3	18.4	16.2	60.2	29.6	803.6	1997
172.3	119.6	116.8	59.0	19.1	18.8	54.7	31.2	821.7	1998
178.5	116.2	115.7	62.0	19.6	19.6	59.0	11.0	815.8	1999
191.1	125.4	134.8	64.0	18.5	20.8	61.7	-	852.3	2000
187.4	92.0	139.7	69.5	17.3	19.5	57.8	-	810.5	2001
186.2	87.9	138.2	66.5	16.9	20.0	59.9	-	790.7	2002
192.1	96.0	109.3	66.5	16.7	21.1	60.9	-	788.4	2003
195.2	111.6	81.7	66.5	16.8	22.0	62.6	-	800.9	2004
186.8	102.2	115.9	68.0	16.4	17.0	60.0	10.0	806.4	2005
174.4	101.3	112.8	61.5	14.6	15.5	57.0	10.0	765.7	2006p

See "silver statistical position" table for related statistics. NA-Not Available.
Sources: U.S. Bureau of Mines, Handy & Harman, trade sources, CPM Group.
March 3, 2006

European Silver Fabrication Demand

Million Troy Ounces

	1979	1980	1981	1982	1983	1984	1985
Jewelry/Silverware	50.3	27.5	28.7	32.7	23.9	27.3	33.1
Photography	47.9	41.4	43.2	44.9	45.6	47.6	48.1
Electronics	33.4	29.8	25.6	23.2	23.8	26.2	27.2
Brazing Alloys/Solders	20.8	15.2	13.0	12.0	9.9	10.5	10.4
Dental	1.3	1.6	1.3	1.2	1.1	1.1	1.1
Mirrors	2.3	2.5	2.6	2.2	1.9	1.9	1.8
Miscellaneous	6.6	5.3	4.8	4.4	3.6	4.3	3.9
Total	162.0	123.2	119.3	121.1	109.8	118.9	125.7
% Change Year Ago	--	-24.0%	-3.2%	1.5%	-9.3%	8.3%	5.7%
Coinage	22.6	5.8	7.0	8.5	5.8	7.8	8.1
Total Including Coinage	184.6	129.0	126.3	129.6	115.6	126.7	133.8
% Change Year Ago	--	-30.1%	-2.1%	2.6%	-10.8%	9.6%	5.6%

	1986	1987	1988	1989	1990	1991	1992
Jewelry/Silverware	47.3	53.3	57.3	63.8	68.3	73.1	71.8
Photography	51.1	52.6	57.0	57.1	59.0	60.0	62.2
Electronics	28.5	29.0	31.5	34.8	34.7	34.8	32.4
Brazing Alloys/Solders	10.9	11.0	11.4	13.0	13.3	13.5	13.4
Dental	1.1	1.1	1.2	1.1	1.0	1.2	1.2
Mirrors	1.8	1.4	1.5	2.0	2.0	2.0	2.0
Miscellaneous	4.2	4.0	4.6	4.8	4.4	4.6	4.6
Total	144.9	152.5	164.3	176.6	182.7	189.2	187.6
% Change Year Ago	15.3%	5.3%	7.8%	7.5%	3.4%	3.6%	-0.8%
Coinage	5.3	11.1	10.2	9.0	7.5	11.9	7.5
Total Including Coinage	150.2	163.5	174.6	185.6	190.2	201.1	195.1
% Change Year Ago	12.2%	8.9%	6.7%	6.3%	2.5%	5.7%	-3.0%

	1993	1994	1995	1996	1997	1998	1999
Jewelry/Silverware	68.7	74.3	80.9	74.0	78.0	92.4	90.4
Photography	63.9	70.6	72.6	74.4	77.5	81.8	85.6
Electronics	32.1	31.5	32.2	30.6	31.3	34.0	35.1
Brazing Alloys/Solders	12.9	12.6	11.9	11.5	11.7	12.6	13.1
Dental	1.1	1.1	1.1	1.1	1.1	1.2	1.3
Mirrors	2.3	2.5	2.8	2.9	3.1	3.5	3.5
Miscellaneous	4.2	4.6	4.2	4.2	4.3	4.8	5.1
Total	185.3	197.2	205.7	198.7	207.0	230.3	234.2
% Change Year Ago	-1.2%	6.4%	4.3%	-3.4%	4.2%	11.2%	1.7%
Coinage	6.3	6.6	8.2	7.2	7.63	8.6	8.1
Total Including Coinage	191.6	203.8	213.9	205.9	214.7	238.9	242.3
% Change Year Ago	-1.8%	6.4%	5.0%	-3.7%	4.2%	11.3%	1.4%

	2000	2001	2002	2003	2004	2005	2006p
Jewelry/Silverware	86.5	82.4	69.0	71.2	72.7	67.7	64.3
Photography	88.6	88.3	89.3	88.8	89.8	81.0	72.2
Electronics	37.1	34.4	33.1	34.0	34.9	34.6	35.1
Brazing Alloys/Solders	12.9	11.9	11.5	11.7	11.6	11.3	11.5
Dental	1.3	1.3	1.3	1.3	1.4	1.4	1.4
Mirrors	3.4	3.1	2.9	3.0	3.2	3.2	3.2
Miscellaneous	6.2	5.9	5.6	5.9	5.9	5.9	5.9
Super Conducters			2.5	10	25	25	25
Total	236.0	227.3	215.1	225.8	244.5	230.1	218.6
% Change Year Ago	0.8%	-3.7%	-5.4%	5.0%	8.3%	-5.9%	-5.0%
Coinage	-	-	-	-	-	-	-
Total Including Coinage	236.0	227.3	215.1	225.8	244.5	230.1	218.6
% Change Year Ago	-2.6%	-3.7%	-5.4%	5.0%	8.3%	-5.9%	-5.0%

Notes: Totals may not equal the sums of categories due to rounding. Consumption of silver in semi-fabricated form is excluded.
Sources: European trade sources, CPM Group.
March 3, 2006

Italian Silver Fabrication Demand
Million Troy Ounces

	1986	1987	1988	1989	1990	1991	1992
Sterlingware	18.5	23.2	23.2	28.9	32.2	37.0	38.6
Silverplate	0.4	0.4	0.4	0.4	0.6	0.6	0.6
Jewelry	4.1	5.0	5.4	5.0	5.5	5.5	5.5
Photography	4.2	3.5	1.9	1.6	2.3	2.3	2.5
Electronics	4.2	4.2	4.5	4.5	4.0	4.1	4.0
Brazing Alloys/Solders	1.1	1.1	1.2	1.3	1.6	1.8	1.9
Mirrors	0.3	0.3	0.3	0.3	0.8	0.8	0.8
Miscellaneous	0.9	0.9	1.0	1.1	1.0	1.0	1.0
Total	33.5	38.6	37.9	43.0	47.9	53.0	54.9
% Change Year Ago	39.9%	15.2%	-2.0%	13.7%	11.3%	10.6%	3.6%
Coinage	0.2	0.2	0.2	0.2	0.1	—	0.2
Total Including Coinage	33.7	38.8	38.0	43.3	48.0	53.0	55.1
% Change Year Ago	37.9%	15.1%	-2.0%	13.8%	10.9%	10.4%	4.0%

	1993	1994	1995	1996	1997	1998	1999
Sterlingware	36.3	40.7	46.6	43.8	46.4	56.6	54.7
Silverplate	0.6	0.8	0.9	0.8	0.9	1.1	1.0
Jewelry	5.2	6.0	6.7	6.1	7.0	8.8	7.9
Photography	2.5	2.7	2.8	2.8	2.8	3.0	3.1
Electronics	4.0	4.0	4.0	4.0	4.0	4.4	4.5
Brazing Alloys/Solders	1.9	2.0	2.1	2.1	2.1	2.3	2.3
Mirrors	0.8	0.9	1.0	1.0	1.0	1.1	1.1
Miscellaneous	1.0	1.0	1.0	1.0	1.0	1.1	1.1
Total	52.3	58.0	65.1	61.5	65.2	78.4	75.7
% Change Year Ago	-4.7%	10.9%	12.2%	-5.8%	6.0%	20.2%	-3.4%
Coinage	—	—	—	—	—	—	—
Total Including Coinage	52.3	58.0	65.1	61.5	65.2	78.4	75.7
% Change Year Ago	-5.1%	10.9%	12.2%	-5.8%	6.0%	20.2%	-3.4%

	2000	2001	2002	2003	2004	2005	2006p
Sterlingware	53.0	51.1	41.0	42.2	42.8	38.5	36.5
Silverplate	1.0	0.9	0.7	0.8	1.0	1.0	1.0
Jewelry	7.5	7.2	6.0	6.2	6.5	6.0	5.8
Photography	3.0	2.9	2.5	2.5	2.4	2.0	1.6
Electronics	4.8	4.4	4.5	4.6	4.8	4.5	4.6
Brazing Alloys/Solders	2.2	2.1	2.2	2.3	2.3	2.0	2.0
Mirrors	1.0	0.8	0.8	0.8	1.0	1.0	1.0
Miscellaneous	1.0	1.0	1.0	1.0	1.0	1.0	1.0
Total	73.5	70.4	58.7	60.4	61.8	56.0	53.5
% Change Year Ago	-2.9%	-4.2%	-16.6%	2.9%	2.3%	-9.4%	-4.5%
Coinage	—						
Total Including Coinage	73.5						
% Change Year Ago	-2.9%						

Notes: Totals may not equal the sums of categories due to rounding. Consumption of silver in semi-fabricated form is excluded.
Sources: European trade sources, CPM Group.
March 7, 2006

German Silver Fabrication Demand

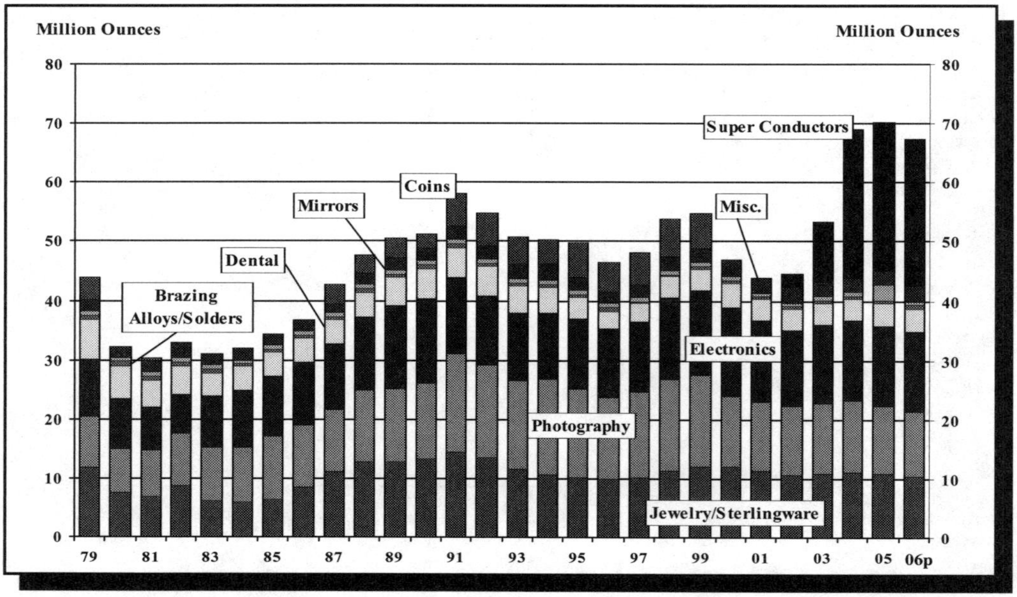

German Silver Fabrication Demand
Million Troy Ounces

	1979	1980	1981	1982	1983	1984	1985
Jewelry/Silverware	11.8	7.6	6.9	8.7	6.1	5.9	6.4
Photography	8.7	7.3	7.8	8.9	9.2	9.2	10.6
Electronics	9.6	8.7	7.4	6.7	8.6	9.7	10.1
Brazing Alloys/Solders	6.7	5.3	4.5	4.7	3.9	4.0	4.2
Dental	0.5	0.7	0.5	0.5	0.4	0.3	0.3
Mirrors	0.5	0.5	0.5	0.5	0.5	0.5	0.5
Miscellaneous	2.0	1.8	1.8	2.4	1.9	2.1	2.0
Total	39.8	31.9	29.3	32.7	30.3	32.2	34.6
% Change Year Ago	—	-19.8%	-8.2%	11.6%	-7.3%	6.2%	7.5%
Coinage	3.7	—	0.5	0.3	—	—	—
Total Including Coinage	43.5	31.9	29.8	33.0	30.3	32.2	34.6
% Change Year Ago	—	-26.7%	-6.6%	10.7%	-8.2%	6.2%	7.5%

	1986	1987	1988	1989	1990	1991	1992
Jewelry/Silverware	8.5	11.2	12.7	12.7	13.2	14.5	13.5
Photography	10.4	10.5	12.1	12.5	12.9	16.7	15.7
Electronics	10.6	10.9	12.3	13.8	14.3	12.7	11.6
Brazing Alloys/Solders	4.0	4.1	4.2	4.8	5.0	5.1	5.0
Dental	0.4	0.3	0.3	0.3	0.4	0.5	0.5
Mirrors	0.5	0.5	0.5	0.5	0.5	0.5	0.5
Miscellaneous	1.9	1.6	1.9	2.1	2.1	2.3	2.4
Total	36.3	39.1	44.1	46.9	48.4	52.3	49.1
% Change Year Ago	5.0%	7.6%	12.8%	6.2%	3.3%	8.1%	-6.1%
Coinage	—	3.2	3.2	3.2	2.4	5.5	5.3
Total Including Coinage	36.3	42.3	47.3	50.1	50.8	57.8	54.4
% Change Year Ago	5.0%	16.5%	11.8%	5.8%	1.5%	13.9%	-6.0%

	1993	1994	1995	1996	1997	1998	1999
Jewelry/Silverware	11.6	10.7	10.3	10.0	10.1	11.5	12.0
Photography	15.1	16.1	14.8	13.8	14.5	15.4	15.5
Electronics	11.3	11.2	11.9	11.6	11.9	13.7	14.2
Brazing Alloys/Solders	4.5	4.2	3.5	2.9	3.1	3.5	3.6
Dental	0.4	0.4	0.4	0.4	0.4	0.4	0.5
Mirrors	0.5	0.5	0.5	0.5	0.6	0.7	0.7
Miscellaneous	2.4	2.7	2.2	2.0	2.1	2.3	2.3
Total	45.8	45.8	43.6	41.1	42.7	47.5	48.8
% Change Year Ago	-6.7%	0.1%	-4.8%	-5.6%	3.8%	11.2%	2.7%
Coinage	4.5	4.2	5.8	5.1	5.5	6.5	6.0
Total Including Coinage	50.3	50.0	49.4	46.2	48.2	54.0	54.8
% Change Year Ago	-7.5%	-0.6%	-1.2%	-6.4%	4.2%	12.0%	1.5%

	2000	2001	2002	2003	2004	2005	2006p
Jewelry/Silverware	12.0	11.4	10.6	10.9	11.1	11.0	10.5
Photography	12.0	11.7	11.6	11.9	12.1	11.4	10.8
Electronics	15.0	13.6	13.0	13.3	13.6	13.5	13.7
Brazing Alloys/Solders	4.0	3.6	3.4	3.6	3.6	3.7	3.8
Dental	0.5	0.5	0.5	0.5	0.5	0.5	0.5
Mirrors	0.7	0.6	0.5	0.5	0.5	0.5	0.5
Miscellaneous	2.8	2.6	2.5	2.6	2.6	2.6	2.6
Super Conducters	-	-	2.5	10.0	25.0	25.0	25.0
Total	47.0	44.0	44.6	53.3	69.0	68.2	67.4
% Change Year Ago	-3.7%	-6.4%	1.4%	19.5%	29.5%	-1.2%	-1.2%

Notes: Totals may not equal the sums of categories due to rounding.
Sources: European trade sources, CPM Group.
March 7, 2006

U.K. Silver Fabrication Demand

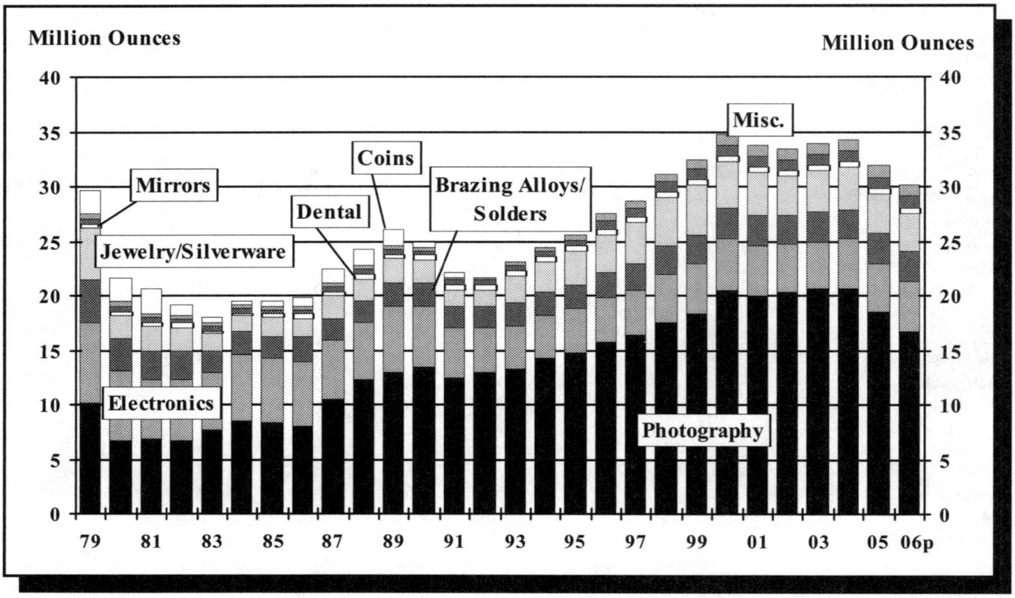

United Kingdom Silver Fabrication Demand

Million Troy Ounces

	1979	1980	1981	1982	1983	1984	1985
Jewelry/Silverware	4.9	2.1	2.3	2.2	1.5	1.4	1.8
Photography	10.2	6.7	6.9	6.8	7.7	8.6	8.3
Electronics	7.3	6.4	5.4	5.5	5.3	5.9	5.9
Brazing Alloys/Solders	3.9	3.0	2.6	2.6	2.0	2.2	2.1
Dental	0.3	0.4	0.4	0.4	0.3	0.3	0.3
Mirrors	0.5	0.4	0.4	0.4	0.4	0.4	0.4
Miscellaneous	0.5	0.5	0.4	0.3	0.3	0.3	0.3
Total	27.6	19.5	18.4	18.1	17.7	19.2	19.1
% Change Year Ago	—	-29.3%	-5.6%	-1.6%	-2.2%	8.3%	-0.5%
Coinage	2.0	2.1	2.2	0.9	0.6	0.3	0.4
Total Including Coinage	29.6	21.6	20.6	19.1	18.3	19.5	19.5
% Change Year Ago	—	-27.0%	-4.6%	-7.3%	-4.2%	6.4%	-0.1%
	1986	**1987**	**1988**	**1989**	**1990**	**1991**	**1992**
Jewelry/Silverware	1.7	2.0	2.0	2.2	2.1	1.5	1.5
Photography	8.1	10.4	12.3	13.0	13.4	12.5	13.0
Electronics	5.8	5.5	5.4	5.9	5.6	4.5	4.0
Brazing Alloys/Solders	2.3	2.0	1.9	2.3	2.1	2.0	2.0
Dental	0.4	0.5	0.5	0.5	0.5	0.5	0.5
Mirrors	0.4	0.4	0.4	0.4	0.4	0.4	0.4
Miscellaneous	0.3	0.3	0.3	0.3	0.3	0.3	0.3
Total	19.1	21.1	22.7	24.5	24.4	21.7	21.7
% Change Year Ago	0.2%	10.5%	7.7%	7.9%	-0.5%	-11.1%	0.0%
Coinage	0.8	1.3	1.6	1.6	0.3	0.2	—
Total Including Coinage	19.8	22.4	24.3	26.1	24.7	21.9	21.7
% Change Year Ago	1.8%	13.1%	8.7%	7.4%	-5.5%	-11.3%	-0.9%
	1993	**1994**	**1995**	**1996**	**1997**	**1998**	**1999**
Jewelry/Silverware	2.6	2.7	3.0	3.4	3.8	4.4	4.5
Photography	13.2	14.3	14.8	15.7	16.4	17.5	18.3
Electronics	4.0	4.0	4.0	4.1	4.1	4.5	4.6
Brazing Alloys/Solders	2.1	2.1	2.2	2.4	2.4	2.6	2.7
Dental	0.5	0.5	0.5	0.5	0.5	0.5	0.5
Mirrors	0.5	0.5	0.6	0.8	0.9	1.0	1.0
Miscellaneous	0.3	0.4	0.5	0.6	0.6	0.7	0.9
Total	23.2	24.4	25.6	27.5	28.7	31.2	32.5
% Change Year Ago	6.7%	5.5%	4.9%	7.3%	4.4%	8.7%	4.2%
Coinage	—	—	—	—	—	—	—
Total Including Coinage	23.2	24.4	25.6	27.5	28.7	31.2	32.5
% Change Year Ago	6.9%	5.2%	4.9%	7.3%	4.4%	8.7%	4.2%
	2000	**2001**	**2002**	**2003**	**2004**	**2005**	**2006p**
Jewelry/Silverware	4.3	4.0	3.7	3.8	3.9	3.7	3.5
Photography	20.5	20.0	20.4	20.6	20.7	18.5	16.7
Electronics	4.7	4.6	4.3	4.4	4.5	4.5	4.6
Brazing Alloys/Solders	2.8	2.7	2.6	2.7	2.7	2.7	2.8
Dental	0.5	0.5	0.5	0.5	0.5	0.5	0.5
Mirrors	1.0	1.0	0.9	1.0	1.0	1.0	1.0
Miscellaneous	1.0	1.0	1.0	1.0	1.0	1.0	1.0
Total	34.8	33.8	33.4	34	34.3	31.9	30.1
% Change Year Ago	7.1%	-2.9%	-1.2%	1.8%	0.9%	-7.0%	-5.6%
Coinage	—	—	—	—	—	—	—
Total Including Coinage	34.8	33.8	33.4	34	34.3	31.9	30.1
% Change Year Ago	7.1%	-2.9%	-1.2%	1.8%	0.9%	-7.0%	-5.6%

Notes: Totals may not equal the sums of categories due to rounding.
Sources: European trade sources, CPM Group.
March 7, 2006

Belgian Silver Fabrication Demand

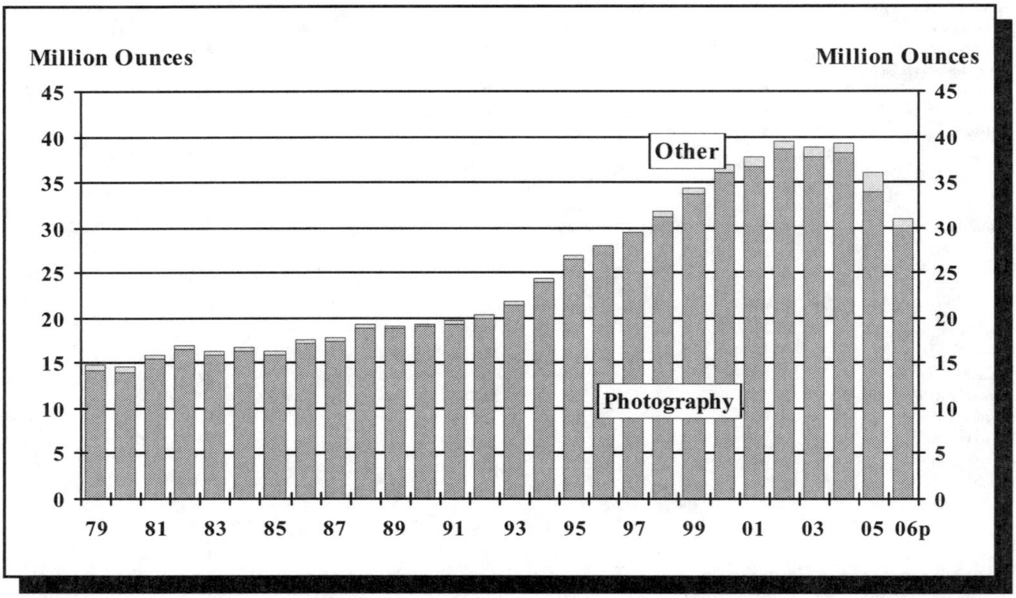

Belgian Silver Fabrication Demand

Million Troy Ounces

	1979	1980	1981	1982	1983	1984	1985
Photography	14.2	14.1	15.5	16.6	15.9	16.4	16.0
Mirrors	0.1	0.1	0.1	0.3	0.3	0.3	0.3
Sterlingware/Jewelry	0.1	0.1	0.1				
Electronics	0.1	0.1	*	*	*	*	*
Dental	*	*	*	*			
Miscellaneous	0.2	0.2	0.2	0.1	0.1	0.1	0.1
Total	14.8	14.6	16.0	17.0	16.3	16.8	16.4
% Change Year Ago	-----	-1.4%	9.5%	6.4%	-4.1%	3.4%	-2.4%

	1986	1987	1988	1989	1990	1991	1992
Photography	17.2	17.4	18.8	18.8	19.0	19.3	20.0
Mirrors	0.3	0.3	0.3	0.3	0.3	0.3	0.3
Sterlingware/Jewelry							
Electronics	*	*	*	*	*	*	*
Dental							
Miscellaneous	0.1	0.2	0.1	0.1	0.1	0.1	0.1
Total	17.6	17.9	19.2	19.2	19.4	19.7	20.4
% Change Year Ago	7.3%	1.7%	7.3%	-0.2%	1.0%	1.5%	3.6%

	1993	1994	1995	1996	1997	1998	1999
Photography	21.5	24.1	26.5	28.0	29.4	31.2	33.8
Mirrors	0.3	0.3	0.4	0.4	0.4	0.5	0.5
Sterlingware/Jewelry							
Electronics	*	*	*	*	*	*	*
Dental							
Miscellaneous	0.1	0.1	0.1	0.1	0.1	0.2	0.2
Total	21.9	24.5	26.9	28.5	29.9	31.8	34.5
% Change Year Ago	7.4%	11.7%	10.0%	6.1%	4.7%	6.4%	8.3%

	2000	2001	2002	2003	2004	2005	2006p
Photography	36.0	36.8	38.6	37.8	38.2	34.0	30.0
Mirrors	0.5	0.5	0.5	0.5	0.5	0.5	0.5
Sterlingware/Jewelry							
Electronics	*	*	*	*	*	*	*
Dental							
Miscellaneous	0.5	0.5	0.4	0.5	0.5	0.5	0.5
Total	37.0	37.8	39.5	38.8	39.2	35.0	31.0
% Change Year Ago	7.4%	2.2%	4.5%	-1.8%	1.0%	-10.7%	-11.4%

Notes: Totals may not equal the sums of categories due to rounding. Asterisks indicate that consumption in individual industries totaled less than 100,000 ounces.
Sources: European trade sources, CPM Group.
March 7, 2006

French Silver Fabrication Demand

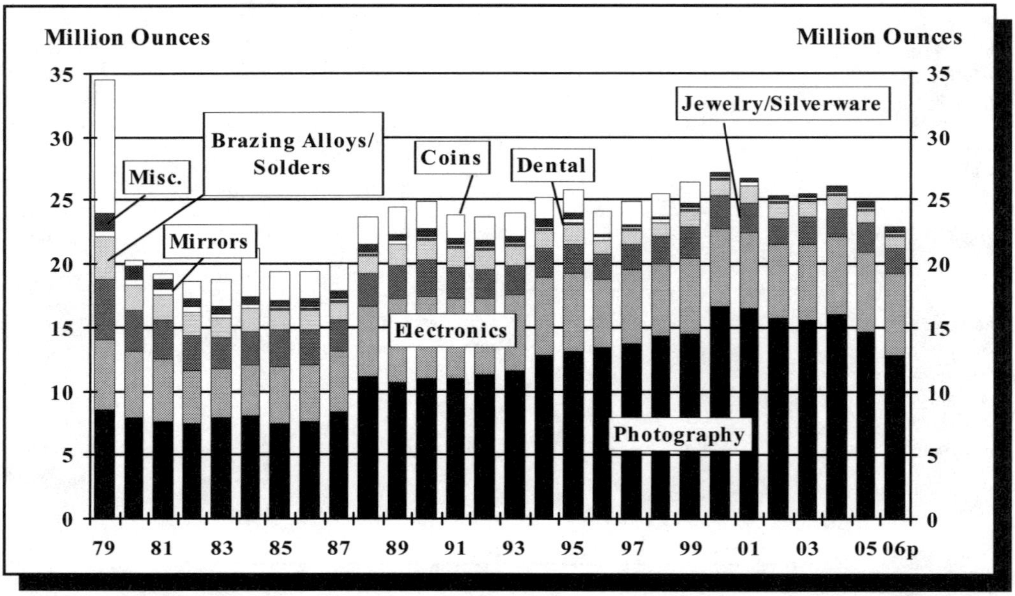

French Silver Fabrication Demand

Million Troy Ounces

	1979	1980	1981	1982	1983	1984	1985
Jewelry/Silverware	4.7	3.2	3.0	2.8	2.4	2.6	2.8
Photography	8.5	7.9	7.7	7.5	7.9	8.1	7.6
Electronics	5.6	5.3	4.9	4.1	3.9	3.9	4.4
Brazing Alloys/Solders	3.4	2.0	2.0	1.8	1.5	1.8	1.6
Dental	—	—	—	—	0.1	0.1	0.1
Mirrors	0.4	0.4	0.4	0.4	0.3	0.3	0.2
Miscellaneous	1.4	1.0	0.8	0.5	0.4	0.3	0.3
Total	24.1	19.8	18.9	17.1	16.5	17.1	16.9
% Change Year Ago	—	-17.8%	-4.5%	-9.5%	-3.5%	3.7%	-0.9%
Coinage	10.6	0.1	0.1	1.4	2.2	3.9	2.2
Total Including Coinage	34.7	19.9	19.0	18.5	18.7	21.0	19.1
% Change Year Ago	—	-42.7%	-4.5%	-2.6%	1.1%	12.3%	-8.9%

	1986	1987	1988	1989	1990	1991	1992
Jewelry/Silverware	2.8	2.3	2.5	2.7	2.8	2.5	2.3
Photography	7.7	8.4	11.2	10.8	11.0	10.9	11.3
Electronics	4.4	4.8	5.5	6.4	6.5	6.3	6.0
Brazing Alloys/Solders	1.6	1.5	1.5	1.6	1.6	1.6	1.5
Dental	0.1	0.1	0.1	0.1	0.1	0.1	0.1
Mirrors	0.2	0.2	0.2	0.2	0.2	0.2	0.2
Miscellaneous	0.3	0.3	0.3	0.3	0.3	0.3	0.3
Total	17.0	17.6	21.3	22.1	22.5	21.9	21.7
% Change Year Ago	0.4%	3.4%	20.9%	3.9%	1.9%	-2.8%	-0.9%
Coinage	2.2	2.2	2.2	2.2	2.2	1.8	1.8
Total Including Coinage	19.2	19.8	23.4	24.3	24.7	23.7	23.5
% Change Year Ago	0.3%	3.0%	18.5%	3.6%	1.8%	-4.2%	-0.7%

	1993	1994	1995	1996	1997	1998	1999
Jewelry/Silverware	2.3	2.3	2.4	2.1	2.1	2.2	2.4
Photography	11.6	12.9	13.2	13.5	13.8	14.3	14.5
Electronics	6.0	6.0	6.0	5.3	5.7	5.7	6.0
Brazing Alloys/Solders	1.5	1.5	1.5	1.0	1.0	1.0	1.3
Dental	0.1	0.1	0.1	0.1	0.1	0.1	0.1
Mirrors	0.2	0.2	0.3	0.2	0.2	0.2	0.2
Miscellaneous	0.3	0.3	0.3	0.2	0.2	0.2	0.2
Total	22.0	23.3	23.8	22.4	23.1	23.7	24.7
% Change Year Ago	1.4%	5.8%	2.2%	-6.0%	3.3%	2.6%	4.2%
Coinage	1.8	1.8	1.8	1.8	1.8	1.8	1.8
Total Including Coinage	23.8	25.1	25.6	24.2	24.9	25.5	26.5
% Change Year Ago	1.3%	5.4%	2.1%	-5.6%	3.1%	2.4%	3.9%

	2000	2001	2002	2003	2004	2005	2006p
Jewelry/Silverware	2.5	2.3	2.0	2.1	2.1	2.2	2.0
Photography	16.7	16.5	15.8	15.6	16.0	14.7	12.8
Electronics	6.1	6.0	5.8	6.0	6.2	6.3	6.4
Brazing Alloys/Solders	1.3	1.3	1.2	1.2	1.1	1.0	1.0
Dental	0.1	0.1	0.1	0.1	0.1	0.1	0.1
Mirrors	0.2	0.2	0.2	0.2	0.2	0.2	0.2
Miscellaneous	0.3	0.3	0.3	0.4	0.4	0.4	0.4
Total	27.2	26.7	25.4	25.6	26.1	24.9	22.9
% Change Year Ago	10.1%	-1.8%	-4.9%	0.8%	2.0%	-4.6%	-8.0%

Notes: Totals may not equal the sums of categories due to rounding. Asterisks indicate that consumption in individual industries totaled less than 100,000 ounces.

Sources: European trade sources, CPM Group.

March 7, 2006

Austrian Silver Fabrication Demand

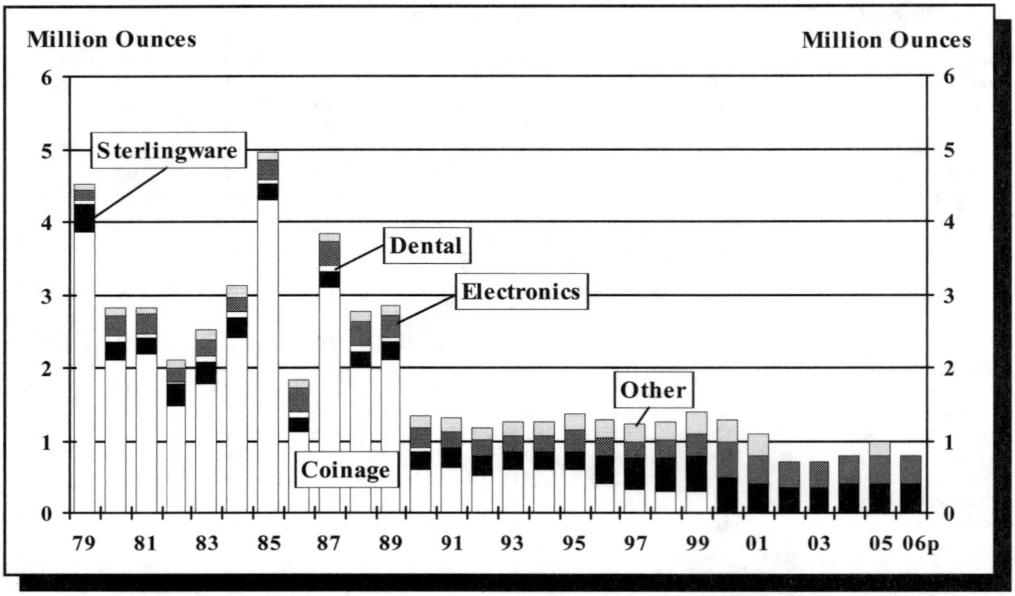

Austrian Silver Fabrication Demand
Million Troy Ounces

	1979	1980	1981	1982	1983	1984	1985
Sterlingware/Jewelry	0.40	0.26	0.21	0.29	0.30	0.28	0.21
Dental	0.06	0.07	0.06	0.05	0.07	0.07	0.07
Electronics	0.13	0.30	0.26	0.18	0.24	0.21	0.26
Brazing Alloys/Solders	*	0.06	0.06	0.06	0.06	0.10	0.11
Medals/Medallions	*	*	*	*	*	*	*
Miscellaneous	*	*	*	*	*	0.1	*
Total	0.59	0.69	0.59	0.58	0.67	0.73	0.66
% Change Year Ago	—	17.5%	-14.0%	-2.2%	15.5%	8.1%	-9.3%
Coinage	3.85	2.10	2.20	1.48	1.78	2.40	4.30
Total Including Coinage	4.44	2.79	2.79	2.06	2.46	3.13	4.96
% Change Year Ago	—	-37.2%	0.1%	-26.1%	19.0%	27.3%	58.6%

	1986	1987	1988	1989	1990	1991	1992
Sterlingware/Jewelry	0.21	0.21	0.23	0.24	0.26	0.27	0.26
Dental	0.09	0.08	0.07	0.06	0.06	*	*
Electronics	0.32	0.32	0.33	0.30	0.26	0.23	0.23
Brazing Alloys/Solders	0.10	0.11	0.12	0.15	0.18	0.19	0.18
Medals/Medallions	*	*	*	*	*	*	*
Miscellaneous	*	*	*	*	*	*	*
Total	0.71	0.73	0.76	0.76	0.75	0.68	0.67
% Change Year Ago	7.8%	2.3%	4.0%	0.4%	-0.8%	-9.4%	1.5%
Coinage	1.11	3.10	2.00	2.10	0.60	0.62	0.52
Total Including Coinage	1.82	3.83	2.76	2.86	1.35	1.30	1.19
% Change Year Ago	-63.2%	109.8%	-28.0%	3.7%	-52.7%	-3.5%	-8.7%

	1993	1994	1995	1996	1997	1998	1999
Sterlingware/Jewelry	0.26	0.26	0.26	0.40	0.42	0.46	0.50
Dental	*	*	*	*	*	*	*
Electronics	0.22	0.22	0.30	0.23	0.23	0.25	0.30
Brazing Alloys/Solders	0.18	0.18	0.20	0.09	0.09	0.10	0.10
Medals/Medallions	*	*	*	*	*	*	*
Miscellaneous	*	*	*	0.17	0.15	0.16	0.20
Total	0.66	0.66	0.76	0.89	0.89	0.97	1.10
% Change Year Ago	-1.5%	0.0%	15.2%	17.1%	0.4%	8.5%	13.4%
Coinage	0.60	0.60	0.60	0.40	0.33	0.30	0.30
Total Including Coinage	1.26	1.26	1.36	1.29	1.22	1.27	1.40
% Change Year Ago	6.1%	0.0%	7.6%	-5.1%	-5.1%	3.8%	10.2%

	2000	2001	2002	2003	2004	2005	2006p
Sterlingware/Jewelry	0.50	0.40	0.35	0.35	0.40	0.40	0.40
Dental	*	*	*	*	*	*	*
Electronics	0.50	0.40	0.35	0.36	0.40	0.40	0.40
Brazing Alloys/Solders	0.10	0.10	0.10	0.10	0.10	0.10	0.10
Medals/Medallions	*	*	*	*	*	*	*
Miscellaneous	0.20	0.20	0.10	0.10	0.10	0.10	0.10
Total	1.30	1.10	0.90	0.91	1.00	1.00	1.00
% Change Year Ago	18.2%	-15.4%	-18.2%	1.1%	9.9%	-	-

Notes: Totals may not equal the sums of categories due to rounding. Asterisks indicate that consumption in individual industries totaled less than 50,000 ounces.
Sources: European trade sources, CPM Group.
March 7, 2006

Netherlands Silver Fabrication Demand

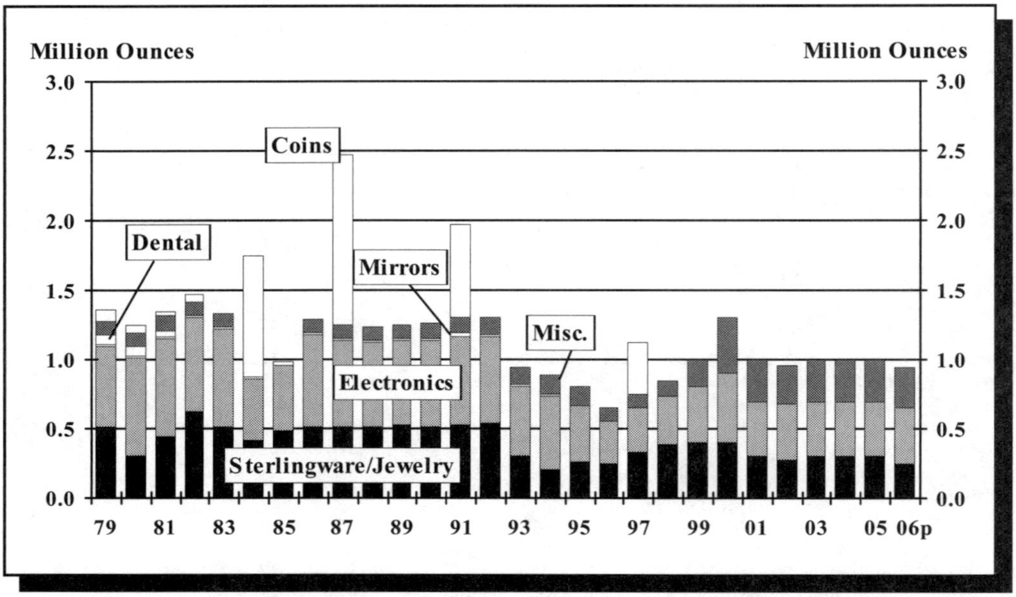

Netherlands Silver Fabrication Demand

Million Troy Ounces

	1979	1980	1981	1982	1983	1984	1985
Sterlingware/Jewelry	0.52	0.31	0.44	0.62	0.52	0.41	0.48
Electronics	0.58	0.71	0.71	0.68	0.71	0.45	0.48
Mirrors	*	*	*	*	*	*	*
Dental	0.06	0.06	0.05	—	—	—	—
Miscellaneous	0.10	0.10	0.10	0.10	0.10	—	—
Total	1.26	1.18	1.30	1.40	1.32	0.86	0.98
% Change Year Ago	—	-6.5%	10.0%	8.3%	-5.7%	-34.4%	11.5%
Coinage	0.08	0.05	0.02	0.03	—	0.87	—
Total Including Coinage	1.34	1.23	1.32	1.44	1.32	1.74	0.98
% Change Year Ago	—	-8.5%	7.5%	8.9%	-7.8%	30.8%	-43.5%

	1986	1987	1988	1989	1990	1991	1992
Sterlingware/Jewelry	0.52	0.52	0.51	0.52	0.52	0.53	0.54
Electronics	0.66	0.62	0.61	0.61	0.62	0.64	0.62
Mirrors	*	*	*	*	*	*	*
Dental	—	—	—	—	—	—	—
Miscellaneous	0.10	0.10	0.10	0.10	0.10	0.11	0.13
Total	1.28	1.29	1.23	1.29	1.29	1.29	1.29
% Change Year Ago	32.1%	-3.0%	-1.4%	1.2%	0.6%	3.3%	0.3%
Coinage	—	1.21	—	—	—	0.67	—
Total Including Coinage	1.28	2.50	1.23	1.29	1.29	1.96	1.29
% Change Year Ago	30.4%	95.9%	-51.0%	4.9%	0.5%	51.9%	-34.2%

	1993	1994	1995	1996	1997	1998	1999
Sterlingware/Jewelry	0.30	0.28	0.27	0.25	0.34	0.39	0.40
Electronics	0.50	0.53	0.40	0.30	0.31	0.35	0.40
Mirrors	*	*	*	*	*	*	*
Dental	—	—	—	—	—	—	—
Miscellaneous	0.13	0.13	0.13	0.10	0.10	0.11	0.20
Total	0.98	0.99	0.80	0.65	0.75	0.85	1.00
% Change Year Ago	-24.0%	1.0%	-19.3%	-18.7%	15.4%	13.3%	17.6%
Coinage	—	—	—	—	0.38		
Total Including Coinage	0.98	0.99	0.80	0.65	1.13		
% Change Year Ago	-24.0%	1.0%	-19.2%	-18.8%	73.6%		

	2000	2001	2002	2003	2004	2005	2006p
Sterlingware/Jewelry	0.40	0.30	0.28	0.30	0.30	0.30	0.25
Electronics	0.50	0.40	0.40	0.40	0.40	0.40	0.40
Mirrors	*	*	*	*	*	*	*
Dental	—	—	—	—	—	—	—
Miscellaneous	0.40	0.30	0.28	0.30	0.30	0.30	0.30
Total	1.30	1.00	0.96	1.00	1.00	1.00	0.95
% Change Year Ago	30.0%	-23.1%	-4.0%	4.2%	0.0%	0.0%	-5.0%

Notes: Totals may not equal the sums of categories due to rounding. *Mirrors absorb around 2,000 ounces annually.
Sources: European trade sources, CPM Group.
March 7, 2006

Annual U.S. Silver Fabrication Demand, 1986 - 1997

Million Troy Ounces

	1986	1987	1988	1989	1990	1991
Photography	55.4	60.2	62.5	65.2	68.0	66.0
Electrical Contacts and Conductors	27.4	22.7	23.0	23.5	22.8	18.3
Batteries	3.7	2.4	2.5	2.8	3.0	3.1
Sterling Ware	3.9	3.8	3.5	3.4	3.5	3.5
Jewelry	4.6	4.2	2.9	2.4	2.0	2.0
Silverplate	3.7	2.5	2.6	2.7	2.8	2.8
Brazing Alloys and Solders	6.4	5.6	5.5	6.0	6.2	6.4
Catalysts	2.3	2.4	2.6	2.8	3.0	3.3
Medallions and Commemorative Objects	4.0	4.2	—	—	—	—
Dental and Medical Supplies	1.5	1.3	1.4	1.7	1.8	—
Mirrors	1.0	1.0	1.1	1.1	1.2	1.1
Bearings	0.4	0.3	—	—	—	—
Miscellaneous	4.6	4.5	4.4	8.4	11.0	12.2
Total Industrial	118.9	115.3	112.0	120.0	125.3	118.7
% Change Year Ago	0.3%	-3.1%	-2.8%	7.1%	4.4%	-5.3%
Coinage	10.3	12.2	7.9	6.8	9.1	9.1
Total Fabrication	129.2	127.5	119.9	126.8	134.4	127.8
% Change Year Ago	8.7%	-1.4%	-5.9%	5.8%	6.0%	-4.9%

	1992	1993	1994	1995	1996	1997
Photography	64.4	65.0	71.0	72.9	78.3	84.6
Electrical Contacts and Conductors	18.3	18.8	19.5	20.9	22.3	26.5
Batteries	3.1	3.3	3.6	4.1	4.5	4.8
Sterling Ware	3.9	4.0	4.2	4.4	4.8	5.1
Jewelry	3.0	3.3	3.7	4.1	4.4	4.9
Silverplate	2.9	3.0	3.1	3.5	3.9	4.1
Brazing Alloys and Solders	7.1	7.2	7.5	7.7	8.2	8.9
Catalysts	3.8	4.0	4.2	4.9	5.5	5.7
Medallions and Commemorative Objects	—	—	—	—	—	—
Dental and Medical Supplies	—	—	—	—	—	—
Mirrors	1.2	1.3	1.5	1.7	2.1	2.4
Biocides	—	—	—	—	—	—
Miscellaneous	11.2	11.2	11.8	12.0	12.7	13.5
Total Industrial	118.9	121.1	130.1	136.2	146.7	160.5
% Change Year Ago	0.2%	1.9%	7.4%	4.7%	7.7%	9.4%
Coinage	8.1	8.9	8.1	7.5	5.0	5.3
Total Fabrication	127.0	130.0	138.2	143.7	151.7	165.8
% Change Year Ago	-0.6%	2.4%	6.3%	4.0%	5.6%	9.3%

Annual U.S. Silver Fabrication Demand, 1998 - 2006p

Million Troy Ounces

	1998	1999	2000	2001	2002	2003
Photography	91.0	96.0	104.0	102.0	104.0	103.0
Electrical Contacts and Conductors	28.4	29.2	32.7	29.5	27.3	28.3
Batteries	4.9	5.0	5.2	5.3	5.4	5.5
Sterling Ware	5.7	5.8	5.6	4.6	4.4	4.5
Jewelry	5.5	5.7	6.1	4.9	4.2	5.0
Silverplate	4.5	4.4	4.5	4.0	3.8	4.0
Brazing Alloys and Solders	9.3	9.1	8.6	8.5	8.2	8.0
Catalysts	5.9	5.9	6.3	6.1	6.0	6.3
Medallions and Commemorative Objects	—	—	—	—	—	—
Dental and Medical Supplies	—	—	—	—	—	—
Mirrors	2.6	2.6	2.6	2.5	2.4	2.5
Bearings	—	—	—	—	1.0	3.0
Miscellaneous	14.5	14.8	15.5	20.0	19.5	22.0
Total Industrial	172.3	178.5	191.1	187.4	186.2	192.1
% Change Year Ago	7.4%	3.6%	7.1%	-1.9%	-0.6%	3.2%
Coinage	5.6	9.9	10.3	10.2	11.5	10.5
Total Fabrication	177.9	188.4	201.4	197.6	197.7	202.6
% Change Year Ago	7.3%	5.9%	6.9%	-1.9%	0.0%	2.5%

	2004	2005	2006p
Photography	99.0	88.0	76.6
Electrical Contacts and Conductors	29.4	30.7	32.0
Batteries	5.5	5.8	6.0
Sterling Ware	4.7	4.7	4.4
Jewelry	5.3	5.5	5.2
Silverplate	4.1	4.2	4.0
Brazing Alloys and Solders	8.2	8.5	8.6
Catalysts	6.5	6.7	6.8
Medallions and Commemorative Objects	—	—	—
Dental and Medical Supplies	—	—	—
Mirrors	2.5	2.5	2.4
Biocides	5.0	5.2	5.4
Miscellaneous	25.0	25.0	23.0
Total Industrial	195.2	186.8	174.4
% Change Year Ago	1.6%	-4.3%	-6.6%
Coinage	11.1	9.9	10.0
Total Fabrication	206.3	196.7	174.4
% Change Year Ago	1.9%	-4.7%	-11.3%

Notes: Totals may not equal the sums of components due to rounding.
Categories marked with dashes are included in miscellaneous.
Sources: U.S. Bureau of Mines, trade sources, CPM Group.
March 7, 2006

Japanese Silver Fabrication Demand, 1973-1990
Million Troy Ounces

	1973	1974	1975	1976	1977	1978	1979	1980	1981
Photography	25.0	22.6	23.0	27.3	31.2	31.4	32.2	32.6	33.9
Electrical Contacts	11.1	9.2	5.6	6.8	6.9	7.0	8.9	7.6	6.4
Caustic Silver	4.4	2.9	2.6	4.7	5.8	6.5	6.6	5.6	5.6
Brazing Alloys and Solders	7.3	5.9	2.9	4.7	4.3	4.7	5.3	3.5	3.1
Tube, Sheet, and Bar	6.5	4.8	3.5	5.9	5.6	5.1	4.9	3.2	3.0
Electroplating	4.3	2.8	2.3	3.4	2.8	2.9	2.8	2.5	2.4
Jewelry and Silverware	3.9	1.8	1.4	2.0	2.2	2.5	2.2	1.0	1.1
Miscellaneous	6.5	7.7	5.1	6.0	4.4	4.8	5.9	5.5	4.1
Total	69.0	57.7	46.4	60.8	63.2	64.9	68.8	61.5	59.6
% Change Year Ago		-16.4%	-19.6%	31.0%	3.9%	2.7%	6.0%	-10.6%	-3.1%
Coinage	—	—	—	—	—	—	—	—	—
Total Including Coinage	69.0	57.7	46.4	60.8	63.2	64.9	68.8	61.5	59.6
% Change Year Ago	—	-16.4%	-19.6%	31.0%	3.9%	2.7%	6.0%	-10.6%	-3.1%

	1982	1983	1984	1985	1986	1987	1988	1989	1990
Photography	36.6	40.9	41.3	42.2	47.0	51.3	56.8	54.8	56.5
Electrical Contacts	6.6	7.7	7.8	7.5	6.8	7.0	8.4	9.5	9.7
Caustic Silver	5.5	6.7	7.6	6.8	7.6	8.3	9.6	9.0	9.0
Brazing Alloys and Solders	3.3	3.2	3.9	3.7	3.7	3.8	4.4	4.6	4.5
Tube, Sheet, and Bar	3.6	3.2	3.9	3.6	4.1	5.3	5.6	6.9	7.6
Electroplating	2.3	2.8	3.7	3.2	3.2	4.9	3.6	3.8	4.1
Jewelry and Silverware	1.3	1.1	1.0	1.4	1.7	2.2	3.0	3.5	3.8
Dental	—	—	—	—	—	1.4	1.6	1.7	1.4
Miscellaneous	4.0	6.5	9.6	4.2	4.4	8.1	9.0	8.7	10.3
Total	63.2	72.1	78.8	72.6	78.5	92.3	102.0	102.5	106.9
% Change Year Ago	6.0%	14.1%	9.3%	-7.9%	8.1%	17.6%	10.5%	0.5%	4.3%
Coinage	—	—	—	—	6.4	—	—	—	8.9
Total Including Coinage	63.2	72.1	78.8	72.6	84.9	92.3	102.0	102.5	115.8
% Change Year Ago	6.0%	14.1%	9.3%	-7.9%	16.9%	8.7%	10.5%	0.5%	13.0%

Notes: Totals may not equal the sums of components due to rounding. There was no silver use in coinage in Japan prior to 1986. * - unidentified uses included.
Sources: Japanese trade sources, CPM Group.
March 10, 2006

Japanese Silver Fabrication Demand, 1991-2006p

Million Troy Ounces

	1991	1992	1993	1994	1995	1996	1997	1998	1999
Photography	57.8	58.0	58.5	61.1	63.6	65.7	67.3	71.0	71.5
Electrical Contacts	9.7	8.4	8.7	8.9	10.1	9.3	11.3	7.9	6.0
Caustic Silver	8.4	7.9	7.5	8.9	10.9	10.0	9.1	8.0	7.4
Brazing Alloys and Solders	4.8	4.2	3.8	4.5	4.9	4.7	5.2	5.0	5.5
Tube, Sheet, and Bar	7.5	7.2	7.2	7.1	6.8	6.0	4.8	4.5	4.3
Electroplating	4.1	3.4	3.5	3.6	3.3	3.2	3.0	2.5	2.0
Jewelry and Silverware	3.5	2.8	2.9	2.7	2.4	2.7	2.7	2.3	2.0
Dental	1.7	1.6	1.4	1.6	1.7	1.8	1.8	1.6	1.5
Miscellaneous	11.4	13.0	18.2	17.1	18.8	20.1	21.5	16.8	16.0
Total	108.9	106.5	111.7	115.5	122.5	123.5	126.7	119.6	116.2
% Change Year Ago	1.9%	-2.2%	4.9%	3.4%	6.1%	0.8%	2.6%	-5.6%	-2.8%
Coinage	—	—	—	—	—	—	—	—	—
Total Including Coinage	108.9	106.5	111.7	115.5	122.5	123.5	126.7	119.6	116.2
% Change Year Ago	-6.0%	-2.2%	4.9%	3.4%	6.1%	0.8%	2.6%	-5.6%	-2.8%

	2000	2001	2002	2003	2004	2005	2006p
Photography	55.5	53.5	49.2	43.9	40.0	31.8	28.0
Electrical Contacts	10.8	4.8	4.9	7.0	8.3	6.6	7.0
Caustic Silver	10.0	6.5	7.1	9.5	9.9	9.4	9.8
Brazing Alloys and Solders	4.9	3.6	3.2	3.1	3.4	3.0	3.0
Tube, Sheet, and Bar	5.5	2.8	6.9	7.3	8.0	7.0	7.3
Electroplating	3.0	1.6	—	—	—	—	—
Jewelry and Silverware	3.0	2.8	2.6	2.9	3.0	3.1	3.2
Dental	2.0	1.0	—	—	—	—	—
Miscellaneous	30.7	15.4	11.5	12.3	14.0	11.3	13.0
Super Conductors	—	—	2.5	10.0	25.0	30.0	30.0
Total	125.4	92.0	87.9	96.0	111.6	102.2	101.3
% Change Year Ago	7.9%	-26.6%	-4.5%	9.2%	16.2%	-8.4%	-0.9%
Coinage	—	—	—	—	—	—	—
Total Including Coinage	125.4	92.0	87.9	96.0	111.6	102.2	101.3
% Change Year Ago	7.9%	-26.6%	-4.5%	9.2%	16.2%	-8.4%	-0.9%

Thai Silver Fabrication Demand

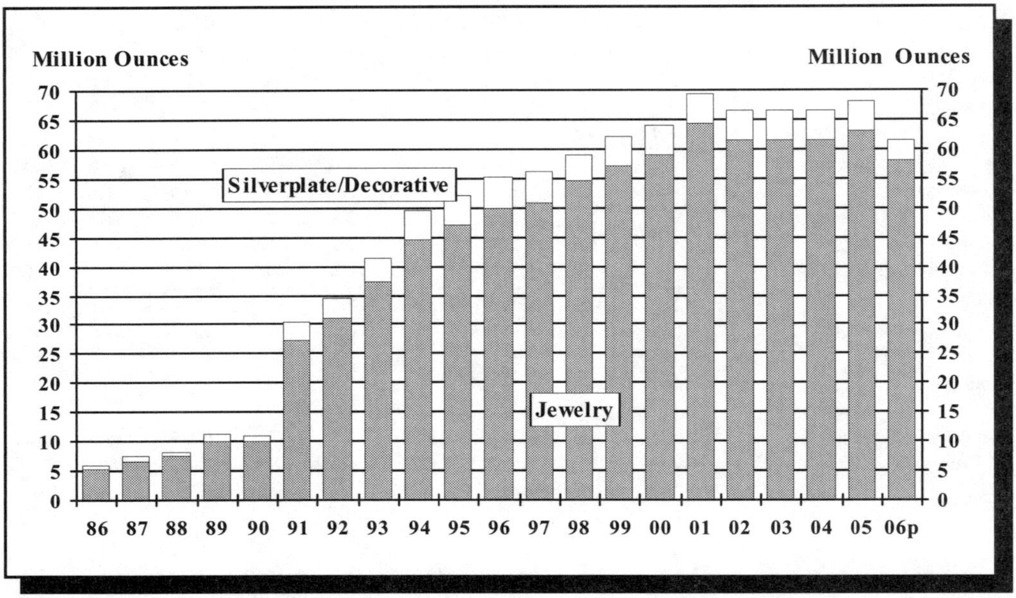

Thai Silver Fabrication Demand
Million Troy Ounces

	1986	1987	1988	1989	1990	1991
Jewelry	5.3	6.6	7.4	10.1	9.9	27.3
Silverplate/Decorative	0.6	0.7	0.8	1.1	1.1	3.0
Total Demand	5.9	7.4	8.2	11.2	11.0	30.4
% Change Year Ago	—	25.0%	11.1%	36.7%	-1.9%	176.2%

	1992	1993	1994	1995	1996	1997
Jewelry	31.0	37.3	44.7	46.9	49.8	50.8
Silverplate/Decorative	3.4	4.1	5.0	5.1	5.4	5.5
Total Demand	34.5	41.4	49.7	52.0	55.1	56.3
% Change Year Ago	13.5%	20.0%	20.0%	4.7%	6.0%	2.1%

	1998	1999	2000	2001	2002	2003
Jewelry	54.5	57.0	59.0	64.2	61.5	61.5
Silverplate/Decorative	4.5	5.0	5.0	5.3	5.0	5.0
Total Demand	59.0	62.0	64.0	69.5	66.5	66.5
% Change Year Ago	4.8%	5.1%	3.2%	8.6%	-4.3%	0.0%

	2004	2005	2006p
Jewelry	61.5	63.0	58.0
Silverplate/Decorative	5.0	5.0	3.5
Total Demand	66.5	68.0	61.5
% Change Year Ago	0.0%	2.3%	-9.6%

Notes: Totals may not equal the sums of categories due to rounding.
Sources: Thai trade sources, CPM Group.
March 7, 2006

South Korean Silver Fabrication Demand

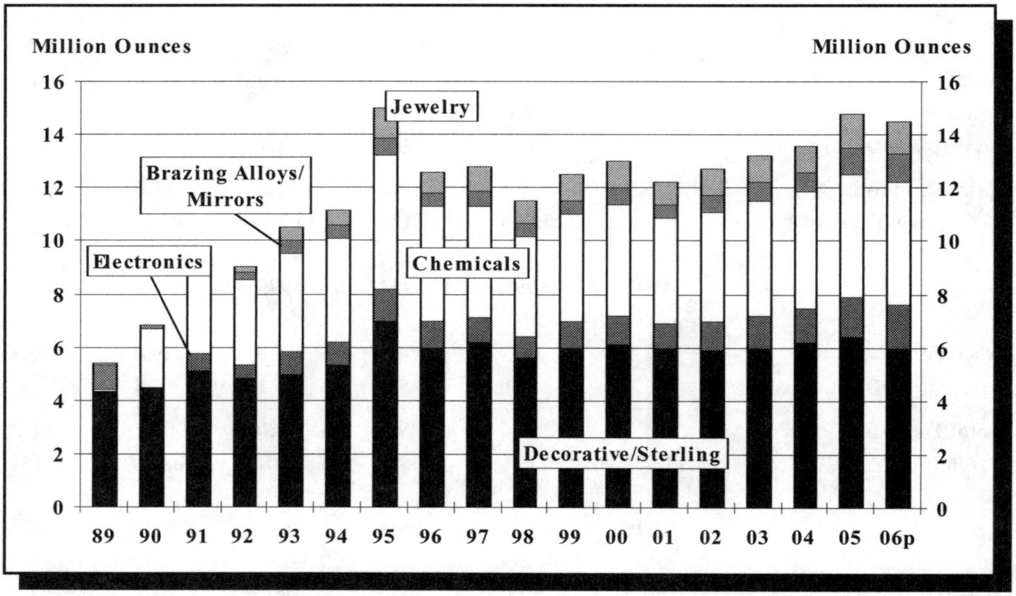

South Korean Silver Fabrication Demand
Million Troy Ounces

	1989	1990	1991	1992	1993	1994	1995
Decorative/Sterling	4.3	4.5	5.1	4.8	5.0	5.3	7.0
Electronics	0.0	0.0	0.6	0.5	0.8	0.9	1.2
Chemicals	0.0	2.2	3.2	3.2	3.7	3.9	5.0
Brazing Alloys	1.0	0.1	0.2	0.3	0.5	0.5	0.7
Jewelry	0.0	0.0	0.2	0.2	0.5	0.6	1.1
Total	5.4	6.8	9.3	9.0	10.5	11.2	15.0
% Change Year Ago	—	27.4%	36.2%	-3.1%	16.2%	6.7%	33.9%

	1996	1997	1998	1999	2000	2001	2002
Decorative/Sterling	6.0	6.2	5.6	6.0	6.1	6.0	5.9
Electronics	1.0	0.9	0.8	1.0	1.1	0.9	1.1
Chemicals	4.3	4.2	3.8	4.0	4.2	4.0	4.1
Brazing Alloys	0.5	0.6	0.5	0.5	0.6	0.5	0.6
Jewelry	0.8	0.9	0.8	1.0	1.0	0.8	1.0
Total	12.6	12.8	11.5	12.5	13.0	12.2	12.7
% Change Year Ago	-16.0%	1.6%	-10.2%	8.7%	4.0%	-6.2%	4.1%

	2003	2004	2005	2006p
Decorative/Sterling	6.0	6.2	6.4	6.0
Electronics	1.2	1.3	1.5	1.6
Chemicals	4.3	4.4	4.6	4.6
Mirrors	-	-	-	-
Brazing Alloys	0.7	0.7	1.0	1.1
Jewelry	1.0	1.0	1.3	1.2
Total	13.2	13.6	14.8	14.5
% Change Year Ago	3.9%	3.0%	8.8%	-2.0%

Notes: Totals may not equal sums of categories due to rounding. Consumption in individual industries prior to 1989 totaled less than 100,000 ounces. Dashes indicate that consumption was less than 100,000 ounces.
Sources: Trade sources, CPM Group
March 7, 2006

Taiwan Silver Fabrication Demand

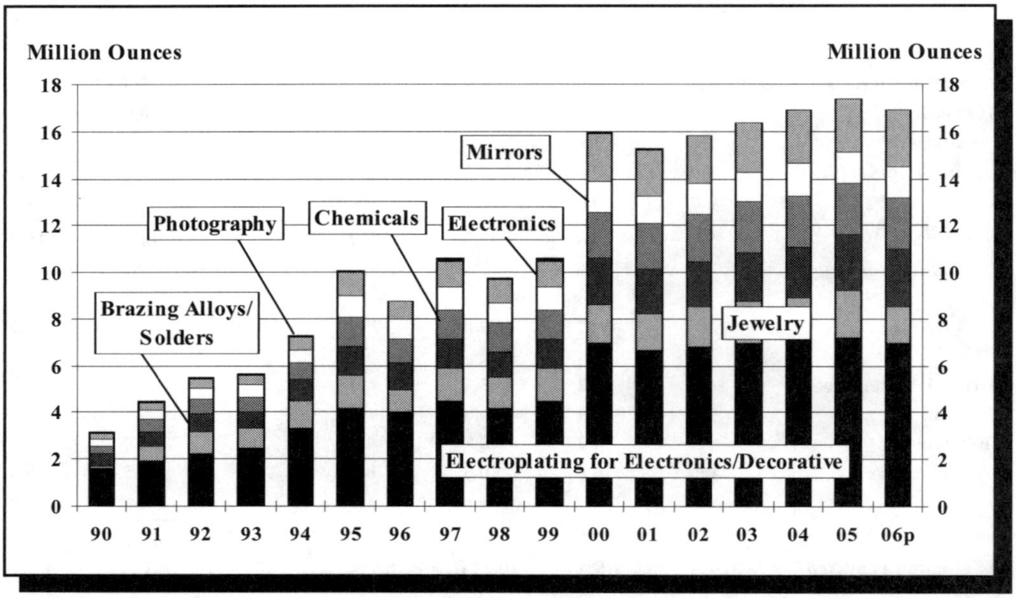

Taiwan Silver Fabrication Demand
Million Troy Ounces

	1990	1991	1992	1993	1994	1995	1996	1997
Photography	0.1	0.1	0.1	0.1	0.1	0.1	0.0	0.1
Electronics	0.3	0.3	0.4	0.4	0.5	1.0	0.8	1.1
Electroplating for								
Electronics and Decorative	1.6	1.9	2.3	2.5	3.3	4.2	4.0	4.5
Chemicals	0.3	0.5	0.6	0.6	0.7	1.3	1.0	1.3
Mirrors	0.3	0.4	0.5	0.5	0.6	0.9	0.9	1.0
Brazing Alloys and Solders	0.5	0.6	0.7	0.7	0.9	1.2	1.1	1.2
Jewelry	0.1	0.6	1.0	0.9	1.2	1.4	1.0	1.4
Total	3.2	4.5	5.5	5.6	7.3	10.1	8.8	10.6
% Change Year Ago	—	40.5%	23.0%	2.2%	29.5%	38.4%	-12.9%	20.5%

	1998	1999	2000	2001	2002	2003	2004	2005
Photography	0.1	0.1	0.1	0.1	0.0	0.0	0.0	0.0
Electronics	1.0	1.1	2.0	1.9	2.0	2.1	2.2	2.3
Electroplating for								
Electronics and Decorative	4.2	4.5	7.0	6.7	6.8	7.0	7.1	7.2
Chemicals	1.2	1.3	2.0	1.9	2.0	2.1	2.2	2.2
Mirrors	0.9	1.0	1.3	1.2	1.3	1.3	1.4	1.3
Brazing Alloys and Solders	1.1	1.2	2.0	2.0	2.0	2.1	2.2	2.4
Jewelry	1.3	1.4	1.6	1.5	1.7	1.8	1.8	2.0
Total	9.8	10.6	16.0	15.3	15.8	16.4	16.9	17.4
% Change Year Ago	-7.5%	8.2%	50.9%	-4.4%	3.3%	3.8%	3.0%	3.0%

	2006p
Photography	0.0
Electronics	2.4
Electroplating for	
Electronics and Decorative	7.0
Chemicals	2.2
Mirrors	1.3
Brazing Alloys and Solders	2.5
Jewelry	1.5
Total	16.9
% Change Year Ago	-2.9%

Notes: Totals may not equal sums of categories due to rounding. Consumption in individual industries prior to 1990 totaled less than 100,000 ounces.
Sources: Trade sources, CPM Group.
March 7, 2006

Hong Kong Silver Fabrication Demand

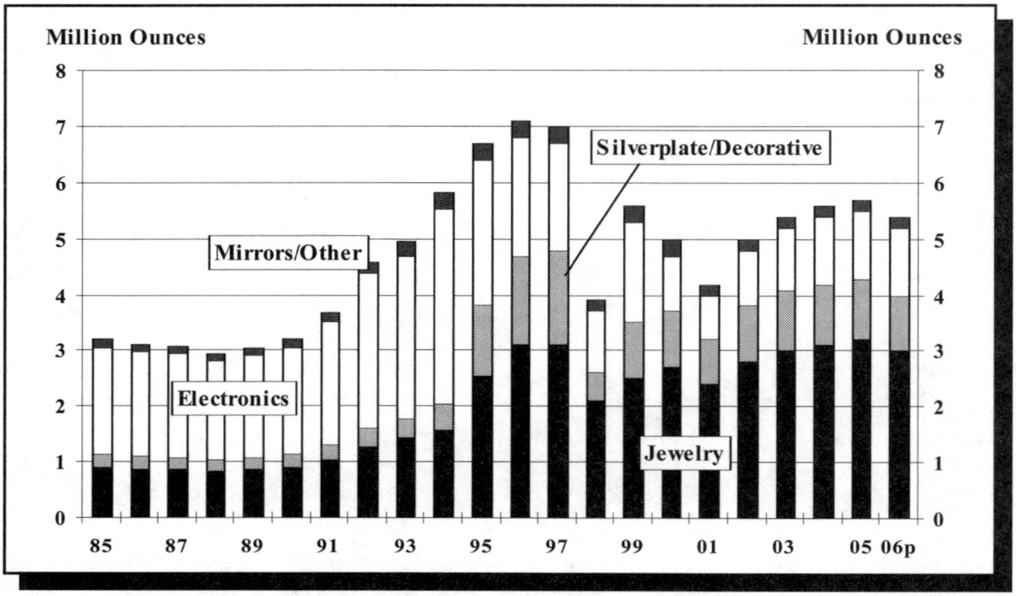

Hong Kong Silver Fabrication Demand

Million Troy Ounces

	1985	1986	1987	1988	1989	1990
Jewelry	0.9	0.9	0.9	0.8	0.9	0.9
Silverplate/decorative	0.2	0.2	0.2	0.2	0.2	0.2
Electronics	1.9	1.9	1.9	1.8	1.8	1.9
Mirrors/other	0.2	0.2	0.2	0.1	0.2	0.2
Total Demand	3.2	3.1	3.1	3.0	3.1	3.2
% Change Year Ago	—	-3.0%	-1.0%	-4.2%	3.3%	5.3%

	1991	1992	1993	1994	1995	1996
Jewelry	1.0	1.3	1.4	1.6	2.5	3.1
Silverplate/decorative	0.3	0.3	0.4	0.5	1.3	1.6
Electronics	2.2	2.8	2.9	3.5	2.6	2.1
Mirrors/other	0.2	0.2	0.3	0.3	0.3	0.3
Total Demand	3.7	4.6	4.9	5.8	6.7	7.1
% Change Year Ago	15.0%	24.4%	7.5%	17.9%	14.9%	6.0%

	1997	1998	1999	2000	2001	2002
Jewelry	3.1	2.1	2.5	2.7	2.4	2.8
Silverplate/decorative	1.7	0.5	1.0	1.0	0.8	1.0
Electronics	1.9	1.1	1.8	1.0	0.8	1.0
Mirrors/other	0.3	0.2	0.3	0.3	0.2	0.2
Total Demand	7.0	3.9	5.6	5.0	4.2	5.0
% Change Year Ago	-1.4%	-44.3%	43.6%	-10.7%	-16.0%	19.0%

	2003	2004	2005	2006p
Jewelry	3.0	3.1	3.2	3.0
Silverplate/decorative	1.1	1.1	1.1	1.0
Electronics	1.1	1.2	1.2	1.2
Mirrors/other	0.2	0.2	0.2	0.2
Total Demand	5.4	5.6	5.7	5.4
% Change Year Ago	8.0%	3.7%	1.8%	-5.3%

Notes: Totals may not equal the sums of categories due to rounding. Consumption in individual industries prior to 1985 totaled less than 100,000 ounces.
Sources: Hong Kong trade sources, CPM Group.
March 7, 2006

Indian Silver Fabrication Demand

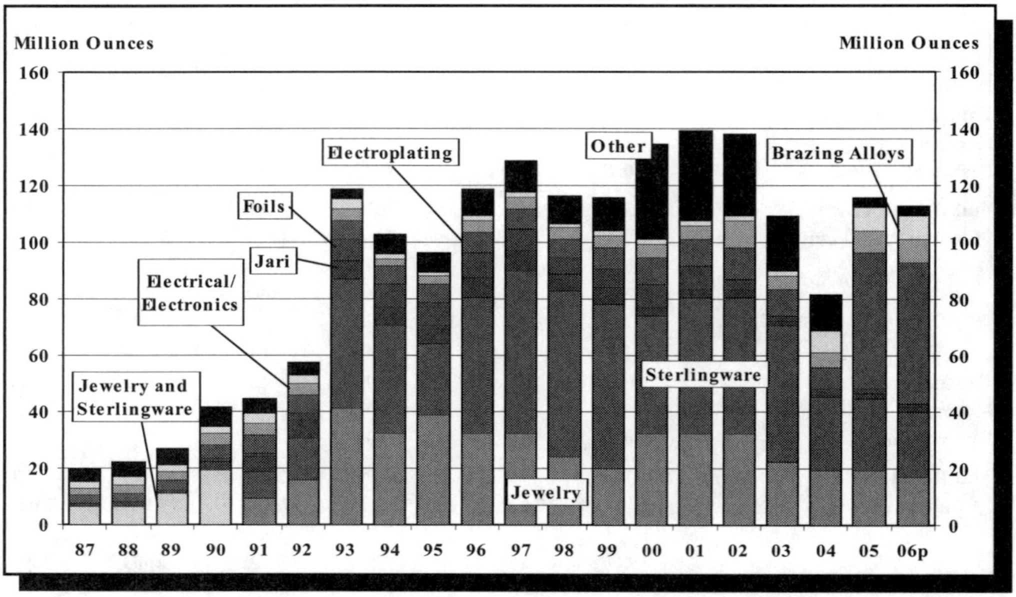

Indian Silver Fabrication Demand
Million Troy Ounces

	1987	1988	1989	1990	1991	1992	1993	1994	1995	1996
Industrial Uses										
Photography	4.1	4.8	4.8	5.6	2.6	2.6	2.3	1.6	0.6	0.6
Electoplating	2.7	3.2	3.2	4.8	6.4	6.4	6.4	6.4	6.4	7.2
Electrical/Electronics	2.7	3.2	3.2	4.0	4.2	4.2	4.2	2.6	3.2	4.0
Brazing Alloys	2.2	2.4	2.4	2.4	3.2	3.2	3.2	1.6	1.0	1.6
Jari	1.4	1.6	1.6	3.2	5.1	6.4	6.4	6.4	6.4	7.1
Foils	—	—	—	1.0	1.6	2.3	8.0	8.0	8.0	8.8
Chemicals	—	—	—	—	—	—	—	2.3	3.2	3.2
Mirrors and Bangels										1.6
Miscellaneous	0.7	0.8	0.8	1.4	2.6	2.3	1.6	3.2	3.2	4.3
Subtotal	13.8	16.0	16.1	22.5	25.7	27.3	32.2	32.1	32.2	38.6
% Change Year Ago	-	15.9%	0.5%	39.8%	-12.5%	6.2%	18.0%	-0.3%	0.3%	20.0%
Jewelry and Silverware										
Jewelry	—	—	—	—	9.6	16.1	41.3	32.2	38.6	32.2
Silverware	—	—	—	—	9.2	14.4	45.5	38.6	25.7	48.2
Subtotal	6.3	6.4	10.9	19.3	18.8	30.5	86.8	70.7	64.3	80.4
% Change Year Ago	—	1.6%	70.3%	77.1%	-2.6%	62.2%	184.6%	-18.5%	-9.1%	25.0%
Total	20.1	22.4	27.0	41.8	44.5	57.8	119.0	102.9	96.5	119.0
% Change Year Ago	—	11.4%	20.4%	54.8%	6.5%	29.9%	105.9%	-13.5%	-6.2%	23.3%

	1997	1998	1999	2000	2001	2002	2003	2004	2005	2006p
Industrial Uses										
Photography	0.6	0.6	1.0	—	—	—	—	—	—	—
Electroplating	7.2	6.6	7.4	9.6	9.6	11.3	9.6	8.0	48.2	50.0
Electrical/Electronics	4.2	4.0	4.5	4.8	4.8	9.7	4.8	4.8	8.0	8.0
Brazing Alloys	1.6	1.3	1.7	1.6	1.6	1.6	1.6	8.0	8.0	8.0
Jari	7.1	6.0	6.0	3.2	3.2	3.2	1.6	0.8	1.6	1.6
Foils	7.6	5.7	6.5	8.0	8.0	3.2	1.6	2.3	1.6	1.6
Chemicals	4.0	3.8	4.5	20.9	19.3	16.1	9.6	7.7	0.6	1.0
Mirrors & Bangles	1.9	1.6	2.3	3.2	3.2	3.2	2.4	2.3	—	—
Miscellaneous	4.3	4.0	3.7	9.6	9.6	9.7	7.2	2.7	2.6	2.6
Total	38.6	33.6	37.6	60.9	59.3	57.9	38.6	36.7	70.7	72.8
% Change Year Ago	0.0%	-12.9%	11.8%	62.0%	-2.6%	-2.4%	-33.4%	-5.0%	93.0%	2.9%
Jewelry and Silverware										
Jewelry	32.2	24.0	20.2	32.1	32.1	32.2	22.5	19.3	19.3	17.0
Silverware	57.9	59.2	57.9	41.8	48.3	48.2	48.2	25.7	25.7	23.0
% Change Year Ago	90.0	83.1	78.1	73.9	80.4	80.4	70.7	45.0	45.0	40.0
	12.0%	-7.7%	-6.0%	-5.4%	8.8%	0.0%	-12.0%	-36.4%	0.0%	-11.1%
Total	128.6	116.8	115.7	134.8	139.7	138.3	109.3	81.7	115.7	112.8
% Change Year Ago	8.1%	-9.2%	-0.9%	16.5%	3.6%	-1.0%	-20.9%	-25.3%	41.7%	-2.5%

Note: Totals may not equal the sums of categories due to rounding. Photography included in chemical from 2000.
Silver Nitrate in miscellaneous, mirrors and bangles in plating, 2005-2006.
Silverware includes some kilo bars, tola bars, coins, and medallions for investment purposes
Sources: Indian trade sources, CPM Group.
March 7, 2006

Pakistan Silver Fabrication Demand

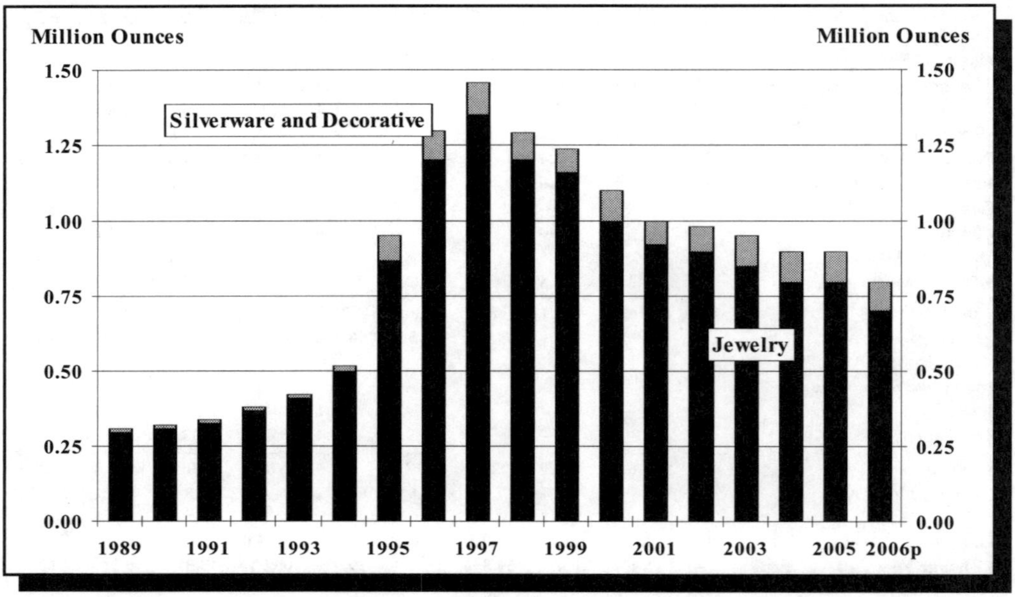

Pakistan Silver Fabrication Demand
Million Troy Ounces

	1989	1990	1991	1992	1993	1994
Jewelry	0.90	0.91	0.94	1.08	1.21	1.60
Silverware and Decorative	0.30	0.32	0.35	0.35	0.40	0.43
Total	1.20	1.23	1.29	1.43	1.61	2.03
% Change Year Ago	—	2.5%	4.9%	10.9%	12.5%	26.2%
	1995	**1996**	**1997**	**1998**	**1999**	**2000**
Jewelry	3.40	6.70	7.50	7.00	6.80	6.20
Silverware and Decorative	0.50	0.10	0.15	0.13	0.10	0.10
Total	3.90	6.80	7.65	7.13	6.90	6.30
% Change Year Ago	92.1%	74.4%	12.5%	-6.8%	-3.2%	-8.7%
	2001	**2002**	**2003**	**2004**	**2005**	**2006p**
Jewelry	5.60	5.75	4.75	5.00	4.70	4.50
Silverware and Decorative	0.10	0.25	0.25	0.25	0.30	0.20
Total	5.70	6.00	5.00	5.25	5.00	4.70
% Change Year Ago	-9.5%	5.3%	-16.7%	5.0%	-4.8%	-6.0%

Note: Totals may not equal the sums of categories due to rounding.
Sources: Trade sources, CPM Group.
March 7, 2006

Bangladesh Silver Fabrication Demand

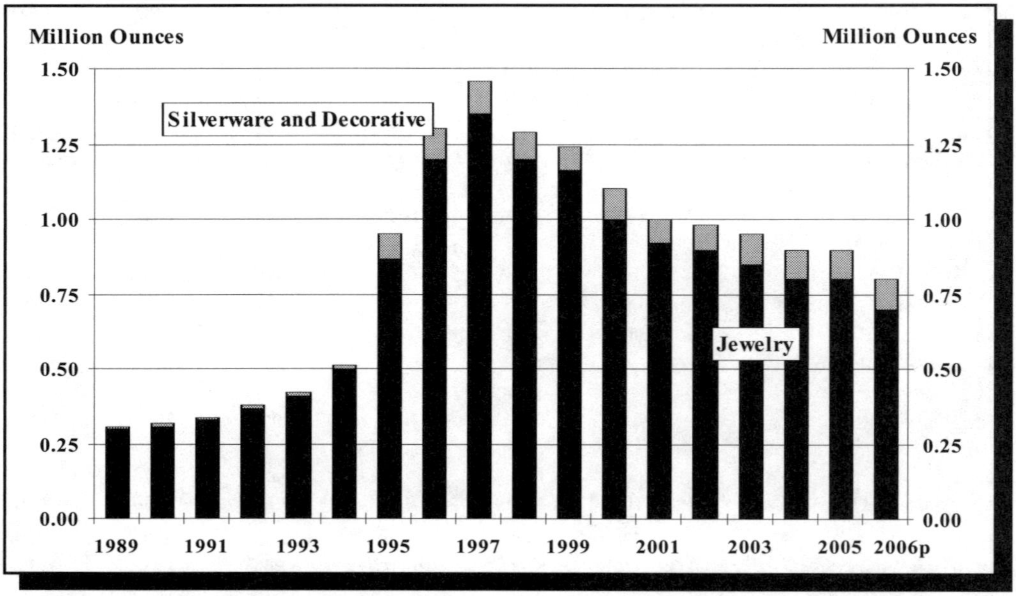

Bangladesh Silver Fabrication Demand
Million Troy Ounces

	1989	1990	1991	1992	1993
Jewelry	0.30	0.31	0.33	0.37	0.41
Silverware and Decorative	0.01	0.01	0.01	0.01	0.01
Total	0.31	0.32	0.34	0.38	0.42
% Change Year Ago	—	3.2%	6.3%	11.8%	10.5%

	1994	1995	1996	1997	1998
Jewelry	0.50	0.87	1.20	1.35	1.20
Silverware and Decorative	0.02	0.08	0.10	0.11	0.09
Total	0.52	0.95	1.30	1.46	1.29
% Change Year Ago	23.8%	82.7%	36.8%	12.3%	-11.6%

	1999	2000	2001	2002	2003
Jewelry	1.16	1.00	0.92	0.90	0.85
Silverware and Decorative	0.08	0.10	0.08	0.08	0.10
Total	1.24	1.10	1.00	0.98	0.95
% Change Year Ago	-3.9%	-11.3%	-9.1%	-2.0%	-3.1%

	2004	2005	2006p
Jewelry	0.80	0.80	0.70
Silverware and Decorative	0.10	0.10	0.10
Total	0.90	0.90	0.80
% Change Year Ago	-5.3%	0.0%	-11.1%

Note: Totals may not equal the sums of categories due to rounding.
Sources: Trade sources, CPM Group.
March 7, 2006

Mexican Silver Fabrication Demand

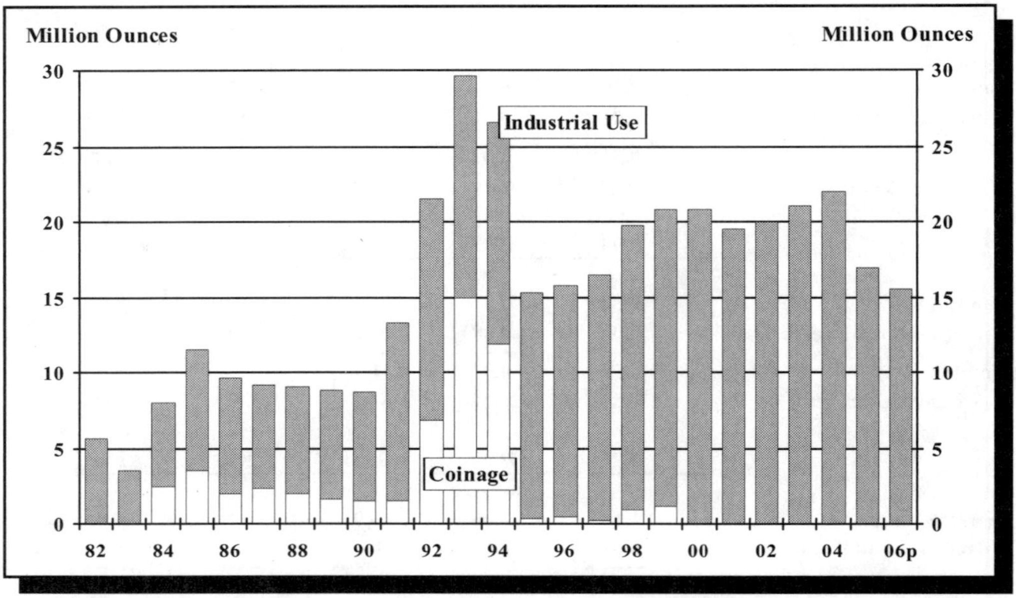

Mexican Silver Fabrication Demand
Million Troy Ounces

	1982	1983	1984	1985	1986	1987	1988	1989
Industrial								
Photography	3.2	2.0	3.1	4.5	4.3	3.9	4.0	4.0
Jewelry and Decorative	1.7	1.0	1.6	2.3	2.2	2.0	2.1	2.1
Electronics and Electrical Contacts	0.9	0.5	0.8	1.2	1.2	1.0	1.0	1.1
Subtotal	5.7	3.5	5.5	8.0	7.7	6.9	7.1	7.1
% Change Year Ago	-	-38.6%	57.1%	45.5%	-3.8%	-10.4%	2.9%	0.0%
Coinage			2.5	3.5	2.0	2.3	2.0	1.7
% Change Year Ago	-	NM	NM	40.0%	-42.9%	15.0%	-13.0%	-15.0%
Total Fabrication Demand	5.7	3.5	8.0	11.5	9.7	9.2	9.1	8.8
% Change Year Ago	-	-38.6%	128.6%	43.8%	-15.7%	-5.2%	-1.1%	-3.3%

	1990	1991	1992	1993	1994	1995	1996	1997
Industrial								
Photography	4.0	6.6	8.1	8.1	8.1	8.3	8.3	8.4
Jewelry and Decorative	2.1	3.4	4.4	4.4	4.4	4.5	4.6	5.1
Electronics and Electrical Contacts	1.1	1.8	2.2	2.2	2.2	2.3	2.4	2.7
Subtotal	7.2	11.8	14.7	14.7	14.7	15.0	15.3	16.2
% Change Year Ago	1.4%	63.2%	25.1%	0.0%		2.0%	2.0%	5.9%
Coinage	1.5	1.5	6.8	15.0	11.9	0.3	0.5	0.3
% Change Year Ago	-11.8%	0.0%	353.3%	120.6%	-20.7%	-97.5%	66.7%	-49.2%
Total Fabrication Demand	8.7	13.3	21.5	29.7	26.6	15.3	15.8	16.5
% Change Year Ago	-1.1%	52.3%	62.3%	38.1%	-10.4%	-42.5%	3.3%	4.1%

	1998	1999	2000	2001	2002	2003	2004	2005
Industrial								
Photography	8.8	9.2	10.0	9.3	9.5	10.0	10.4	5.0
Jewelry and Decorative	7.2	7.5	7.6	7.2	7.5	8.0	8.4	8.8
Electronics and Electrical Contacts	2.8	2.9	3.2	3.0	3.0	3.1	3.2	3.2
Subtotal	18.8	19.6	20.8	19.5	20.0	21.1	22.0	17.0
% Change Year Ago	16.0%	4.3%	6.1%	-6.3%	2.6%	5.5%	4.3%	-22.7%
Coinage	1.0	0.4	0.7	1.4	1.1	1.0	0.9	0.6
% Change Year Ago	293.6%	-60.0%	75.0%	100.0%	-21.4%	-9.1%	-10.0%	-33.3%
Total Fabrication Demand	19.8	20.0	21.5	20.9	21.1	22.1	22.9	17.6
% Change Year Ago	20.3%	1.0%	7.5%	-2.8%	1.0%	4.7%	3.6%	-23.1%

	2006p
Industrial	
Photography	4.0
Jewelry and Decorative	8.3
Electronics and Electrical Contacts	3.2
Subtotal	15.5
% Change Year Ago	-8.8%
Coinage	0.8
% Change Year Ago	33.3%
Total Fabrication Demand	16.3
% Change Year Ago	-7.4%

Notes: Totals may not equal the sums of categories because of rounding. NM - Not Meaningful.
Sources: Industry sources, CPM Group.
March 7, 2006

Brazilian Silver Fabrication Demand

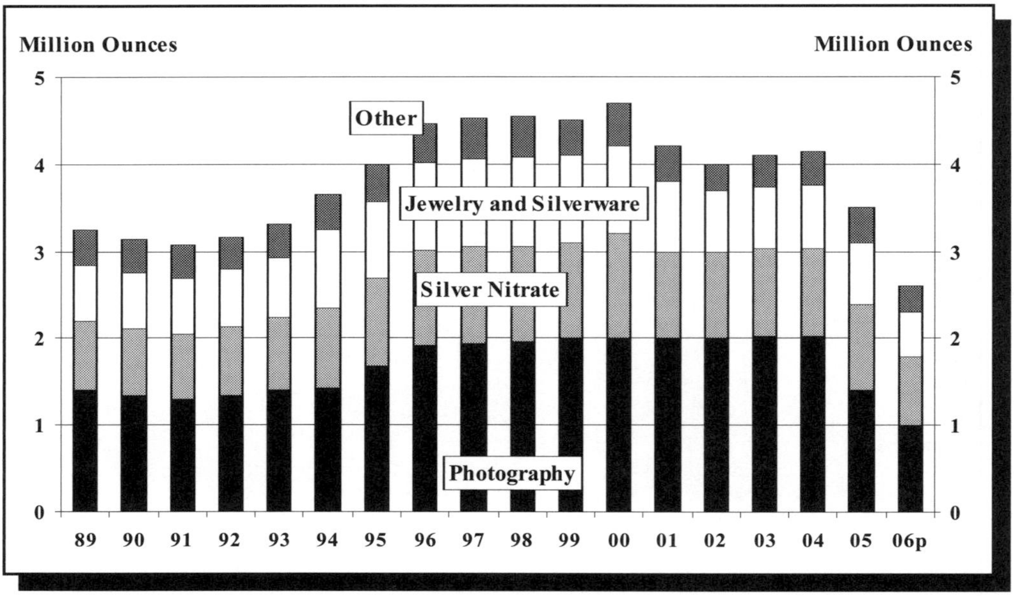

Brazilian Silver Fabrication Demand
Million Troy Ounces

	1989	1990	1991	1992	1993	1994
Photography	1.40	1.34	1.30	1.34	1.41	1.43
Silver Nitrate	0.80	0.78	0.76	0.80	0.84	0.93
Jewelry and Silverware	0.65	0.64	0.64	0.65	0.67	0.89
Other	0.39	0.38	0.37	0.38	0.39	0.41
Total	3.24	3.14	3.07	3.17	3.31	3.66
% Change Year Ago	—	-3.1%	-2.2%	3.3%	4.4%	10.6%

	1995	1996	1997	1998	1999	2000
Photography	1.68	1.92	1.95	1.96	2.00	2.00
Silver Nitrate	1.02	1.09	1.11	1.10	1.10	1.20
Jewelry and Silverware	0.87	1.00	1.01	1.02	1.00	1.00
Other	0.43	0.46	0.47	0.48	0.40	0.50
Total	4.00	4.47	4.54	4.56	4.50	4.70
% Change Year Ago	9.2%	11.9%	1.6%	0.4%	-1.3%	4.4%

	2001	2002	2003	2004	2005	2006p
Photography	2.00	2.00	2.02	2.02	1.40	1.00
Silver Nitrate	1.00	1.00	1.01	1.01	1.00	0.80
Jewelry and Silverware	0.80	0.70	0.71	0.73	0.70	0.50
Other	0.40	0.30	0.36	0.38	0.40	0.30
Total	4.20	4.00	4.10	4.14	3.50	2.60
% Change Year Ago	-10.6%	-4.8%	2.5%	1.0%	-15.5%	-25.7%

Note: Totals may not equal the sums of categories due to rounding.
Sources: Centromin, Doe Run Peru, industry sources, CPM Group.
March 7, 2006

Peruvian Silver Fabrication Demand

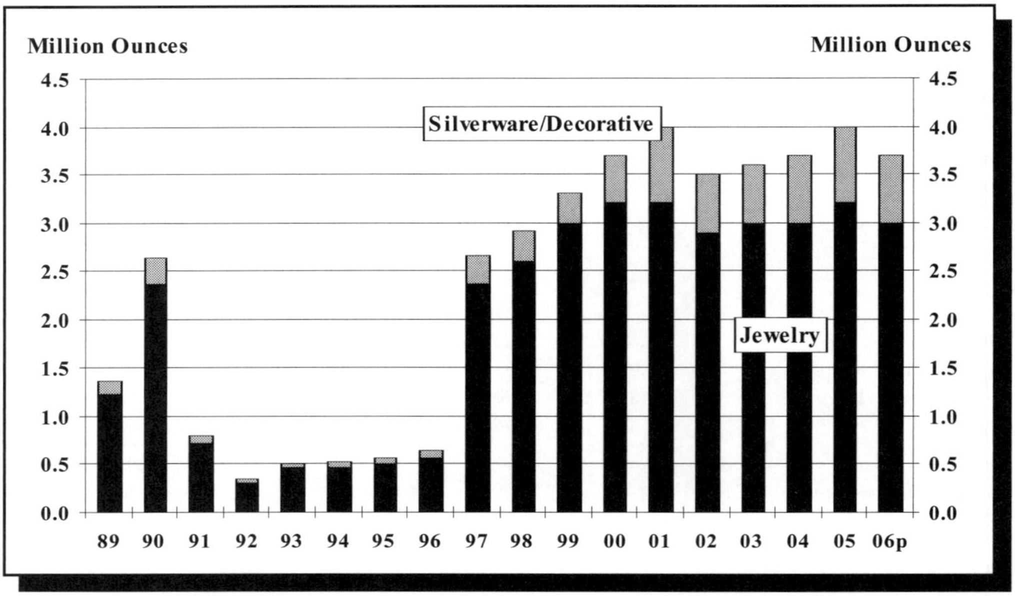

Peruvian Silver Fabrication Demand

Million Troy Ounces

	1989	1990	1991	1992	1993	1994
Jewelry	1.24	2.37	0.72	0.32	0.46	0.47
Silverplate/ Decorative	0.14	0.26	0.08	0.04	0.05	0.05
Total	1.37	2.64	0.80	0.35	0.51	0.52
% Change Year Ago	—	92.0%	-69.5%	-56.0%	45.5%	1.1%

	1995	1996	1997	1998	1999	2000
Jewelry	0.51	0.57	2.37	2.61	3.00	3.20
Silverplate/ Decorative	0.06	0.07	0.29	0.31	0.30	0.50
Total	0.57	0.64	2.66	2.92	3.30	3.70
% Change Year Ago	10.5%	11.6%	314.7%	9.8%	13.0%	12.1%

	2001	2002	2003	2004	2005	2006p
Jewelry	3.20	2.90	3.00	3.00	3.20	3.00
Silverplate/ Decorative	0.80	0.60	0.60	0.70	0.80	0.70
Total	4.00	3.50	3.60	3.70	4.00	3.70
% Change Year Ago	8.1%	-12.5%	2.9%	2.8%	8.1%	-7.5%

Note: Totals may not equal the sums of categories due to rounding.
Sources: Centromin, Doe Run Peru, industry sources, CPM Group.
March 7, 2006

Canadian Silver Fabrication Demand

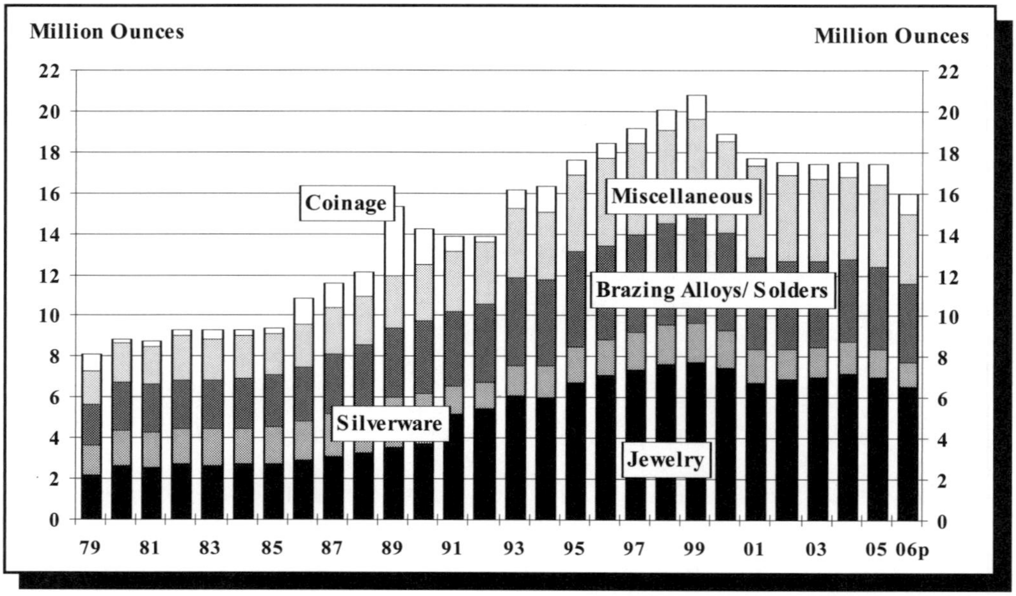

Canadian Silver Fabrication Demand
Million Troy Ounces

	1979	1980	1981	1982	1983	1984	1985	1986	1987
Jewelry	2.2	2.6	2.6	2.7	2.7	2.7	2.7	2.9	3.1
Silverware	1.5	1.7	1.7	1.8	1.8	1.8	1.8	1.9	2.1
Brazing Alloys/Solders	2.0	2.4	2.4	2.3	2.4	2.4	2.5	2.7	2.9
Miscellaneous	1.6	1.9	1.9	2.2	2.0	2.1	2.0	2.1	2.3
Total	7.3	8.7	8.5	9.0	8.9	9.0	9.1	9.6	10.4
% Change Year Ago	—	19.2%	-2.3%	5.9%	-1.1%	1.1%	1.1%	5.5%	8.3%
Coinage	0.8	0.2	0.3	0.3	0.4	0.3	0.3	1.3	1.2
Total Including Coinage	8.1	8.9	8.8	9.3	9.3	9.3	9.4	10.9	11.6
% Change Year Ago	—	9.9%	-1.1%	5.7%	0.0%	0.0%	1.1%	16.0%	6.4%

	1988	1989	1990	1991	1992	1993	1994	1995	1996
Jewelry	3.3	3.6	3.8	5.2	5.4	6.1	6.0	6.8	7.1
Silverware	2.2	2.4	2.5	1.3	1.4	1.5	1.5	1.7	1.8
Brazing Alloys/Solders	3.1	3.4	3.5	3.7	3.8	4.3	4.2	4.7	4.6
Miscellaneous	2.4	2.6	2.8	2.9	3.0	3.3	3.3	3.7	4.2
Total	11.0	12.0	12.5	13.1	13.6	15.2	15.1	16.9	17.7
% Change Year Ago	5.8%	9.1%	4.2%	4.8%	3.8%	11.8%	-0.7%	11.9%	4.7%
Coinage	1.1	3.3	1.7	0.8	0.3	1.0	1.2	0.7	0.7
Total Including Coinage	12.1	15.3	14.2	13.9	13.9	16.2	16.3	17.6	18.4
% Change Year Ago	4.3%	26.4%	-7.2%	-2.1%	0.0%	16.5%	0.6%	8.0%	4.5%

	1997	1998	1999	2000	2001	2002	2003	2004	2005
Jewelry	7.4	7.6	7.8	7.5	6.8	6.9	7.0	7.2	7.0
Silverware	1.8	1.9	1.9	1.8	1.6	1.5	1.5	1.6	1.4
Brazing Alloys/Solders	4.8	5.0	5.1	4.8	4.5	4.3	4.2	4.0	4.0
Miscellaneous	4.4	4.6	4.8	4.4	4.4	4.2	4.0	4.0	4.0
Total	18.4	19.1	19.6	18.5	17.3	16.9	16.7	16.8	16.4
% Change Year Ago	4.0%	3.8%	2.6%	-5.6%	-6.5%	-2.3%	-1.2%	0.6%	-2.4%
Coinage	0.8	1.0	1.2	0.4	0.4	0.6	0.7	0.7	1.0
Total Including Coinage	19.2	20.1	20.8	18.9	17.7	17.5	17.4	17.5	17.4
% Change Year Ago	4.2%	4.9%	3.5%	-9.1%	-6.3%	-1.1%	-0.6%	0.6%	-0.6%

	2006p
Jewelry	6.6
Silverware	1.2
Brazing Alloys/Solders	3.8
Miscellaneous	3.4
Total	15.0
% Change Year Ago	-8.5%
Coinage	1.0
Total Including Coinage	16.0
% Change Year Ago	-8.0%

Notes: Totals may not equal the sums of categories due to rounding.
Sources: Statistics Canada, trade sources, CPM Group.
March 7, 2006

Australian Silver Fabrication Demand

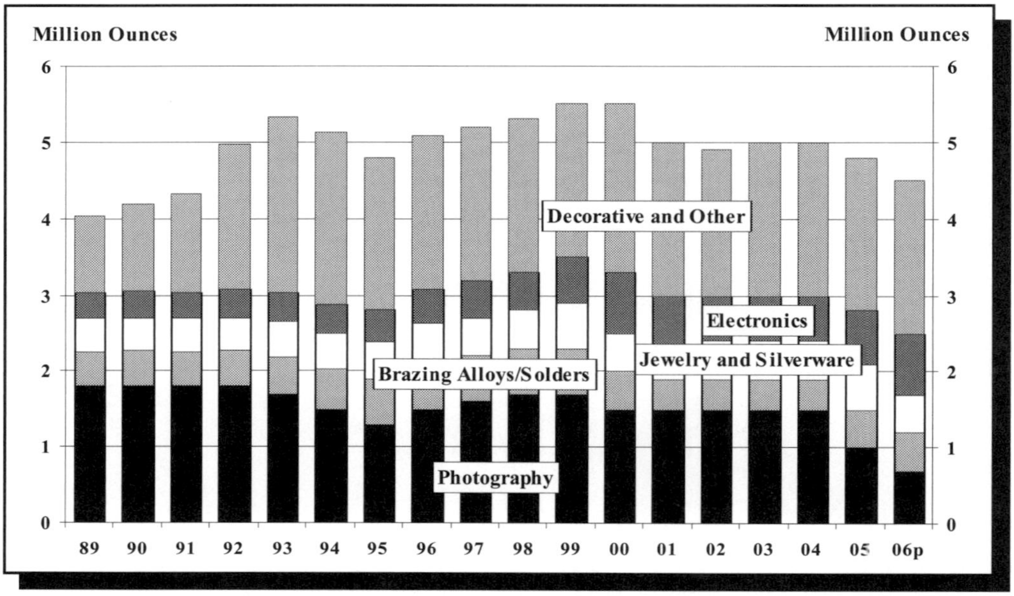

Australian Silver Fabrication Demand
Million Troy Ounces

	1989	1990	1991	1992	1993	1994
Photography	1.8	1.8	1.8	1.8	1.7	1.5
Brazing Alloys and Solders	0.5	0.5	0.5	0.5	0.5	0.5
Jewelry and Silverware	0.4	0.4	0.4	0.4	0.5	0.5
Electrical/Electronics	0.3	0.4	0.4	0.4	0.4	0.4
Other	1.0	1.1	1.3	1.9	2.3	2.2
Total	4.0	4.2	4.3	5.0	5.3	5.1
% Change Year Ago	—	5.0%	2.4%	16.3%	6.0%	-3.9%

	1995	1996	1997	1998	1999	2000
Photography	1.3	1.5	1.6	1.7	1.7	1.5
Brazing Alloys and Solders	0.6	0.6	0.6	0.6	0.6	0.5
Jewelry and Silverware	0.5	0.5	0.5	0.5	0.6	0.5
Electrical/Electronics	0.4	0.5	0.5	0.5	0.6	0.8
Other	2.0	2.0	2.0	2.0	2.0	2.2
Total	4.8	5.1	5.2	5.3	5.5	5.5
% Change Year Ago	-6.3%	6.0%	2.2%	1.9%	3.8%	0.0%

	2001	2002	2003	2004	2005	2006p
Photography	1.5	1.5	1.5	1.5	1.0	0.7
Brazing Alloys and Solders	0.4	0.4	0.4	0.4	0.5	0.5
Jewelry and Silverware	0.4	0.5	0.5	0.5	0.6	0.5
Electrical/Electronics	0.7	0.6	0.6	0.6	0.7	0.8
Other	2.0	1.9	2.0	2.0	2.0	2.0
Total	5.0	4.9	5.0	5.0	4.8	4.5
% Change Year Ago	-9.1%	-2.0%	2.0%	0.0%	-4.0%	-6.3%

Note: Other includes small amount of decorative silver use. Totals may not equal the sums of categories due to rounding.
Sources: Australian trade sources, CPM Group.
March 7, 2006

Investment Demand

Investment Demand

Investors clearly have been buying silver. The price of silver would not have risen from $6.45 at the start of 2005 to $9.10 by the end of the year, and $10.74 by 24 March 2006, if someone had not been buying silver. Much of the buying came from investors, ranging from institutional fund management companies and private individuals around the world to proprietary traders at banks and brokerage companies. These diverse entities all were buying silver as an investment.

Even as investor interest in silver was rising sharply, other investors continued to sell silver, taking advantage of higher prices. The net deficit of newly refined silver entering the market relative to fabrication demand, estimated at 15.7 million ounces, had to have been compensated for with sales of metal from inventories. Those inventories may have included some stocks held by industrial producers, users, refiners, and traders. Some of it also represented sales by investors who were taking the opportunity of the highest prices since the early 1980s to sell their long-held silver inventories.

The definitions of who an investor is, what they are investing in, and what their time horizons are all are critical to understanding the mechanics involved in silver investment demand. Sometimes an investor is an individual or institution that approaches the silver market in the

Annual Net Investment Demand and Prices

Prices Through 21 March 2006.

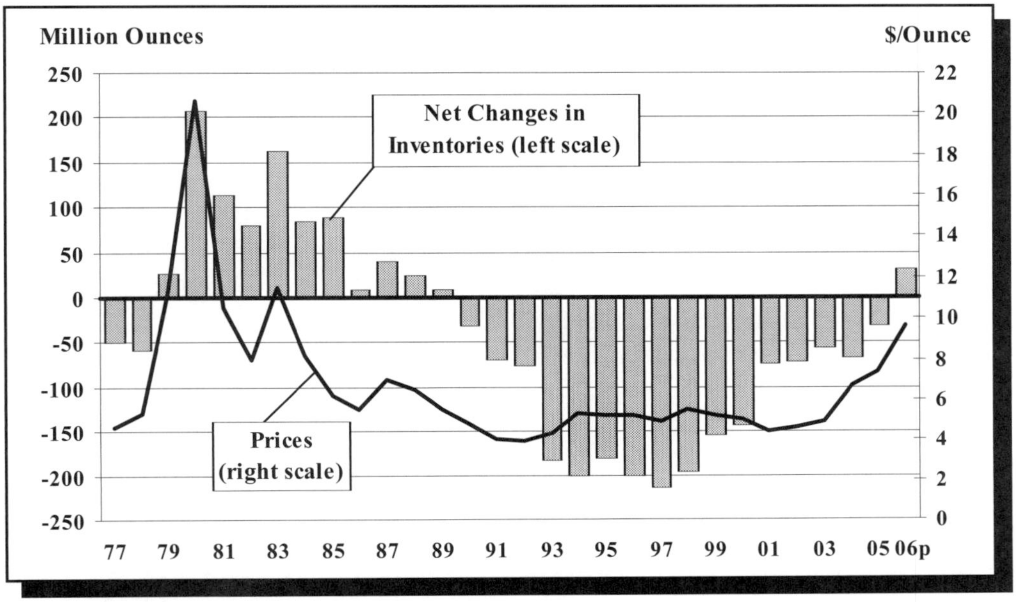

same way it approaches any other investment: As a more or less dispassionate investor seeking either capital appreciation or capital preservation. Within this broad category there are many types of investors. The silver market traditionally has had a core group of investors, many of whom reside in the North America, the Middle East, South Asia, and other parts of Asia. These investors have been joined in recent years by institutional money managers ranging from hedge funds and commodities funds to pension funds and generalist money management companies that are seeking to diversify their portfolio and take advantage of the current upward price trends in silver and other commodities.

Other times an investor may be a company involved in silver - a producer, consumer, refiner, or dealer that concludes it should hold inventories of silver, perhaps in expectation of higher prices. While these entities do not fit the classic definition of an investor, they are in fact investing in silver if they are holding inventories beyond what they require on a working inventory basis.

Similar distinctions need to be made between investors that purchase physical silver and those who purchase derivative investment products. The latter range from futures and options to silver-indexed notes and structured products. There are various silver-related derivative investments that have attracted a fair bit of interest, especially from institutional investment managers. These products generally speaking have little or no physical silver involved in their structure and management, but rather derive their value from changes in the underlying silver price without engaging in any physical silver market transactions. Other investors purchase silver mining company stocks.

The third set of distinctions relates to the intended maturity of silver investments taken up by various types of investors. Investors have investment horizons ranging from less than a day to perpetuity. Those investors with shorter time frames tend to focus on futures and options, or forwards traded in the interbank market. Longer term investors tend to buy physical silver.

Much of the investment activity in 2005 appeared to be from two major sets of investors. One set was physical investors, especially in India and Middle Eastern countries. The other was more futures and options oriented institutional investors. Investors in the Middle East have been buying silver and gold held in disparate locations, as a safe haven for some of their wealth in the event of invasion or revolution in their countries. They have shunned North America, Europe, and Japan as locations for holding this metal, apparently in order to avoid the risks of having their assets frozen by governments in those areas as Iranian and Soviet assets were frozen in 1979 and 1980.

Another interesting trend that has emerged since November 2004 has been a move by high net worth individuals, especially in the United States, to hold silver in non-bank vaulting facilities on an allocated basis, often outside of the United States. There has been a simultaneous move on the part of smaller investors to move metal from unallocated accounts managed by banks and brokerage companies to allocated accounts. In some cases these are investors that have held their metal for a long time, and now are revising the mechanics of how they hold their metal. In other cases these are investors new to silver.

Interestingly, at present smaller investors in the United States, long a major source of demand for silver, appear to be a relatively mild force in the current period of investor interest in silver. Many of these investors buy silver in 100-ounce bars or coins. Coins often have tax advantages, and the U.S. Silver Eagle, created in 1986, is a major form of investment for these investors.

Silver Eagle sales totaled 9.9 million ounces in 2005. That was down from 11.1 million ounces in 2004. In fact, Silver Eagle sales have risen on a longer term basis. Silver Eagle sales were running around 5.0 - 5.6 million ounces per year from 1996 through 1998. They rose to 9.9 million ounces in 1999, and then ranged between 10.2 and 11.5 million ounces per year from 2000 through

Recent Trends in U.S. Eagle Sales

Monthly, Through February 2006.

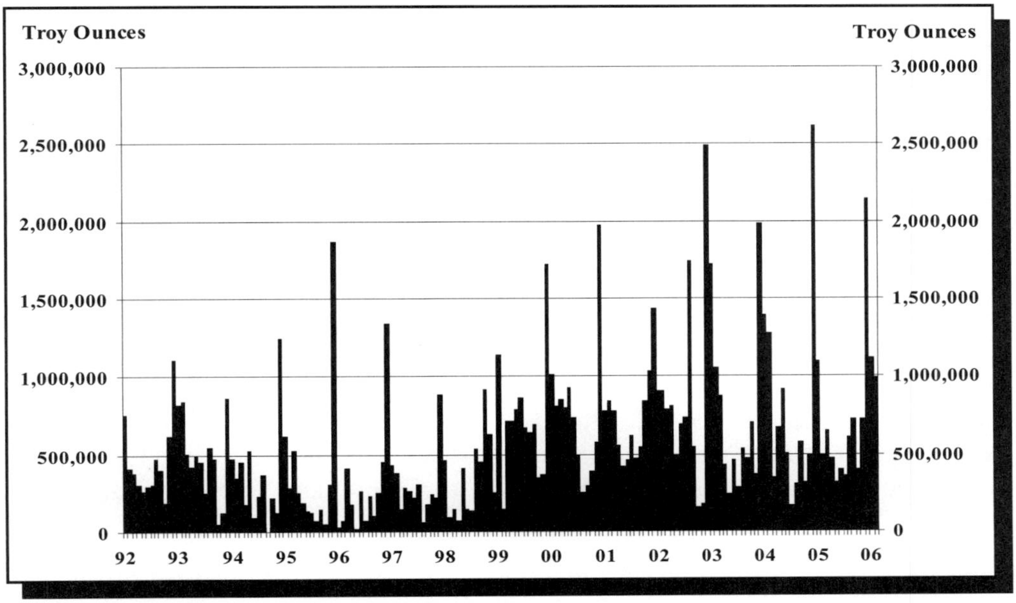

2004. The decline in sales in 2005, to 9.9 million ounces, needs to be viewed in the context of the longer term rise in sales since the late 1990s.

However, given the strong interest in silver on the part of a wide range of investors, it might have seemed reasonable to expect a larger increase in Silver Eagle sales. Part of the explanation may be that the sales figures, shown in tables later in this chapter, are sales of new Silver Eagles by the U.S. Mint, which strikes and sells the coins. In fact, coin dealers report a fair level of investor buying of Silver Eagles, but they also report a substantial volume of sales of older Silver Eagles by other investors. The increased levels of demand for Eagles from new buyers is being met by older coins in the secondary market, the flow of which has been substantial enough to warrant relatively stable new coin requirements in this market. Additionally, the U.S. Mint does not market the Eagles, in gold, silver, and platinum, as dynamically as it did prior to 2000, which may account for the lack of focus on these coins by investors seeking to buy silver.

A Silver ETF

In the middle of 2005 Barclays Global Investors submitted plans to create a silver exchange traded fund, to be called the iShares Silver Trust and to be traded on the American Stock Exchange. The Amex submitted a formal proposal to the U.S. Securities and Exchange Commission in early 2005. The SEC, as per its procedures, posted a notice of this proposal in the Federal Register on 23 January 2006, seeking public comment. When the SEC posted the Amex proposal in the Federal Register on 23 January 2006, opening the period for public comment, the prices of silver was \$9.073. The price of silver immediately began rising, as many investors and bullion traders built long positions in anticipation of the Silver Shares being approved.

The SEC approved the American Stock Exchange's proposal to list iShares Silver Trust shares, to be issued by Barclays Global Investors. The ruling was dated 20 March and was released on the morning of 21 March 2006. In the intervening weeks silver prices rose to around \$10.50, largely on speculative anticipation that the silver ETF would be approved. The silver market reacted by rising a further 20.3 cents to \$10.565 in afternoon trading on 21 March. By the end of that week silver was trading at \$10.74.

Following the positive ruling by the SEC Barclays needs to submit a Registration Statement to the SEC for approval, before the Silver Shares, as it will be called in the market, can start trading. Such a document should be submitted shortly after the 20 March ruling. Approval could take a couple of days or a matter of months. Typically in such a situation the document is prepared for submission, and approval can come quick quickly.

The market is seeking to assess the short and long term implications for silver prices of the arrival of the Silver Shares. The law of unintended consequences suggests caution be applied to such analyses. Several points can be made considering what the Silver Shares mean to the market.

They represent a way for investors to buy silver. As such, they could be thought of as creating a new form of demand for silver, a sub-sector of investment demand. The gold ETFs that have been launched progressively around the world since 2003 have seen an influx of new investors who formerly did not invest in gold. That may be the case for silver, but to a far lesser extent. Silver is not so much a mainstream investment product or asset as is gold. There are a lot of investors who like to buy silver. Many are deeply suspicious of financial institutions, however, and may avoid the silver ETF, preferring physical control over their silver. Some institutional investors are likely to buy into the silver ETF, however, and that alone should increase demand for physical silver measurably. The silver ETF will be backed by physical silver held in allocated accounts.

How much silver will be purchased via the ETF is anyone's guess. The gold ETFs have attracted around 15 million ounces of gold, roughly three times what most observers had expected them to

Silver Equity Prices

Month-end, Through February 2006

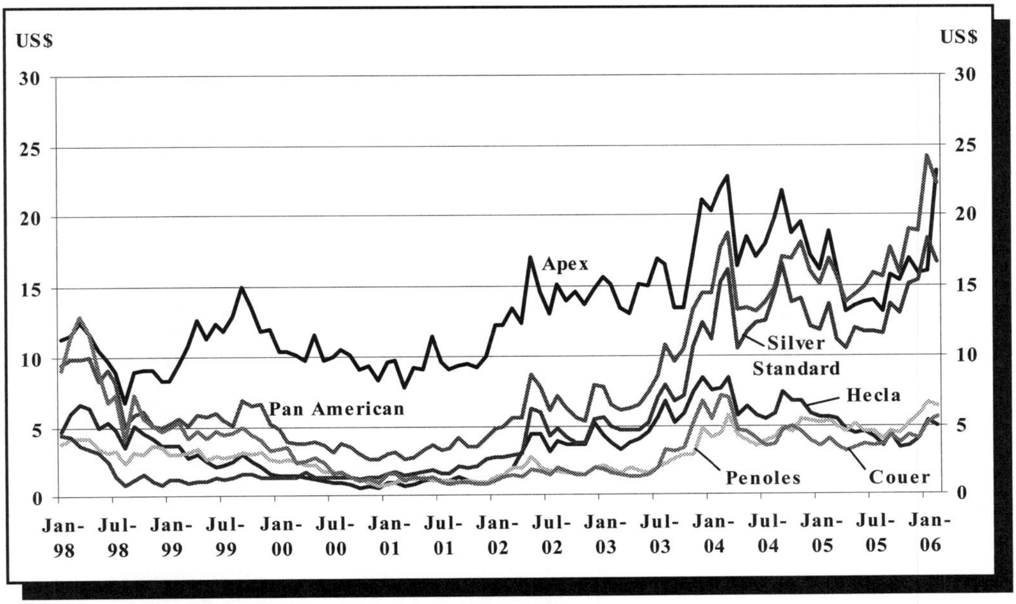

attract. They came out in 2003 and 2004, however, at a good time in the current bull market for precious metals. The Silver Shares will be coming to market at a time when silver prices already have roughly doubled over the past few years. That may limit the interest in them, along with the more exotic nature of silver for some institutional money managers.

The proposal for the Silver Shares suggests an initial inventory of at least 1.5 million ounces backing the shares. That is very little. In reality, the demand for these shares may take 30 million ounces or more. No one can know exactly what the demand level could be. There will continue to be some speculative buying of silver between now and the actual launch of the ETF. Once the ETF is launched the market will be better able to assess the level of demand, and the sustainability of demand, for silver investing via the ETF. The proposal used a figure of 130 million ounces, but that was just an indicative figure. It is possible that the demand for silver for allocation against the Silver Shares may be significant enough to drive silver prices sharply higher on a sustained basis. It also is possible that the silver ETF may prove to be of relatively less significance to the price of silver.

Large Speculative Comex Silver Positions

Weekly, Through 14 March 2006.

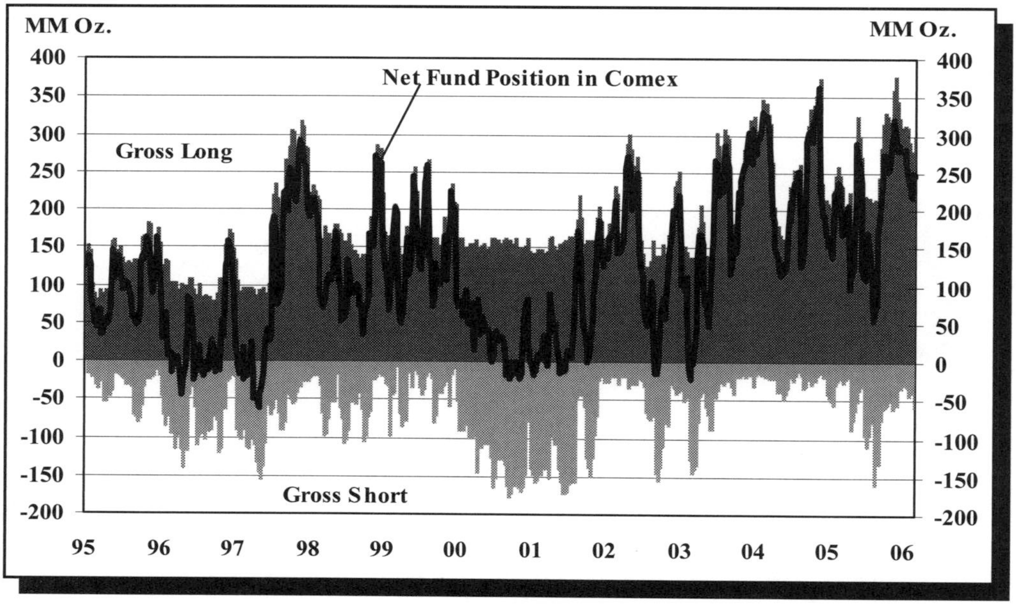

Comparative Investments

	1968-2006		1984-2006		1991-2006	
	Average Return	Average Risk	Average Return	Average Risk	Average Return	Average Risk
DJIA	8.06%	8.78%	11.37%	8.36%	10.36%	7.23%
S&P 500	8.33%	8.95%	10.77%	8.67%	10.23%	7.83%
T-Bills	6.06%	0.46%	5.07%	0.36%	3.98%	0.34%
T-Bonds	7.57%	0.41%	7.52%	0.42%	6.41%	0.34%
Gold	10.19%	10.78%	1.11%	5.99%	1.79%	4.90%
Silver	9.54%	18.36%	0.02%	11.39%	4.42%	9.80%
Platinum	7.26%	12.82%	5.61%	10.50%	6.08%	8.64%
CRB	4.07%	6.06%	1.52%	5.05%	2.60%	4.96%
TWDollar	-0.76%	3.44%	-1.36%	3.63%	-0.44%	3.42%

Note: Calculated on a 12-month moving basis. Risk is defined as the first-order standard deviation of the return over any given 12-month period. Returns based on capital appreciation only. 2006 through February.
Source: CPM Group
March 14, 2006

Silver Coinage

Million Troy Ounces

Year	United States	Canada	Austria	France	Germany	Mexico	Other	Transitional Economies	Total
1960	46.0	7.5	-i-	12.2	-i-	-i-	38.2	-	103.9
1961	56.0	5.1	-i-	23.8	-i-	-i-	51.1	-	136.0
1962	78.0	10.9	-i-	13.7	-i-	-i-	25.0	-	127.6
1963	112.0	13.0	-i-	12.2	-i-	-i-	29.2	-	166.4
1964	203.0	13.7	-i-	10.7	-i-	-i-	39.7	-	267.1
1965	320.3	24.4	2.7	7.2	2.7	-i-	27.8	-	385.1
1966	53.6	15.5	3.3	8.7	2.9	-i-	45.5	-	129.5
1967	43.8	8.8	3.2	9.6	3.1	-i-	36.8	-	105.3
1968	36.8	7.4	2.2	2.9	4.2	-i-	35.8	-	89.3
1969	19.6	0.0	1.9	0.7	2.9	-i-	7.6	-	32.7
1970	0.7	0.0	4.0	3.5	7.4	-i-	7.8	-	23.4
1971	2.5	0.2	3.2	0.4	19.2	-i-	2.3	-	27.8
1972	2.3	0.1	5.8	0.3	22.6	-i-	7.0	-	38.1
1973	0.9	6.6	6.3	0.1	7.0	-i-	7.6	-	28.5
1974	1.0	9.0	5.7	3.6	7.6	-i-	4.7	-	31.6
1975	2.7	10.4	9.1	1.8	5.4	-i-	4.0	-	33.4
1976	1.3	8.4	6.9	6.2	1.8	-i-	5.4	-	30.0
1977	0.1	0.5	8.9	7.1	4.6	4.2	9.1	-	34.5
1978	0.0	1.0	9.6	9.0	3.6	6.6	9.7	-	39.5
1979	0.2	0.8	4.0	10.6	3.7	5.0	6.7	-	31.0

Notes: Excludes transitional economies prior to 1990.
i -- included in Other. na -- not available.
Sources: U.S. Mint; Energy, Mines, and Resources Canada;
Silver Institute; Handy & Harman; Bank of Mexico; trade sources;
CPM Group.
March 20, 2006

Silver Coinage

Million Troy Ounces

Year	United States	Canada	Austria	France	Germany	Mexico	Other	Transitional Economies	Total
1980	0.1	0.2	2.3	0.1	0.0	6.1	6.2	-	15.0
1981	0.2	0.3	3.1	0.1	0.5	0.0	5.3	-	9.5
1982	1.8	0.3	4.5	1.4	0.3	0.0	3.7	-	12.0
1983	2.1	0.4	1.8	2.2	0.0	0.0	3.7	-	10.2
1984	2.0	0.3	2.4	3.9	0.0	2.5	2.6	-	13.7
1985	0.4	0.3	4.6	2.2	0.0	3.5	2.4	-	13.4
1986	10.3	1.3	1.1	2.2	0.0	2.0	9.9	-	26.8
1987	12.2	1.2	3.1	2.2	3.2	2.3	6.2	-	30.4
1988	7.9	1.1	2.0	2.2	3.2	2.0	6.9	-	25.3
1989	6.8	3.3	2.1	2.2	3.2	1.7	7.0	-	26.3
1990	9.1	1.7	0.6	2.2	2.4	1.5	10.9	1.4	29.8
1991	9.1	0.8	0.6	1.8	5.5	1.5	7.5	0.9	27.7
1992	8.1	0.3	0.5	1.8	5.3	6.8	6.0	0.6	29.4
1993	8.9	1.0	0.6	1.8	4.5	15.0	5.6	0.6	38.0
1994	8.1	1.2	0.6	1.8	4.2	11.9	5.2	0.5	33.5
1995	7.5	0.7	0.6	1.8	5.8	0.3	5.0	0.3	22.0
1996	5.0	0.7	0.4	1.8	5.1	0.5	4.4	0.2	18.1
1997	5.3	0.8	0.3	1.8	5.5	0.3	4.7	0.2	18.9
1998	5.6	1.0	0.3	1.8	6.3	1.0	8.8	0.2	25.0
1999	9.9	1.2	0.3	1.8	6.0	0.4	9.7	0.2	29.5
2000	10.3	0.4	na	na	na	0.7	13.8	na	25.2
2001	10.2	0.4	na	na	na	1.4	5.6	na	17.6
2002	11.5	0.6	na	na	na	1.1	7.3	na	20.5
2003	10.5	0.7	na	na	na	1.0	5.5	na	17.7
2004	11.1	0.7	na	na	na	0.9	5.5	na	18.2
2005	9.9	1.0	na	na	na	0.6	5.0	na	16.5
2006p	10.0	1.0	na	na	na	0.8	5.0	na	16.8

U.S. Mint Silver Coin Sales
Troy Ounces

	1986	1987	1988	1989	1990	1991
Uncirculated Eagles						
January	-	715,000	790,000	416,000	1,616,000	1,800,000
February	-	775,000	700,000	700,000	450,000	1,235,000
March	-	1,355,000	130,000	1,755,000	700,000	880,000
April	-	1,060,000	780,000	325,000	250,000	508,000
May	-	1,280,000	650,000	500,000	340,000	210,000
June	-	1,125,000	50,000	460,000	360,000	170,000
July	-	0	100,000	150,000	160,000	210,000
August	-	100,000	226,000	365,000	420,000	160,000
September	-	300,000	353,000	450,000	250,000	150,000
October	-	800,000	305,000	350,000	955,000	260,000
November	1,400,000	1,250,000	400,000	150,000	330,000	250,000
December	3,696,000	660,000	215,000	150,000	1,416,000	1,119,000
Subtotal	5,096,000	9,420,000	4,699,000	5,771,000	7,247,000	6,952,000
% Change	-	84.9%	-50.1%	22.8%	25.6%	-4.1%
Proof Eagles	1,446,778	904,732	557,370	617,694	695,510	511,924
Commemoratives	-	-	-	-	1,172,463	1,645,499
% Change	-	-	-	-	-	40.3%
Proof Coin Sets	-	-	-	-	-	-
Total	6,542,778	10,324,732	5,256,370	6,388,694	9,114,973	9,109,423
% Change	-	57.8%	-49.1%	21.5%	42.7%	-0.1%

	1992	1993	1994	1995	1996	1997
Uncirculated Eagles						
January	756,000	825,000	480,000	625,000	30,000	435,000
February	415,000	850,000	345,000	285,000	75,000	385,000
March	385,000	510,000	450,000	525,000	413,000	150,000
April	310,000	425,000	175,000	250,000	175,000	286,000
May	260,000	500,000	525,000	185,000	25,000	265,000
June	300,000	455,000	100,000	135,000	260,000	220,000
July	310,000	250,000	230,000	125,000	75,000	305,000
August	480,000	550,000	375,000	75,000	230,000	65,000
September	400,000	480,000	0	150,000	105,000	180,000
October	195,000	50,000	225,000	50,000	250,000	240,000
November	625,000	125,000	125,000	310,000	450,000	225,000
December	1,108,000	870,000	1,250,500	1,875,000	1,343,000	890,000
Subtotal	5,544,000	5,890,000	4,280,500	4,590,000	3,431,000	3,646,000
% Change	-20.3%	6.2%	-27.3%	7.2%	-25.3%	6.3%
Proof Eagles	498,543	405,913	372,168	437,924	498,293	440,315
Commemoratives	1,305,112	2,081,825	2,606,920	2,000,000	553,872	727,933
% Change	-20.7%	59.5%	25.2%	-23.3%	-72.3%	31.4%
Proof Coin Sets	792,040	449,677	700,000	458,989	522,713	498,260
Total	8,139,695	8,827,415	7,959,588	7,486,913	5,005,878	5,312,508
% Change	-10.6%	8.4%	-9.8%	-5.9%	-33.1%	6.1%

U.S. Mint Silver Coin Sales
Troy Ounces

	1998	1999	2000	2001	2002	2003
Uncirculated Eagles						
January	460,000	1,145,000	1,011,500	779,500	913,500	1,725,000
February	100,000	149,000	808,500	846,500	905,000	1,055,000
March	145,000	718,000	851,500	786,000	797,000	876,000
April	75,000	716,000	804,500	562,000	815,000	434,000
May	410,000	792,000	925,000	426,000	495,000	245,000
June	150,000	863,000	738,500	467,000	695,000	468,000
July	140,000	678,500	499,500	624,500	740,000	280,000
August	535,000	644,500	255,500	474,500	1,745,000	535,000
September	450,000	694,000	296,500	550,000	550,000	475,000
October	920,000	349,000	386,500	843,500	155,000	705,500
November	635,000	366,000	580,500	1,031,500	175,000	370,000
December	250,000	1,718,000	1,975,000	1,436,500	2,490,000	1,985,000
Subtotal	4,270,000	8,833,000	9,133,000	8,827,500	10,475,500	9,153,500
% Change	17.1%	106.9%	3.4%	-3.3%	18.7%	-12.6%
Proof Eagles	450,728	549,330	600,743	746,398	647,342	747,831
Commemoratives	400,000	300,000	474,073	611,256	347,665	571,740
% Change	-45.0%	-25.0%	58.0%	28.9%	-43.1%	64.5%
Proof Coin Sets	492,828	200,000	100,000			
Total	5,613,556	9,882,330	10,307,816	10,185,154	11,470,507	10,473,071
% Change	5.7%	76.0%	4.3%	-1.2%	12.6%	-8.7%

	2004	2005	2006
Uncirculated Eagles			
January	1,392,500	1,095,000	1,115,000
February	1,281,000	500,000	993,000
March	348,000	650,000	
April	680,000	480,000	
May	914,500	315,000	
June	505,000	400,000	
July	170,000	355,000	
August	311,000	615,000	
September	580,000	725,000	
October	320,000	400,000	
November	492,500	725,000	
December	2,622,500	2,145,000	
Subtotal	9,617,000	8,405,000	2,108,000
% Change	5.1%	-12.6%	-6.1%
Proof Eagles	801,602	711,606	
Commemoratives	717,488	776,097	
% Change	25.5%	8.2%	
Proof Coin Sets			
Total	11,136,090	9,892,703	2,108,000
% Change	6.3%	-11.2%	-78.7%

Notes: The U.S. Eagle program was introduced in November 1986.
Proof coin sets and commemoratives end-year. NA - not available.
Proof Eagles as of 30 September 2005, year-end through 2004.
Source: U.S. Mint, CPM Group.
March 14, 2006

Inventories

Inventories

Inventories are the fourth set of fundamentals that exert important influences on silver. Silver, like gold, is unique among commodities in that it has served as a monetary asset for governments and a financial asset for individuals for more than five millennia. This means that there has been a tendency to hold on to these metals more so than with other commodities, such as copper, lead, or timber. This creates a critical and enormous extra aspect of the market, as there could be untold and unmeasured metal that would be more or less available to the market at any given price. As discussed below, most of this silver probably is lost or otherwise not available to the market. Even a small mount, in percentage terms, can be crucial to silver prices, however.

Unlike gold, most of the silver mined over the past 5,000 years is presumed either to be lost to history or tied up in jewelry, silverware, and religious objects. Also unlike gold, silver bullion inventories have been declining rapidly over the past 16 years. Gold inventories in bullion form have been increasing during this period.

It is estimated that more than 2.1 billion ounces or so of silver existed in bullion inventories as of 1990. The figure could have been around 2.3 billion ounces. Since that time, a large amount of this metal is estimated to have been used in a wide range of fabricated products. The measured deficits in the silver market between identified supply and fabrication demand have totaled 1.96 billion

Market Inventories and Prices

Quarterly, Through Fourth Quarter 2005.

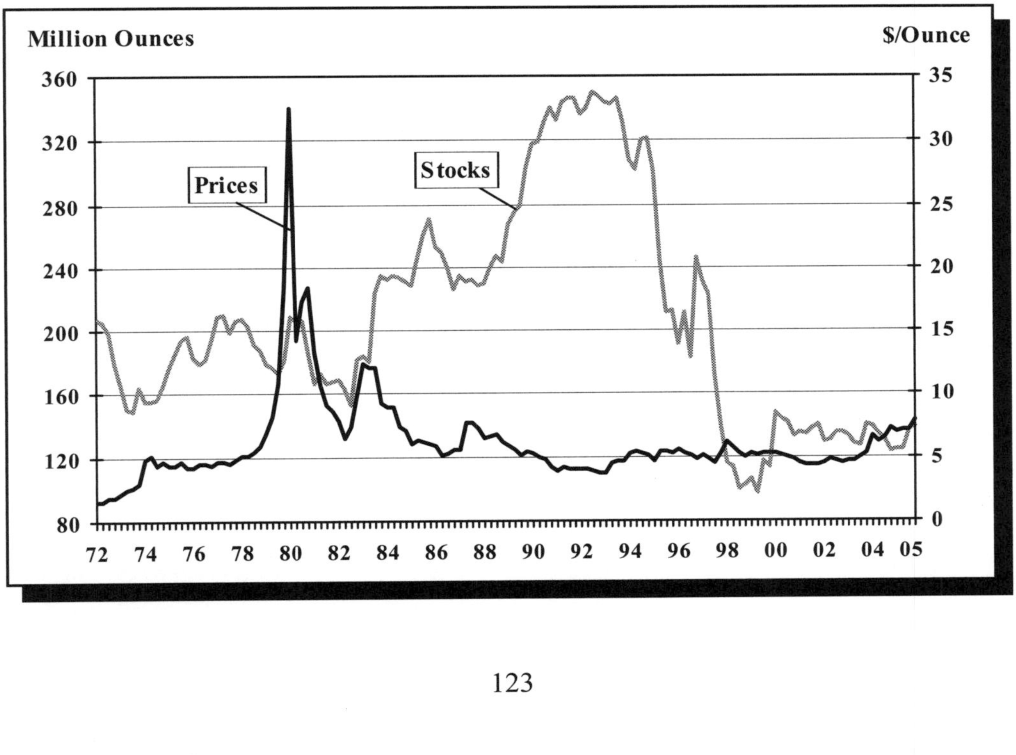

ounces from 1990 through 2005. This excludes investment demand, of course, since it is the investors, whatever sort of entity they are, that for the most part hold silver inventories. (Silver market making bullion dealers and banks also hold silver, as do industrial users, mining companies, refineries, and other trading companies.) Of that 1.96 billion ounce reduction, 387.5 million ounces went into bullion coins, which have been bought by investors. Thus, the drawdown in investor holdings of silver, including both bullion and coins, has not been quite as dramatic as the higher number suggests. Still, there has been a 1.57 billion ounce reduction in bullion inventories during the past 16 years.

Bullion inventories are estimated to be somewhere between 300 and 500 million ounces at present. Another 523 million ounces exists in bullion coin form. There is, of course, a great margin of error for such estimates. These are estimates of metal inventories built up, drawn down, won, lost, bought, and sold over 5,000 years. Most of the transactions were secret, although the Colonial powers did a remarkably thorough job counting much of the silver, gold, and precious stones they shipped from the Americas to Europe, and then on to India and China, in the period from the 17th century through the middle of the last century.

Adding to the margin for error is the leakage between metal held in bullion form, on the one hand, and metal held in the form of old circulating coins, newer bullion coins, jewelry, decorative objects, religious statues, and other fabricated forms. Every precious metals refiner in the world knows that there is a flow of silver in these forms that comes into their melting pots, is refined, and then used as new silver. Attempts are made to measure the secondary recovery of silver from such scrap, but it is clear that in most parts of the world there is a sizable volume of silver that goes unreported and uncounted.

There are, of course, enormous amounts of silver that have been mined through past centuries. The first chapter of this report puts the number at 42.6 billion ounces, give or take a few billion ounces. Most of this silver has been used, lost, or is tied up in jewelry, or in decorative and religious objects that have value far beyond their silver content. It is not readily available to the market for use as silver.

In the period from 1978 through 1984, when silver prices rose from $4.80 to $50 and then stayed above $10 for extended periods of time, perhaps around 400 million ounces of these objects were melted down and refined for their silver content. That was perhaps one or two percent of the tens of billions of ounces of silver ostensibly out there. In other words, much of the silver in product form most likely is not available to the silver bullion market, at least up to prices around $50. At some point, most people have a price, it would seem. In 1980, holders of the vast majority of these materials did not feel that the price of $30 - $50 was sufficient to warrant selling their silverware for its silver content.

For a variety of reasons, silver in product forms should not be considered as metal inventories that are readily available to the market, without a significant increase in prices. Just as copper in power transmission lines should not be viewed as copper market inventories, silver in jewelry and silverware should not be considered silver market inventories.

There are several problems with this. For one thing, the flow of silver from such products into the silver bullion market clearly does happen, albeit probably at a relatively low level. Second, this metal is ostensibly available to the market at some price.

A more important problem is not with the silver in product form, however, but rather with silver in bullion and coin form held in unreported inventories by investors and others around the world. This number is subject to a high margin of error, and is affected by the leakage of metal melted down from product forms and used as bullion. As mentioned above, it is estimated that silver bullion inventories may be down to around 300 - 500 million ounces. First, that is an enormous range. Second, much of it is not reported.

Reported inventories totaled 139.3 million ounces at the end of 2005. That was up from 123.2 million ounces at the end of 2004. It also was down from a peak of 350.6 million ounces at the end of the third quarter 1992, early in the period of investors and bullion banks selling their inventories.

Of this total of 139.3 million ounces as of the end of 2005, 120.0 million ounces were held in Comex-registered depositories. Another 600,000 ounces were held against futures positions in the Tokyo Commodities Exchange, and around 18.8 million ounces were estimated to have been held by industrial refiners, producers, and trading companies.

Unreported inventories may have totaled another 180 - 380 million ounces. Berkshire Hathaway purchased 129.7 million ounces of silver as a strategic investment in 1997 - 1998. The company has not made any statements about the disposition of any of this metal since then, leading most market observers to conclude that the company probably still holds most if not all of this metal. It may have sold some metal in 2004 and 2005, but whether or not it did is utter conjecture and ought not be the subject of this report.

Another 50 - 250 million ounces is estimated to be held by other investors around the world. The low end of this range appears too low to be probable, suggesting that stocks are somewhat higher than this number would indicate.

In addition to these stocks, around 523 million ounces are held by investors in coin form.

Comex-reported silver stocks represent the vast majority of publicly disclosed silver inventories. Comex-reported stocks are broken down into two categories: Silver which is in one of the four Comex-registered silver depositories that meets Comex delivery specifications and has been registered with the Comex Clearinghouse against silver futures positions. These registered stocks totaled 68,048,244 ounces as of the end of 2005. That was up from 61,287,203 ounces at the end of 2004. Since the beginning of 2006 these stocks have risen further, reaching 72,295,794 ounces at the end of February. The four Comex-approved silver depositories are three vaults in New York City run by HSBC, Scotiabank, and Brinks, along with a depository operated by Delaware Depository Service Co. in Wilmington, Delaware.

Comex also reports eligible, but unregistered stocks. It does this so that there is a bit more transparency to the market about how much metal is in these depositories that could be delivered into Comex futures contracts. These eligible inventories totaled 51,925,748 ounces at the end of 2005, up from 42,302,549 ounces. It is believed that much of the silver that is eligible but not registered with the Comex Clearinghouse represents metal passing through these vaulting facilities on its way from refiners to industrial users. Some of this metal also appears to belong to investors who want to own physical silver but do not engage in futures trading on the Comex; they just happen to store their metal in the same depositories.

In addition to the reported metal in these vaults, these facilities also hold metal in forms that are not deliverable against Comex positions, including 100-ounce bars and coins. The volumes of these holdings are not disclosed by the vault managers.

Governments also hold silver, although not as much as they used to hold. At one point in the 1950s the U.S. Treasury held more than two billion ounces. It used silver in circulating coins, and had silver-backed Treasury bills in circulation. As the silver market began to experience upward pressure on prices, starting in the late 1950s and running through much of the 1960s, the Treasury sold off all but around 170 million ounces. It transferred around 139 million ounces of this to the National Defense Stockpile. It later used the remainder of the National Defense Stockpile silver in manufacturing Silver Eagle coins, from late 1986, to the point where it had used that metal by 2001. The Treasury continues to hold around 20 million ounces of silver that was not transferred to the National Defense Stockpile. The Department of Defense owns a bit of silver as well, which it leases out to defense contractors that need silver for the materiel they are producing for the DoD.

Since the U.S. government largely had liquidated its silver inventories, the largest government holder of silver was

Reported and Estimated Silver Inventories

Million Troy Ounces, Year-End Data								December 2005 Percent Change From Dec. 1996
Mid-Point Estimates	1996	2000	2001	2002	2003	2004	2005	
Market *								
Comex *	203.5	94.0	104.5	107.4	124.3	103.6	120.0	-41.0%
Tocom	3.6	1.7	1.4	1.7	0.7	1.2	0.6	-84.2%
Chicago Board of Trade	6.1	4.0	3.7	3.9	-	-	-	-
U.S. and Japanese Industry	32.7	34.1	30.6	23.2	16.2	18.4	18.8	-42.5%
Total Market	245.8	133.8	140.3	136.3	141.1	123.2	139.3	-43.3%
Inferred, Unreported								
Other U.S. depositories and private holdings	386.0	30-100	30-90	60.0	38.0	30.0	30.0	-92.2%
European depositories * and private holdings	170.0	140-200	140-180	160.0	150.0	125.3	125.0	-26.5%
Asia, Latin America	110.0	100.0	90.0	55.0	35.0	25.0	25.0	-77.3%
Subtotal, Inferred	666.0	400.0	360.0	275.0	223.0	180.3	180.0	-73.0%
Subtotal, Bullion	911.8	670.0-800.0	620.0-720.0	411.3	364.1	303.5	319.3	-65.0%
Unreported Coins*								
Bullion	349.0	448.5	465.5	485.5	495.5	506.0	522.5	49.7%
Bags of U.S. monetized coin	20.0	2.0	2.0	2.0	2.0	2.0	2.0	-90.0%
Subtotal, Coins	369.0	450.5	467.5	487.5	497.5	508.0	524.5	42.1%
Total, Bullion and Coins	1280.8	1120.5-1250.5	1087.5-1187.5	898.8	861.6	811.5	843.8	-34.1%
Government Stocks	172.8	140.4	127.2	123.2	123.2	122.7	87.7	-49.2%
Total, with Government	1453.7	1260.9-1390.9	1214.7-1314.7	1022.0	984.8	934.2	931.6	-35.9%

Notes: The total reported and unreported inventory figures cited in this table represent CPM Group's mid-point estimate of silver stocks, based on discussions with industry sources. CPM Group also derives low-end and high-end estimates from this information. It must be emphasized that these figures represent CPM Group's best estimates. There are no official data regarding unreported silver inventories, and there is a wide range between our high, low, and mid-point estimates. * Market stocks data reported by respective exchanges and industry groups.
Comex includes registered and eligible stocks. European estimates include London and Zurich bullion banks.
Coin bags exclude private holdings of old coins, which are included in private holdings.
Source: CPM Group
March 14, 2006

India. The Indian government held around 86.6 million ounces of silver from the late 1980s into 2004. It began selling silver at the start of 2005. At first the program ran into some logistical problems, but as silver prices rose during the final four months of last year Indian bullion dealers and refiners found ways around these issues and began buying more silver from the government. In the end, the Indian government appears to have sold 35.5 million ounces of silver in 2005. This leaves it with 32.0 million ounces held by the Reserve Bank of India and another 19.1 million ounces of silver held in other inventories. This report assumes the RBI silver will be sold in 2006.

The sales of the Indian government silver are bringing to an end the era in which silver was a metal held by central banks, Treasuries, and other government agencies as a quasi-monetary asset. In total, government inventories may have been down to around 87.7 million ounces as of the end of 2005, of which the Indian government held 51.1 million ounces and the U.S. government around 19.9 million ounces. Other governments may hold no more than around 17.7 million ounces of silver at this point. There are market rumors about large inventories held by the Chinese government, but the government has indicated that it liquidated almost all of those inventories several years ago, around 2001 - 2003, as it was ending the People's Bank of China's role as national gold and silver market maker.

Government Silver Inventories

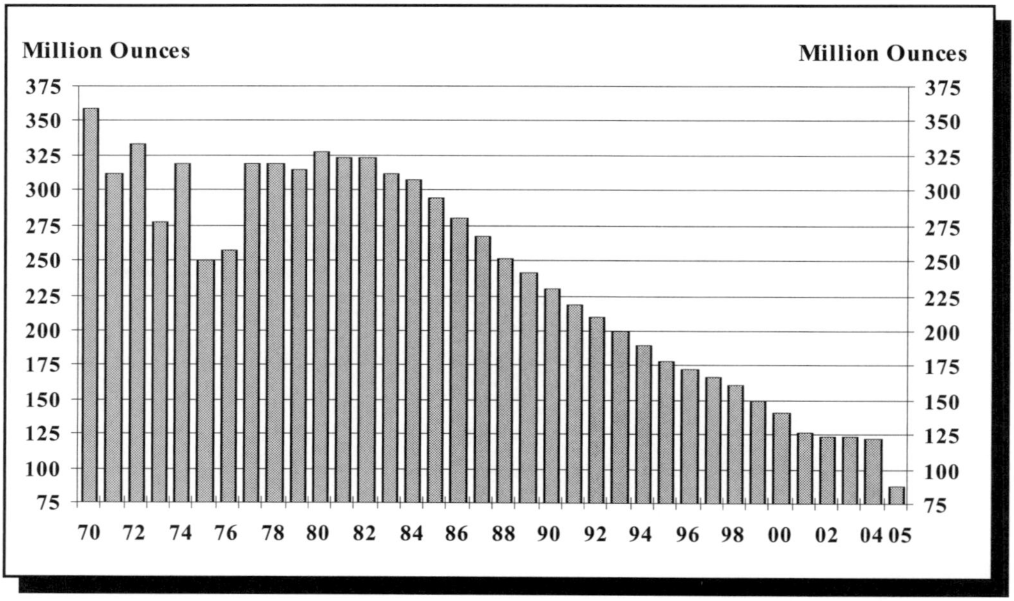

Government Silver Inventories

Million Troy Ounces

	1970	1980	1993	1994	1995	1996	1997	1998	1999	2000	2001	2002	2003	2004	2005
Afghanistan	8.3	8.3	i	i	i	i	i	i	i	i	i	i	i	i	i
Austria	1.1	0.6	i	i	i	i	i	i	i	i	i	i	i	i	i
Belgium	6.3	2.7	i	i	i	i	i	i	i	i	i	i	i	i	i
Australia	1.2	0.0	i	i	i	i	i	i	i	i	i	i	i	i	i
Canada	0.9	0.9	i	i	i	i	i	i	i	i	i	i	i	i	i
Colombia	0.0	0.3	i	i	i	i	i	i	i	i	i	i	i	i	i
Ethiopia	0.2	0.2	i	i	i	i	i	i	i	i	i	i	i	i	i
Finland	1.6	2.5	i	i	i	i	i	i	i	i	i	i	i	i	i
France	3.4	3.4	i	i	i	i	i	i	i	i	i	i	i	i	i
Germany	28.0	6.6	i	i	i	i	i	i	i	i	i	i	i	i	i
Greece	3.6	3.6	i	i	i	i	i	i	i	i	i	i	i	i	i
Guatemala	1.1	1.3	i	i	i	i	i	i	i	i	i	i	i	i	i
India, Reserve Ban	2.6	69.0	67.5	67.5	67.5	67.5	67.5	67.5	67.5	67.5	67.5	67.5	67.5	67.0	32.0
India, non-RBI	-	-	19.1	19.1	19.1	19.1	19.1	19.1	19.1	19.1	19.1	19.1	19.1	19.1	19.1
Italy	9.9	9.9	i	i	i	i	i	i	i	i	i	i	i	i	i
Japan	3.2	3.5	i	i	i	i	i	i	i	i	i	i	i	i	i
Mexico	50.7	11.9	10.0	10.0	6.0	6.0	6.0	6.0	7.0	7.0	7.0	7.0	7.0	7.0	7.0
Nepal	4.4	4.5	i	i	i	i	i	i	i	i	i	i	i	i	i
Netherlands	0.6	0.1	i	i	i	i	i	i	i	i	i	i	i	i	i
Norway	0.2	0.2	i	i	i	i	i	i	i	i	i	i	i	i	i
Philippines	0.2	2.5	i	i	i	i	i	i	i	i	i	i	i	i	i
Pakistan	49.9	0.0	i	i	i	i	i	i	i	i	i	i	i	i	i
Portugal	4.0	1.8	i	i	i	i	i	i	i	i	i	i	i	i	i
Saudia Arabia	4.3	4.7	i	i	i	i	i	i	i	i	i	i	i	i	i
South Africa	1.4	1.2	i	i	i	i	i	i	i	i	i	i	i	i	i
Sweden	0.2	0.2	i	i	i	i	i	i	i	i	i	i	i	i	i
Switzerland	4.6	5.9	i	i	i	i	i	i	i	i	i	i	i	i	i
Taiwan	2.1	2.0	i	i	i	i	i	i	i	i	i	i	i	i	i
Thailand	0.7	0.3	i	i	i	i	i	i	i	i	i	i	i	i	i
United States	163.9	179.6	92.3	83.2	75.5	70.5	65.2	59.2	46.1	37.1	23.9	19.9	19.9	19.9	19.9
Others	0.1	0.1	15.7	9.9	9.7	9.7	9.7	9.7	9.7	9.7	9.7	9.7	9.7	9.7	9.7
Total	359.0	327.8	204.6	189.7	177.8	172.8	167.5	161.5	149.4	140.4	127.2	123.2	123.2	122.7	87.7

Notes: i - included in "Others".
Source: CPM Group.
March 14, 2006

Ratio Between Silver Demand and Reported Stocks

Weeks of Demand Covered by Inventories

Year		Including Eligible Comex Stocks	Excluding Eligible Comex Stocks	Year		Including Eligible Comex Stocks	Excluding Eligible Comex Stocks
1972	1st Qtr.	23.02	-	1981	1st Qtr.	23.46	-
	2nd Qtr.	22.78	-		2nd Qtr.	24.30	-
	3rd Qtr.	22.02	-		3rd Qtr.	23.46	-
	4th Qtr.	19.80	-		4th Qtr.	23.53	-
1973	1st Qtr.	15.63	-	1982	1st Qtr.	22.90	-
	2nd Qtr.	14.25	-		2nd Qtr.	22.05	-
	3rd Qtr.	14.10	-		3rd Qtr.	20.67	-
	4th Qtr.	15.52	-		4th Qtr.	24.44	-
1974	1st Qtr.	16.17	-	1983	1st Qtr.	25.11	-
	2nd Qtr.	16.18	-		2nd Qtr.	24.50	-
	3rd Qtr.	16.24	-		3rd Qtr.	30.55	-
	4th Qtr.	17.19	-		4th Qtr.	31.94	-
1975	1st Qtr.	20.82	-	1984	1st Qtr.	27.92	-
	2nd Qtr.	21.88	-		2nd Qtr.	28.25	-
	3rd Qtr.	22.82	-		3rd Qtr.	27.99	-
	4th Qtr.	23.18	-		4th Qtr.	27.78	-
1976	1st Qtr.	18.49	-	1985	1st Qtr.	28.84	-
	2nd Qtr.	18.11	-		2nd Qtr.	31.10	-
	3rd Qtr.	18.37	-		3rd Qtr.	32.95	-
	4th Qtr.	19.61	-		4th Qtr.	34.25	-
1977	1st Qtr.	22.80	-	1986	1st Qtr.	28.68	-
	2nd Qtr.	23.03	-		2nd Qtr.	28.32	-
	3rd Qtr.	21.73	-		3rd Qtr.	27.17	-
	4th Qtr.	22.50	-		4th Qtr.	25.59	-
1978	1st Qtr.	22.89	-	1987	1st Qtr.	28.68	-
	2nd Qtr.	22.33	-		2nd Qtr.	28.28	-
	3rd Qtr.	21.12	-		3rd Qtr.	28.28	-
	4th Qtr.	20.82	-		4th Qtr.	25.36	-
1979	1st Qtr.	20.25	-	1987	1st Qtr.	26.78	-
	2nd Qtr.	19.99	-		2nd Qtr.	26.33	-
	3rd Qtr.	19.63	-		3rd Qtr.	26.46	-
	4th Qtr.	20.54	-		4th Qtr.	26.14	-
1980	1st Qtr.	28.68	-	1988	1st Qtr.	24.62	-
	2nd Qtr.	28.28	-		2nd Qtr.	25.70	23.67
	3rd Qtr.	28.28	-		3rd Qtr.	26.49	24.31
	4th Qtr.	25.36	-		4th Qtr.	26.07	24.16

Note: Based on end-quarter data.
Sources: CPM Group, New York Commodity Exchange, Tokyo Commodity Exchange, Chicago Board of Trade, London Metal Exchange, Japanese Ministry of Trade and Industry, trade sources.
March 14, 2006

Ratio Between Silver Demand and Reported Stocks
Weeks of Demand Covered by Inventories

Year		Including Eligible Comex Stocks	Excluding Eligible Comex Stocks
1989	1st Qtr.	27.26	24.30
	2nd Qtr.	27.92	24.74
	3rd Qtr.	28.43	24.51
	4th Qtr.	30.81	26.04
1990	1st Qtr.	30.66	25.41
	2nd Qtr.	30.73	23.90
	3rd Qtr.	31.98	25.40
	4th Qtr.	32.77	27.00
1991	1st Qtr.	30.06	24.20
	2nd Qtr.	31.09	26.17
	3rd Qtr.	31.31	26.39
	4th Qtr.	31.24	25.38
1992	1st Qtr.	29.62	22.69
	2nd Qtr.	29.91	23.09
	3rd Qtr.	30.82	22.80
	4th Qtr.	30.60	21.64
1993	1st Qtr.	30.25	22.98
	2nd Qtr.	26.46	20.47
	3rd Qtr.	26.73	19.81
	4th Qtr.	25.61	17.51
1994	1st Qtr.	23.05	15.15
	2nd Qtr.	22.60	15.40
	3rd Qtr.	23.95	17.12
	4th Qtr.	24.08	18.54
1995	1st Qtr.	21.56	16.78
	2nd Qtr.	17.53	14.81
	3rd Qtr.	15.20	12.08
	4th Qtr.	15.27	12.69
1996	1st Qtr.	13.10	10.49
	2nd Qtr.	14.49	11.38
	3rd Qtr.	12.53	9.60
	4th Qtr.	16.86	9.89
1997	1st Qtr.	14.93	9.36
	2nd Qtr.	14.38	8.17
	3rd Qtr.	11.10	5.83
	4th Qtr.	9.05	4.67
1998	1st Qtr.	7.30	4.15
	2nd Qtr.	7.21	4.39
	3rd Qtr.	6.31	3.96
	4th Qtr.	6.50	3.99
1999	1st Qtr.	6.72	4.49
	2nd Qtr.	6.21	3.94
	3rd Qtr.	7.46	5.31
	4th Qtr.	7.23	5.45
2000	1st Qtr.	9.01	6.80
	2nd Qtr.	8.78	7.12
	3rd Qtr.	8.69	7.29
	4th Qtr.	8.17	6.73
2001	1st Qtr.	8.74	6.85
	2nd Qtr.	8.66	6.85
	3rd Qtr.	8.87	6.63
	4th Qtr.	9.00	6.77
2002	1st Qtr.	8.51	6.33
	2nd Qtr.	8.60	6.50
	3rd Qtr.	8.93	5.90
	4th Qtr.	8.93	5.93
2003	1st Qtr.	8.74	5.44
	2nd Qtr.	8.42	4.42
	3rd Qtr.	8.26	4.32
	4th Qtr.	9.22	5.30
2004	1st Qtr.	8.91	4.42
	2nd Qtr.	8.59	4.10
	3rd Qtr.	8.36	3.87
	4th Qtr.	7.88	3.39
2005	1st Qtr.	7.76	3.40
	2nd Qtr.	7.77	3.41
	3rd Qtr.	7.32	2.95
	4th Qtr.	7.50	3.13

Market Silver Inventories
Million Troy Ounces

		Comex	CBT	LME	Tocom	Industry	Total
1972	1st Qtr.	109.1	15.0	6.7	--	77.0	207.8
	2nd Qtr.	98.6	17.3	6.4	--	83.4	205.7
	3rd Qtr.	92.8	19.9	7.7	--	78.4	198.8
	4th Qtr.	77.6	22.8	7.5	--	70.9	178.8
1973	1st Qtr.	69.1	26.5	9.1	--	60.9	165.6
	2nd Qtr.	56.1	23.1	12.3	--	59.5	151.0
	3rd Qtr.	47.5	29.4	15.4	--	57.1	149.4
	4th Qtr.	64.3	27.4	16.3	--	56.4	164.4
1974	1st Qtr.	64.4	25.9	14.8	--	50.9	156.0
	2nd Qtr.	74.3	20.3	13.5	--	48.0	156.1
	3rd Qtr.	68.2	20.0	11.5	--	57.0	156.7
	4th Qtr.	68.0	19.5	12.0	--	66.3	165.8
1975	1st Qtr.	70.3	25.0	12.2	--	69.1	176.6
	2nd Qtr.	78.3	40.3	14.6	--	52.4	185.6
	3rd Qtr.	82.6	42.8	16.4	--	51.8	193.6
	4th Qtr.	85.7	38.5	17.8	--	54.6	196.6
1976	1st Qtr.	79.8	39.4	15.3	--	48.5	183.0
	2nd Qtr.	65.2	47.9	17.5	--	48.7	179.3
	3rd Qtr.	50.0	53.6	29.8	--	48.4	181.8
	4th Qtr.	54.8	61.0	28.5	--	49.8	194.1
1977	1st Qtr.	63.2	64.4	27.5	--	53.5	208.6
	2nd Qtr.	69.4	63.9	25.1	--	52.3	210.7
	3rd Qtr.	64.8	61.3	18.8	--	53.9	198.8
	4th Qtr.	68.4	62.2	19.2	--	56.1	205.9
1978	1st Qtr.	74.1	62.5	19.2	--	51.3	207.1
	2nd Qtr.	72.8	64.0	18.0	--	47.3	202.1
	3rd Qtr.	67.8	62.2	18.2	--	42.9	191.1
	4th Qtr.	58.2	59.9	23.0	--	47.3	188.4
1979	1st Qtr.	49.6	55.3	21.3	--	52.8	179.0
	2nd Qtr.	54.1	56.8	18.8	--	47.0	176.7
	3rd Qtr.	51.5	65.3	15.9	--	40.8	173.5
	4th Qtr.	74.8	58.3	13.1	--	35.4	181.6
1980	1st Qtr.	83.6	57.8	17.8	-	49.7	208.9
	2nd Qtr.	82.0	45.8	28.0	-	50.2	206.0
	3rd Qtr.	82.1	46.1	26.6	-	51.2	206.0
	4th Qtr.	86.6	34.2	27.3	-	36.6	184.7
1981	1st Qtr.	85.4	18.9	24.5	-	38.4	167.2
	2nd Qtr.	86.7	20.4	25.8	-	40.3	173.2
	3rd Qtr.	77.4	21.2	29.7	-	38.9	167.2
	4th Qtr.	77.6	18.9	32.2	-	39.0	167.7
1982	1st Qtr.	77.1	18.6	33.2	-	40.7	169.6
	2nd Qtr.	70.8	15.2	35.7	-	41.6	163.3
	3rd Qtr.	61.5	13.5	36.9	-	41.2	153.1
	4th Qtr.	90.7	15.5	35.2	-	39.6	181.0

Market Silver Inventories
Million Troy Ounces

		Comex	CBT	LME	Tocom	Industry	Total
1983	1st Qtr.	97.2	15.5	34.1	-	37.6	184.4
	2nd Qtr.	90.9	19.0	35.4	-	34.6	179.9
	3rd Qtr.	129.3	21.1	37.7	-	36.2	224.3
	4th Qtr.	127.4	23.8	45.4	-	37.9	234.5
1984	1st Qtr.	116.8	23.4	50.0	-	42.4	232.6
	2nd Qtr.	120.9	21.3	51.7	-	41.5	235.4
	3rd Qtr.	115.0	21.2	52.6	-	44.4	233.2
	4th Qtr.	118.5	19.1	51.6	-	42.3	231.5
1985	1st Qtr.	106.6	17.4	54.1	-	50.2	228.3
	2nd Qtr.	132.4	14.9	50.5	2.1	46.3	246.2
	3rd Qtr.	144.0	16.6	55.0	2.4	42.8	260.8
	4th Qtr.	155.3	17.8	51.2	2.7	44.1	271.1
1986	1st Qtr.	148.2	17.6	40.8	2.9	43.8	253.3
	2nd Qtr.	151.9	17.5	35.8	3.3	41.6	250.1
	3rd Qtr.	157.2	16.5	25.2	3.6	37.4	239.9
	4th Qtr.	145.4	16.7	23.1	4.0	36.8	226.0
1987	1st Qtr.	157.9	15.0	21.8	4.2	35.7	234.6
	2nd Qtr.	152.5	14.0	23.1	4.2	36.8	230.6
	3rd Qtr.	155.7	12.6	21.1	4.4	38.0	231.8
	4th Qtr.	155.3	13.5	20.1	4.5	35.5	228.9
1988	1st Qtr.	155.8	13.5	18.7	4.4	37.8	230.2
	2nd Qtr.	168.2	13.8	14.8	5.3	38.2	240.3
	3rd Qtr.	178.8	13.8	15.1	5.8	34.2	247.7
	4th Qtr.	174.4	12.0	15.0	8.0	34.3	243.7
1989	1st Qtr.	194.8	11.4	11.8	9.8	39.8	267.6
	2nd Qtr.	206.1	13.2	-	10.8	44.0	274.1
	3rd Qtr.	212.3	12.7	-	9.8	44.3	279.1
	4th Qtr.	238.8	11.8	-	10.5	41.4	302.5
1990	1st Qtr.	252.1	11.9	-	10.3	43.6	317.8
	2nd Qtr.	251.6	12.1	-	11.2	43.7	318.6
	3rd Qtr.	260.2	12.9	-	11.4	47.1	331.6
	4th Qtr.	265.4	12.3	-	14.2	47.8	339.7
1991	1st Qtr.	257.9	12.0	-	14.0	48.8	332.7
	2nd Qtr.	266.1	12.1	-	13.9	52.1	344.2
	3rd Qtr.	269.7	12.1	-	13.4	51.5	346.6
	4th Qtr.	270.7	12.1	-	12.1	50.9	345.8
1992	1st Qtr.	262.2	12.1	-	12.1	50.5	336.9
	2nd Qtr.	267.8	11.7	-	10.8	49.9	340.2
	3rd Qtr.	278.6	11.7	-	9.3	51.0	350.6
	4th Qtr.	276.6	11.7	-	8.8	51.0	348.1
1993	1st Qtr.	271.8	11.7	-	7.8	52.8	344.1
	2nd Qtr.	273.9	11.5	-	7.6	50.0	343.1
	3rd Qtr.	276.8	10.7	-	7.6	51.6	346.6
	4th Qtr.	263.1	10.7	-	7.5	50.8	332.1

Market Silver Inventories

Million Troy Ounces

		Comex	CBT	LME	Tocom	Industry	Total
1994	1st Qtr.	239.4	10.7	-	7.5	50.2	307.8
	2nd Qtr.	237.2	10.7	-	7.2	46.6	301.8
	3rd Qtr.	255.2	10.7	-	6.7	47.2	319.8
	4th Qtr.	258.6	10.7	-	6.2	46.0	321.6
1995	1st Qtr.	235.1	10.7	-	6.4	48.3	300.5
	2nd Qtr.	184.6	10.6	-	6.2	43.0	244.4
	3rd Qtr.	156.5	10.2	-	5.1	40.0	211.9
	4th Qtr.	159.1	10.2	-	4.5	39.0	212.8
1996	1st Qtr.	139.7	10.2	-	4.1	37.0	191.0
	2nd Qtr.	167.6	6.4	-	4.0	33.3	211.3
	3rd Qtr.	139.3	6.3	-	3.8	33.3	182.7
	4th Qtr.*	203.5	6.1	-	3.6	32.7	245.8
1997	1st Qtr.	191.7	5.5	-	2.5	31.0	230.7
	2nd Qtr.	185.5	5.5	-	2.4	28.8	222.2
	3rd Qtr.	138.1	5.4	-	2.4	25.5	171.5
	4th Qtr.	109.8	4.8	-	2.2	23.0	139.8
1998	1st Qtr.	86.9	4.4	-	2.0	22.0	115.3
	2nd Qtr.	86.2	4.4	-	1.8	21.5	113.9
	3rd Qtr.	72.8	4.1	-	1.5	21.3	99.7
	4th Qtr.	75.8	4.4	-	1.6	21.0	102.8
1999	1st Qtr.	79.6	4.3	-	1.5	20.0	105.4
	2nd Qtr.	73.5	4.3	-	1.5	18.0	97.4
	3rd Qtr.	79.4	4.2	-	1.5	32.0	117.1
	4th Qtr.	76.0	4.0	-	1.4	32.0	113.4
2000	1st Qtr.	104.3	4.0	-	1.5	38.0	147.7
	2nd Qtr.	102.7	4.0	-	1.7	35.6	144.0
	3rd Qtr.	99.6	4.0	-	1.7	37.2	142.4
	4th Qtr.	94.0	4.0	-	1.7	34.1	133.8
2001	1st Qtr.	96.7	3.9	-	1.6	34.0	136.3
	2nd Qtr.	98.7	3.7	-	1.8	30.8	135.0
	3rd Qtr.	101.5	3.7	-	2.0	30.9	138.2
	4th Qtr.	104.5	3.7	-	1.4	30.6	140.3
2002	1st Qtr.	102.2	3.9	-	1.7	22.0	129.8
	2nd Qtr.	106.6	3.9	-	1.7	19.0	131.2
	3rd Qtr.	107.5	3.9	-	1.7	23.0	136.2
	4th Qtr.	107.4	3.9	-	1.7	23.2	136.3
2003	1st Qtr.	108.7	-	-	1.7	23.4	133.8
	2nd Qtr.	107.2	-	-	1.7	19.9	128.8
	3rd Qtr.	105.9	-	-	0.5	20.1	126.5
	4th Qtr.	124.3	-	-	0.7	16.2	141.1

Market Silver Inventories
Million Troy Ounces

		Comex	CBT	LME	Tocom	Industry	Total
2004	1st Qtr.	122.1	-	-	0.5	16.7	139.2
	2nd Qtr.	118.4	-	-	0.6	15.3	134.3
	3rd Qtr.	107.8	-	-	0.4	22.5	130.7
	4th Qtr.	103.6	-	-	1.2	18.4	123.2
2005	1st Qtr.	103.6	-	-	1.0	20.2	124.8
	2nd Qtr.	104.7	-	-	0.9	19.3	124.9
	3rd Qtr.	116.7	-	-	0.9	18.8	136.4
	4th Qtr.	120.0	-	-	0.6	18.8	139.3

Notes: Industry stocks include dealer, importer, and refiner stocks, in the United States and Japan. The London Metal Exchange ceased its silver contract in June 1989. Stocks formerly registered against the contracts now are held in private hands. The London Metal Exchange re-launched its silver contract in May 1999, but does not publicly report warehouse stocks. *Comex began reporting Wilmington Trust stocks eligible for Comex delivery in the fourth quarter of 1996. Wilmington Trust became a licensed Comex silver depository on January 1, 1997. NA -- not available.
Sources: Comex, Chicago Board of Trade, Tokyo Commodity Exchange, London Metal Exchange, U.S. Bureau of Mines, Japanese Ministry of Trade and Industry, CPM Group.
March 14, 2006

Reported Market Inventories

Quarterly, Through Fourth Quarter 2005.

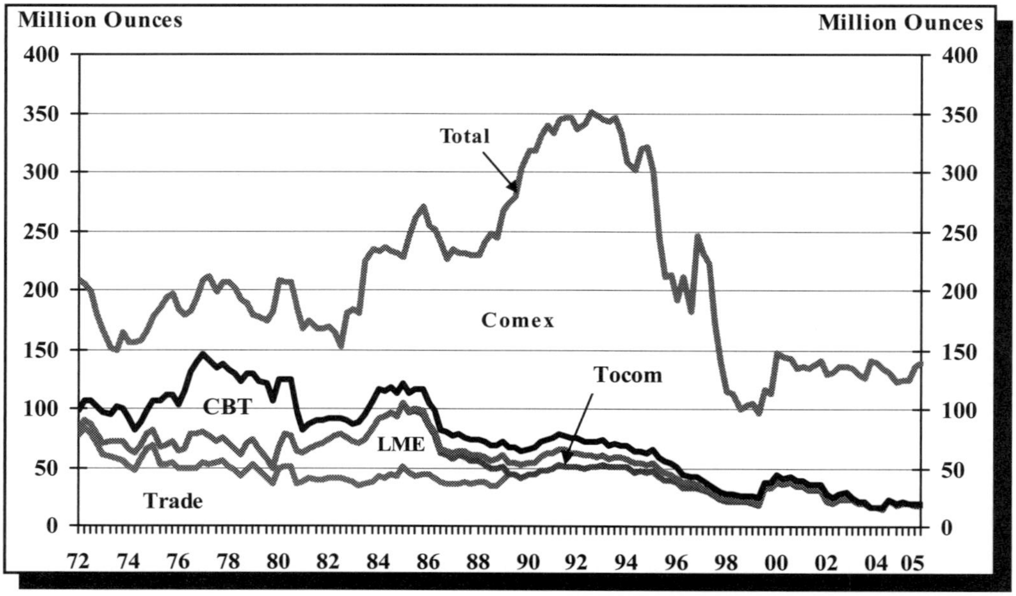

Market Stocks

Quarterly, Through Fourth Quarter 2005.

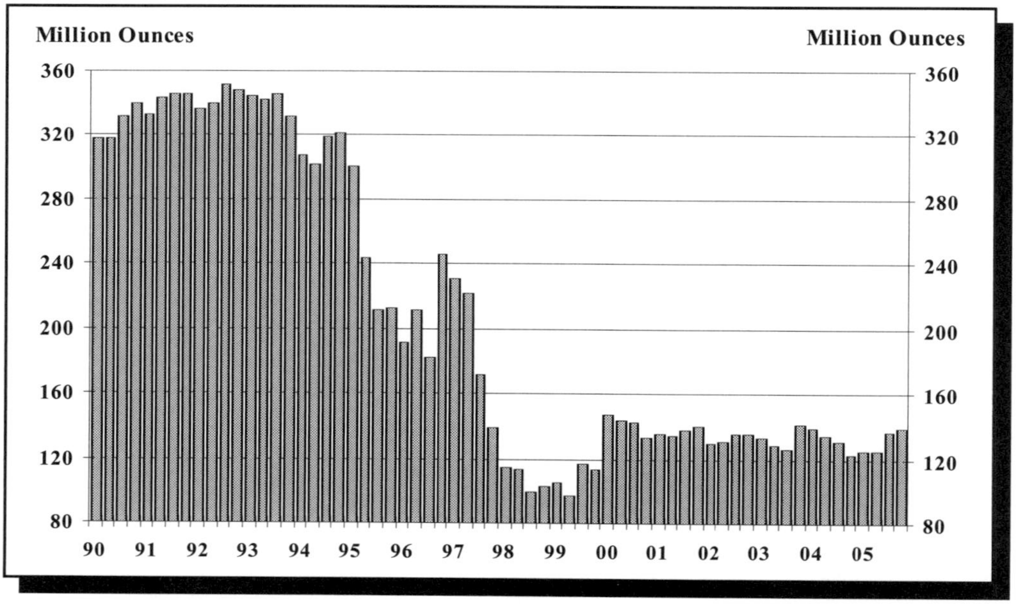

Reported and Unreported Silver Holdings
Million Troy Ounces

	Reported Stock Levels				Year-to-Year Changes		
		Market					
	Government	Exchange	Dealer	Total	Reported Stocks	Unreported Stocks	Total
1970	359.0	135.0	82.2	217.2	NA	NA	NA
1971	311.9	135.7	57.1	192.8	-24.4	-11.6	-36.0
1972	333.6	107.9	70.9	178.8	-14.0	-82.6	-96.6
1973	277.2	108.0	56.4	164.4	-14.4	-114.6	-129.0
1974	319.2	99.5	66.3	165.8	1.4	-53.4	-52.0
1975	250.8	142.0	54.6	196.6	30.8	-40.9	-10.1
1976	257.0	144.3	49.8	194.1	-2.5	-23.2	-25.7
1977	319.0	149.8	56.1	205.9	11.8	-60.9	-49.1
1978	318.8	141.1	47.3	188.4	-17.5	-39.6	-57.1
1979	314.6	146.2	35.4	181.6	-6.8	32.7	25.9
1980	327.8	148.1	50.2	198.3	16.7	190.5	207.2
1981	323.8	128.7	40.3	169.0	-29.3	143.6	114.3
1982	322.8	141.4	41.6	183.0	14.0	66.5	80.5
1983	311.7	196.6	34.6	231.2	48.2	114.3	162.5
1984	307.0	189.2	41.5	230.7	-0.5	86.2	85.7
1985	294.0	227.0	46.3	273.3	42.6	45.6	88.2
1986	280.0	189.2	41.6	230.8	-42.5	50.9	8.4
1987	267.8	193.4	36.8	230.2	-0.6	41.3	40.7
1988	251.6	209.4	38.2	247.6	17.4	6.9	24.3
1989	240.9	261.1	44.0	305.1	57.5	-49.2	8.3
1990	229.9	291.9	43.7	335.6	30.5	-61.3	-30.8
1991	218.4	294.9	52.1	347.0	11.4	-79.5	-68.1
1992	210.3	367.8 *	49.9	417.7	70.7	-146.4 *	-75.7
1993	199.9	373.3	50.0	423.3	5.6	-189.6	-184.0
1994	189.7	347.4	46.0	393.4	-29.9	-170.6	-200.6
1995	177.8	233.2	39.0	272.2	-121.2	-60.3	-181.5
1996	172.8	213.1	32.7	245.8	-26.3	-174.7	-201.0
1997	167.5	116.8	23.0	139.8	-106.0	-107.7	-213.7
1998	161.5	81.8	21.0	102.8	-37.0	-159.7	-196.7
1999	149.4	81.4	32.0	113.4	10.6	-165.2	-154.6
2000	140.4	99.7	34.1	133.8	20.5	-163.0	-142.6
2001	127.2	109.7	30.6	140.3	6.4	-80.5	-74.1
2002	123.2	113.1	23.2	136.3	-4.0	-67.9	-71.9
2003	123.2	124.9	16.2	141.1	4.9	-60.1	-55.2
2004	122.7	104.8	18.4	123.2	-17.9	-40.9	-58.9
2005	87.7	120.5	18.8	139.3	16.2	-44.2	-28.1

Notes: Changes in total stocks represents the change in the supply/demand balance of new metal. Market stocks include reported U.S. dealer inventories and exchange registered stocks. New York Commodity Exchange stocks also include eligible stocks. Changes in market stocks are end-year; 2004 change is through end-December. Changes in unreported stocks is the change in the supply/demand balance of new metal, adjusted for changes in reported inventories. End of year data. *Adjusted to include Wilmington Trust stocks that would have been eligible for Comex delivery. Wilmington Trust became a licensed Comex silver depository on January 1, 1997.
Sources: U.S. Bureau of the Mint; U.S. Bureau of Mines; New York Commodity Exchange; London Metal Exchange; Chicago Board of Trade; Tokyo Commodity Exchange; CPM Group.
Marcg 14, 2006

Comex Inventories
Troy Ounces

		Eligible	Registered	Total
1988	January			
	February			
	March			
	April	20,931,178	137,735,862	158,667,040
	May	23,267,595	141,080,749	164,348,344
	June	19,048,467	149,149,501	168,197,968
	July	22,419,309	147,324,079	169,743,388
	August	20,844,158	154,751,024	175,595,182
	September	20,430,956	158,341,924	178,772,880
	October	20,595,315	154,686,825	175,282,140
	November	18,220,714	160,236,251	178,456,965
	December	17,859,494	158,060,356	175,919,850
1989	January	19,160,193	163,496,673	182,656,866
	February	23,131,632	167,111,383	190,243,015
	March	28,976,762	165,825,629	194,802,391
	April	38,647,464	162,347,967	200,995,431
	May	35,066,425	168,140,357	203,206,782
	June	31,200,288	174,848,870	206,049,158
	July	31,155,105	176,130,744	207,285,849
	August	32,577,746	177,807,340	210,385,086
	September	38,453,219	173,830,263	212,283,482
	October	45,019,114	181,551,266	226,570,380
	November	43,900,831	194,045,589	237,946,420
	December	46,787,483	191,985,060	238,772,543
1990	January	52,157,110	188,639,227	240,796,337
	February	48,801,419	194,619,375	243,420,794
	March	54,362,447	197,741,690	252,104,137
	April	54,149,135	199,623,503	253,772,638
	May	57,134,847	198,286,005	255,420,852
	June	70,866,114	180,759,827	251,625,941
	July	72,595,954	180,730,153	253,326,107
	August	82,219,388	173,594,421	255,813,809
	September	68,279,740	191,904,669	260,184,409
	October	79,486,485	179,127,685	258,614,170
	November	55,330,949	202,354,370	257,685,319
	December	59,768,672	205,570,595	265,339,267
1991	January	61,113,795	205,092,178	266,205,973
	February	58,398,935	205,433,464	263,832,399
	March	64,871,675	192,979,471	257,851,146
	April	66,858,781	196,704,194	263,562,975
	May	62,069,034	201,617,049	263,686,083
	June	54,444,776	211,641,952	266,086,728
	July	60,249,532	216,711,025	276,960,557
	August	56,648,508	214,155,505	270,804,013
	September	54,478,488	215,182,765	269,661,253
	October	58,918,511	206,955,342	265,873,853
	November	57,058,278	205,776,673	262,834,951
	December	64,848,241	205,886,040	270,734,281
1992	January	63,890,330	207,801,743	271,692,073
	February	69,174,680	209,815,116	278,989,796
	March	78,754,912	190,820,207	269,575,119
	April	73,747,831	188,491,645	262,239,476
	May	79,940,269	187,062,531	267,002,800
	June	77,623,785	190,194,292	267,818,077
	July	83,215,228	188,044,215	271,259,443
	August	82,821,967	190,920,787	273,742,754
	September	91,230,401	187,344,698	278,575,099
	October	92,762,047	185,764,386	278,526,433
	November	98,153,181	182,558,939	280,712,120
	December	101,939,323	173,216,882	275,156,205

Comex Inventories
Troy Ounces

		Eligible	Registered	Total
1993	January	106,998,830	165,825,641	272,824,471
	February	86,961,954	186,667,499	273,629,453
	March	82,662,229	189,193,714	271,855,943
	April	80,895,709	185,391,189	266,286,898
	May	77,063,808	193,735,970	270,799,778
	June	77,578,847	196,367,983	273,946,830
	July	85,711,618	191,516,305	277,227,923
	August	87,728,399	191,016,115	278,744,514
	September	89,815,975	187,003,403	276,819,378
	October	97,885,085	177,485,327	275,370,412
	November	112,165,854	165,500,524	277,666,378
	December	105,016,928	158,120,600	263,137,528
1994	January	97,437,653	154,247,251	251,684,904
	February	95,900,884	154,829,493	250,730,377
	March	105,568,497	133,805,368	239,373,865
	April	104,233,160	136,059,600	240,292,760
	May	79,737,856	154,212,232	233,950,088
	June	96,149,822	141,224,293	237,374,115
	July	98,196,337	148,094,476	246,290,813
	August	93,530,348	155,886,182	249,416,530
	September	91,233,359	163,964,469	255,197,828
	October	97,483,828	162,150,002	259,633,830
	November	91,432,535	174,277,752	265,710,287
	December	73,964,895	184,653,457	258,618,352
1995	January	77,729,176	181,925,185	259,654,361
	February	77,301,784	186,743,449	264,045,233
	March	66,693,322	168,421,093	235,114,415
	April	38,952,612	172,075,316	211,027,928
	May	47,374,096	142,293,524	189,667,620
	June	37,984,494	146,585,835	184,570,329
	July	40,169,295	141,099,427	181,268,722
	August	32,983,203	142,780,620	175,763,823
	September	43,442,226	113,101,277	156,543,503
	October	52,007,958	103,983,191	155,991,149
	November	38,836,229	119,188,166	158,024,395
	December	35,831,045	123,280,548	159,111,593
1996	January	36,940,389	107,025,922	143,966,311
	February	33,366,191	117,967,447	151,333,638
	March	38,068,627	101,672,254	139,740,881
	April	34,243,584	107,567,990	141,811,574
	May	43,247,715	106,072,060	149,319,775
	June	45,337,013	122,259,056	167,596,069
	July	49,138,317	107,484,770	156,623,087
	August	38,299,394	112,452,911	150,752,305
	September	38,911,341	100,411,090	139,322,431
	October	42,753,103	87,275,643	130,028,746
	November	39,979,743	108,471,715	148,451,458
	December*	101,619,515	101,831,268	203,450,783
1997	January	101,738,914	93,110,545	194,849,459
	February	87,402,640	105,816,663	193,219,303
	March	86,111,053	105,600,425	191,711,478
	April	85,722,960	104,078,774	189,801,734
	May	101,394,054	98,802,811	200,196,865
	June	95,997,795	89,531,201	185,528,996
	July	90,018,293	79,591,120	169,609,413
	August	83,284,069	81,012,292	164,296,361
	September	81,331,218	56,818,062	138,149,280
	October	74,874,064	58,051,601	132,925,665
	November	70,579,064	56,460,142	127,039,206
	December	67,618,752	42,229,326	109,848,078

Comex Inventories
Troy Ounces

		Eligible	Registered	Total
1998	January	68,780,324	35,324,866	104,105,190
	February	53,563,944	36,531,320	90,095,264
	March	49,746,209	37,179,714	86,925,923
	April	52,506,354	36,050,079	88,556,433
	May	52,985,545	37,347,768	90,333,313
	June	44,538,232	41,707,022	86,245,254
	July	38,926,117	39,581,321	78,507,438
	August	35,148,850	43,532,564	78,681,414
	September	37,194,347	35,602,263	72,796,610
	October	40,196,352	32,862,795	73,059,147
	November	39,129,372	37,688,599	76,817,971
	December	39,731,390	36,076,073	75,807,463
1999	January	41,143,162	34,025,293	75,168,455
	February	45,015,339	33,119,380	78,134,719
	March	34,966,954	44,638,085	79,605,039
	April	34,623,366	44,195,505	78,818,871
	May	34,889,797	42,621,838	77,511,635
	June	35,536,370	37,977,406	73,513,776
	July	35,374,638	42,217,393	77,592,031
	August	34,472,469	45,133,568	79,606,037
	September	33,824,345	45,566,758	79,391,103
	October	33,608,471	45,546,418	79,154,889
	November	33,551,213	44,864,649	78,415,862
	December	27,938,474	48,056,048	75,994,522
2000	January	28,218,317	45,730,145	73,948,462
	February	28,778,744	65,003,696	93,782,440
	March	36,268,761	67,990,735	104,259,496
	April	28,224,388	74,364,580	102,588,968
	May	26,381,397	72,903,682	99,285,079
	June	27,253,384	75,459,430	102,712,814
	July	25,114,032	77,176,922	102,290,954
	August	23,216,925	74,661,578	97,878,503
	September	22,905,824	76,645,930	99,551,754
	October	21,975,302	73,773,921	95,749,223
	November	20,492,787	75,224,472	95,717,259
	December	23,581,876	70,401,291	93,983,167
2001	January	24,818,365	68,376,467	93,194,832
	February	25,978,135	72,680,650	98,658,785
	March	29,548,156	67,145,444	96,693,600
	April	28,577,377	67,167,204	95,744,581
	May	27,393,422	68,696,703	96,090,125
	June	28,204,631	70,495,433	98,700,064
	July	36,392,330	64,102,014	100,494,344
	August	36,440,680	66,328,997	102,769,677
	September	34,839,925	66,698,130	101,538,055
	October	36,640,993	67,340,623	103,981,616
	November	34,934,455	70,300,573	105,235,028
	December	34,715,333	69,832,178	104,547,511
2002	January	34,494,716	67,900,097	102,394,813
	February	32,428,939	68,554,133	100,983,072
	March	33,243,387	68,932,187	102,175,574
	April	32,389,844	71,533,549	103,923,393
	May	33,757,824	74,068,776	107,826,600
	June	32,133,892	74,432,507	106,566,399
	July	42,706,117	63,434,826	106,140,943
	August	46,886,596	61,202,926	108,089,522
	September	46,218,923	61,322,723	107,541,646
	October	48,334,900	59,547,885	107,882,785
	November	47,645,570	59,458,840	107,104,410
	December	45,734,368	61,660,853	107,395,221

Comex Inventories
Troy Ounces

		Eligible	Registered	Total
2003	January	50,562,260	56,514,494	107,076,754
	February	50,484,559	58,647,084	109,131,643
	March	50,500,867	58,189,084	108,689,951
	April	53,168,722	54,999,604	108,168,326
	May	59,025,032	46,067,341	105,092,373
	June	61,179,745	46,042,085	107,221,830
	July	65,315,896	41,186,781	106,502,677
	August	60,982,910	43,861,897	104,844,807
	September	60,407,335	45,451,486	105,858,821
	October	60,061,555	55,401,789	115,463,344
	November	60,430,739	64,104,546	124,535,285
	December	59,970,714	64,300,016	124,270,730
2004	January	72,056,800	52,123,986	124,180,786
	February	70,368,603	52,825,960	123,194,563
	March	70,198,328	51,889,166	122,087,494
	April	72,266,724	50,420,414	122,687,138
	May	71,605,034	46,867,062	118,472,096
	June	52,764,168	65,605,072	118,369,240
	July	52,976,426	63,276,608	116,253,034
	August	52,632,893	56,678,487	109,311,380
	September	45,350,018	62,439,079	107,789,097
	October	42,970,021	61,654,128	104,624,149
	November	41,511,949	61,319,474	102,831,423
	December	42,302,549	61,287,203	103,589,752
2005	January	40,765,019	61,594,562	102,359,581
	February	40,435,337	61,058,686	101,494,023
	March	41,688,765	61,938,594	103,627,359
	April	38,851,493	65,143,967	103,995,460
	May	60,118,068	44,910,706	105,028,774
	June	60,314,695	44,404,436	104,719,131
	July	58,880,816	50,585,264	109,466,080
	August	56,040,938	59,547,308	115,588,246
	September	56,338,376	60,348,359	116,686,735
	October	56,707,193	59,549,790	116,256,983
	November	52,036,979	65,570,801	117,607,780
	December	51,925,748	68,048,244	119,973,992
2006	January	56,693,377	68,099,235	124,792,612
	February	55,602,621	72,295,794	127,898,415

Notes: Stocks are month-end. *Comex began reporting Wilmington Trust stocks eligible for The Comex deliver in the fourth quarter of 1996. Wilmington became a licensed Comex silver depository as of January 1, 1997.
Source: Comex.
March 14, 2006

Comex Stocks

Month-End, Through February 2006.

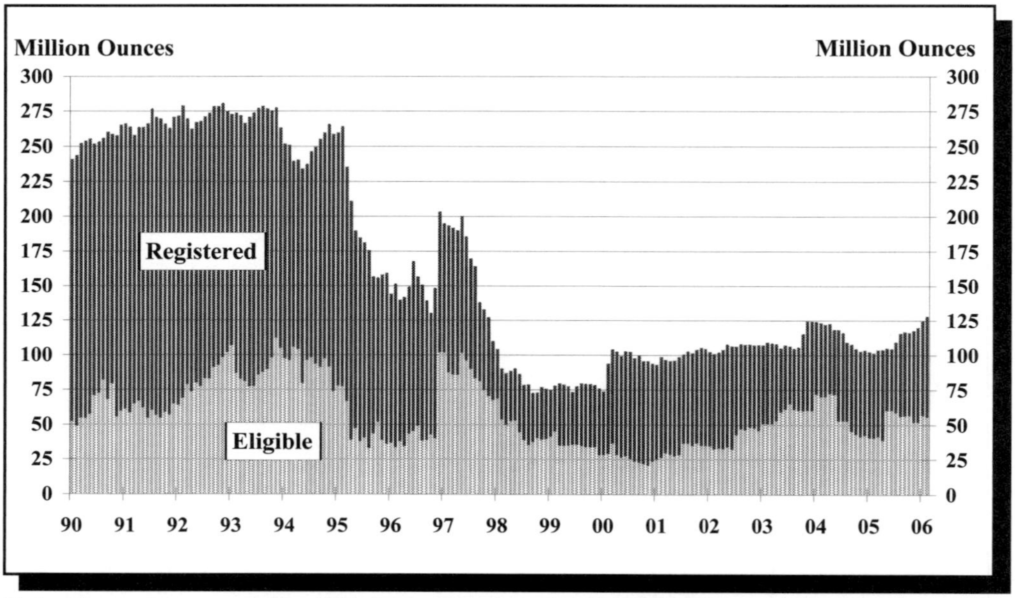

Note: Comex began reporting Wilmington Trust stocks eligible for Comex delivery in the fourth quarter of 1996. Wilmington became a licensed Comex silver depository as of 1 January 1997.

Markets

Markets

The volume of silver traded in the major international markets rose sharply in 2005, led by a 10.8% increase in New York Comex futures volumes and a 5.6% increase in London clearing volumes. The increase in trading in both of these markets, and across the other markets, reflected strong investor demand for silver and increased speculative trading in the metal. It came at a period when silver trading also was beginning on new exchanges, in Mumbai, India, and elsewhere, which may have detracted from the growth in the major markets. The major international markets for silver are the New York Comex and the London interbank market.

Futures and options trading volumes rose 9.1% to 34.7 billion ounces. Silver volumes have been rising since 2001, when they bottomed out at 15.9 billion ounces. Volumes were even higher in the first two months of 2006, running at an annualized rate of 46.4 billion ounces. Volumes may subside later in 2006, so that the full-year volumes may not be as high as that figure.

The volume of silver that cleared through banks that are members of the London Bullion Market Association (LBMA) totaled 27.9 billion ounces in 2005. This was an increase of 5.6% from 2004 levels. While the LBMA clearing volumes have risen, the volumes cleared through LBMA members continued to lose ground compared to the combined trading volumes of the New York Commodity Exchange

The Silver Market

2006 Annualized Through February

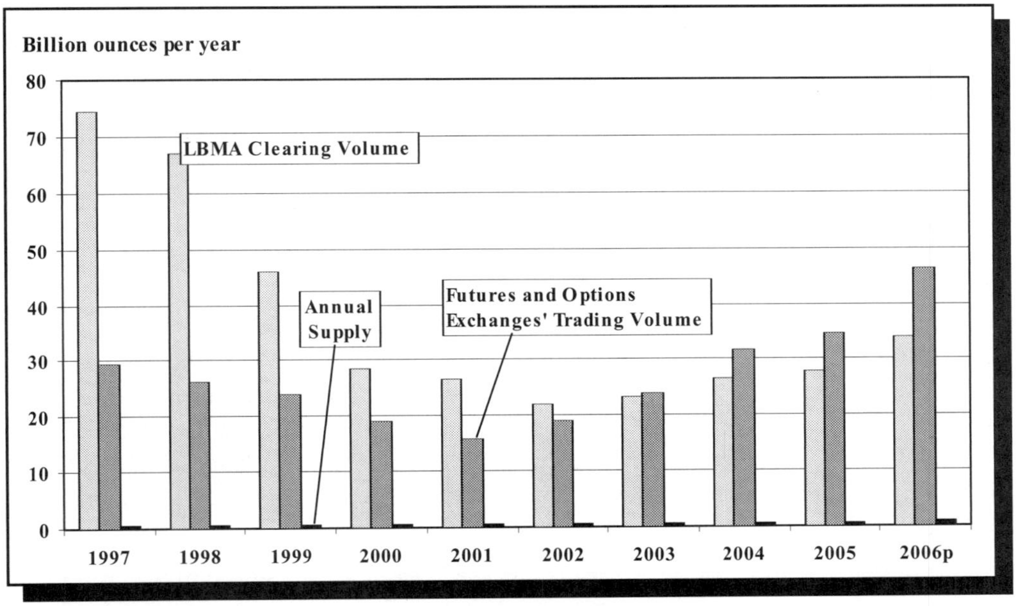

(COMEX), Tokyo Commodity Exchange (TOCOM) and Chicago Board of Trade (CBT). The gap in trading volumes between the two groups has been widening since 2003, as institutional and individual investors have moved sharply back into Comex trading and there has been a revival of silver activity on the CBT.

Comex trading volume for silver rose to 27.6 billion ounces in 2005; this was an increase of 10.6% from 2004 levels. Trading volumes have been rising steadily since 2001. The largest increase since then was in 2003, when volumes increased 27.7% from the previous year. Year-to-date trading volume through February totaled 5.6 billion ounces, up 20.4% from the 4.6 billion ounces during the same period in the previous year.

Comex open interest stood at 656.1 million ounces at the end of 2005. This was an increase of 30.4% compared to the end of 2004. As with trading volume, Comex open interest has been rising since 2001. Open interest has more than doubled from 315.5 million ounces at the end of 2001 range to 656.1 million ounces at the end of 2005 and 639.2 million ounces at the end of February 2006. Open interest in 2005 peaked in November at 704.5 million ounces; this was a 20.4% increase from November 2004 levels.

Annual trading volume on the Tocom fell for the first time since 2000 in 2005. Volumes stood at 788.6 million ounces, down significantly by 44.5% from the 1.4 billion ounces recorded in 2004. Trading volumes in 2004 were the highest since the 1.6 billion witnessed in 1998. December saw the highest level of trading volume for 2005, at 113.5 million ounces, accounting for 14.4% of the year's total trading volume.

Open interest for the Tocom was flat in 2005, with open interest in most months hovering around 16.5 million ounces. Open interest rose briefly to 21.7 million ounces at the end of November 2005, but slipped back quickly to the 16 million ounce range the following month. Open interest on the Tocom earlier had declined steadily through 2004, ending the year at 16.5 million ounces and remained around this level for most part of 2005.

Trading volumes in Comex options have been rising swiftly since 2001. Trading volumes rose to 5.7 billion ounces in 2005, a 10.7% rise from 2004 levels. Trading volumes in 2004 stood at 5.1 billion, 82.0% greater than the 2.8 billion ounces in 2003. The highest monthly trading volume since 1985 was recorded in January 2006, when trading volumes stood at 986.9 million ounces.

Open interest in Comex options stood at 527.6 million ounces at the end of 2005. This was an increase of 65.8% from the 318.1 million ounces at the end of 2004. Open interest in January 2006 rose to a record, standing at 763.1 million ounces.

The LBMA reports monthly data on average daily turnover of silver, the number of trades per day on average, and the value of the transactions. CPM Group calculates the average size of a trade clearing across LBMA member banks. This figure is informative as an indication of the size of the trades being made. Many trades do not appear in the LBMA clearing statistics, as they are cleared within a bank, and not between two banks. This is particularly true of smaller transactions, for which any given bank will have a better chance of being able to clear it within its own book. Larger transactions are more likely to require a bank clearing it with another bank. Additionally, proprietary trading by the banks' own staffs will clear across the market, as they will not trade with themselves.

When the LBMA began publishing its monthly clearing volumes in late 1996 and 1997, the average transaction clearing across the banks was around 500,000 ounces or larger. As the late 1990s progressed this declined to around 400,000 - 450,000 ounces in 1998. After many banks suffered short-term marked to market losses in gold and silver in late 1999, many bullion banks and brokerage companies pulled back sharply from the proprietary trading they had focused on in the 1990s. Many cut back on metals trading, in some cases exiting the precious metals markets entirely. Other banks focused

London Bullion Market Association - Average Transaction Size

Ounces of Silver Transferred Divided by Number of Transfers

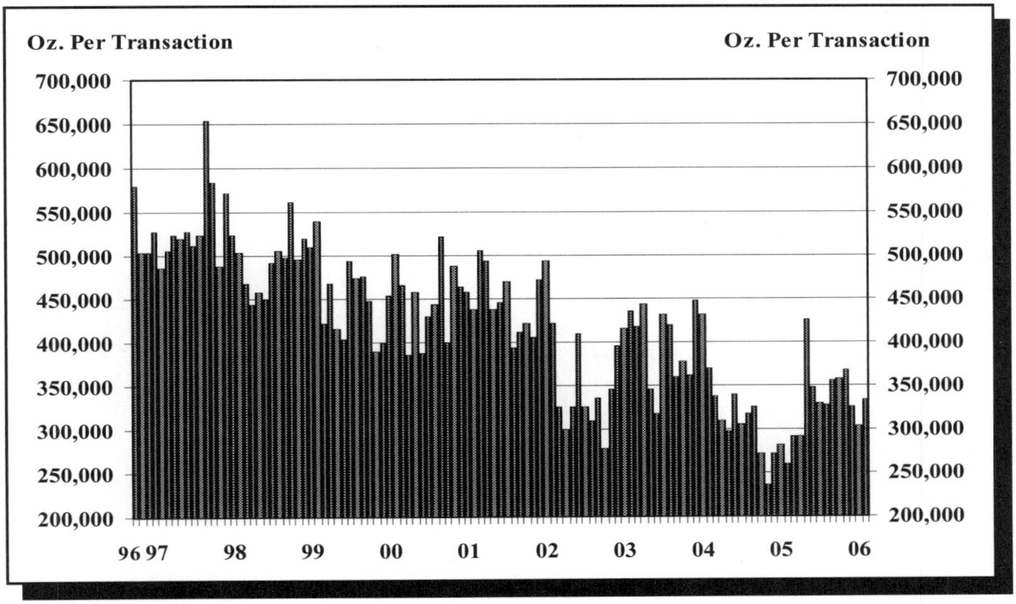

solely on client business for investors and commercial counterparts. The average transaction size declined sharply, to 398,000 ounces on average in 2003 and 318,500 ounces in 2004. November 2004 was a record low average trade size of 236,700 ounces. This was well below typical monthly average trade sizes, which usually are more than 300,000 ounces per trade. It was interesting timing, since November 2004 also saw a sharp increase in silver prices.

Since the end of 2004 the average transaction size has increased. This may reflect some increase in inter-bank proprietary trading, although for the most part many of the banks appear to be continuing to avoid rebuilding those operations. While many banks are rebuilding their precious metals and commodities trading desks, they have tended to continue to focus on client business and not engage in the heavy volumes of proprietary trading that characterized much of the 1990s.

This trend is reflected in the fact that the number of transactions in silver clearing across the London market has risen more sharply than has the trading volume. The typical daily number of transactions was 410 in January of 2006, and 457 in February. This contrasts with daily transaction numbers consistently below 250 from the middle of 2000 through most of 2003. The volume of transactions in terms of the number of ounces has risen since 2003 as well, but not as sharply. This suggests that the increased activity is more focused on commercial transactions, which often tend to be smaller than transactions for institutional investors, funds, or the banks' own propriety trading desks.

The Silver Market 1997 - 2006p
Million Ounces

	1997	1998	1999	2000	2001	2002	2003	2004	2005	2006p
Annual Supply	608.7	650.0	690.7	734.7	753.4	738.9	743.2	752.5	790.7	814.1
Futures and Options Exchanges Trading Volume	29,478.1	26,218.9	23,885.3	19,032.3	15,911.0	19,259.9	23,974.5	31,829.7	34,723.8	46,375.3
London Bullion Market Association Clearing Volume	74,573.9	67,059.3	46,111.9	28,475.4	26,552.5	21,888.9	23,460.0	26,402.5	27,886.4	34,035.0
Total	104,660.7	93,928.2	70,687.9	48,242.4	43,216.9	41,887.7	48,177.7	58,984.7	63,400.9	81,224.4
Ratio: Trading: Annual Supply	171:1	144:1	101:1	65:1	56:1	56:1	64:1	77:1	79:1	99:1

Source: CPM Group
Notes: Tocom through February 2006, Comex Through February 2006.
LBMA Through February 2006. Annualized Data.
March 20, 2006

London Bullion Market Clearing Turnover

Daily Averages

Ounces Transferred (Million Ounces)

	1996	1997	1998	1999	2000	2001	2002	2003	2004	2005	2006
January	-	294.4	330.4	214.2	149.2	105.1	175.7	89.7	143.4	76.9	124.5
February	-	275.0	347.8	277.3	172.7	102.0	108.7	107.5	121.5	77.5	152.9
March	-	284.1	272.1	188.8	134.0	131.3	77.9	90.0	128.7	93.8	
April	-	253.0	230.7	198.2	106.9	121.6	68.8	79.2	133.8	87.6	
May	-	236.6	266.5	189.0	121.0	110.2	99.9	78.9	94.7	152.1	
June	-	270.5	217.9	161.3	97.0	99.8	107.2	61.3	95.1	123.4	
July	-	270.6	233.5	191.3	93.3	99.5	72.9	108.3	93.6	95.1	
August	-	263.3	223.4	196.1	100.5	89.4	66.2	97.8	82.5	104.4	
September	-	314.3	232.2	176.3	117.0	96.7	61.7	96.2	82.3	126.8	
October	279.4	345.5	249.4	182.4	82.2	101.9	67.5	101.3	92.0	124.7	
November	244.3	327.9	169.1	125.9	97.6	91.4	58.2	89.6	75.5	132	
December	248.8	395.8	202.2	119.9	116.4	147.3	79.1	110.1	102.2	131.3	

Value in Billions of Dollars

	1996	1997	1998	1999	2000	2001	2002	2003	2004	2005	2006
January	-	1.4	1.9	1.1	0.77	0.49	0.77	0.43	0.91	0.51	1.14
February	-	1.4	2.4	1.5	0.91	0.46	0.48	0.50	0.78	0.54	1.46
March	-	1.5	1.7	1.0	0.68	0.58	0.35	0.41	0.93	0.68	
April	-	1.2	1.5	1.0	0.54	0.53	0.31	0.36	0.94	0.62	
May	-	1.1	1.5	1.0	0.60	0.49	0.47	0.37	0.55	1.07	
June	-	1.3	1.1	0.8	0.48	0.44	0.52	0.28	0.56	0.9	
July	-	1.2	1.3	1.0	0.46	0.42	0.36	0.52	0.59	0.67	
August	-	1.2	1.2	1.0	0.49	0.38	0.30	0.49	0.55	0.74	
September	-	1.5	1.2	0.9	0.57	0.42	0.28	0.50	0.53	0.91	
October	1.4	1.7	1.2	1.0	0.40	0.45	0.30	0.51	0.65	0.96	
November	1.2	1.7	0.8	0.6	0.46	0.38	0.26	0.46	0.57	1.04	
December	1.2	2.3	1.0	0.6	0.54	0.64	0.37	0.62	0.73	1.13	

Number of Transfers

	1996	1997	1998	1999	2000	2001	2002	2003	2004	2005	2006
January	-	557	630	420	329	229	355	216	332	272	410
February	-	565	690	514	344	233	257	247	329	299	457
March	-	562	581	448	288	260	239	215	380	321	
April	-	482	520	423	277	246	230	178	431	299	
May	-	455	583	454	264	252	307	228	317	357	
June	-	513	484	400	250	224	262	193	280	355	
July	-	528	474	387	217	212	224	251	305	289	
August	-	503	441	413	226	227	214	233	259	318	
September	-	481	466	371	224	235	184	267	252	356	
October	481	592	443	407	205	242	243	268	337	349	
November	484	671	341	322	200	225	168	248	319	359	
December	493	691	389	300	251	312	200	246	375	403	

Note: * partly estimated.
Value is calculated using the monthly average London fixing for silver. Allocations between Clearing Members where the sole purpose is for overnight credit and physical movements arranged by Clearing Members in locations other than London are excluded.
Source: London Bullion Market Association, CPM Group.
March 22, 2006

London Bullion Market Association - Ounces of Silver Transferred

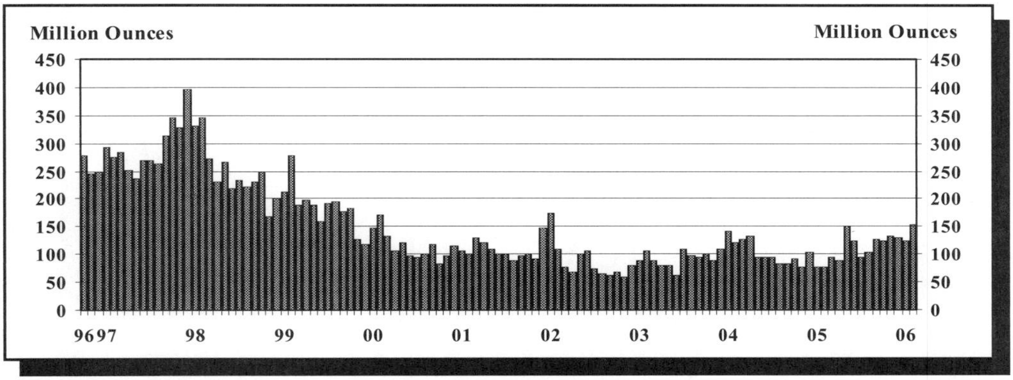

Value of Silver Transferred

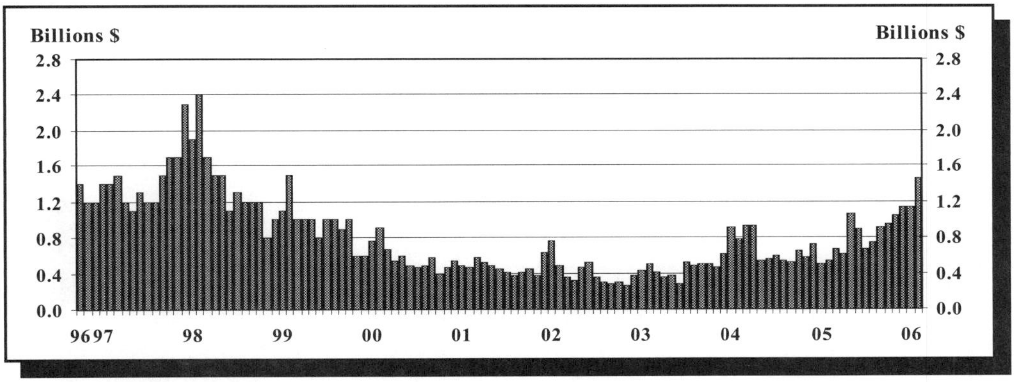

Number of Transfers

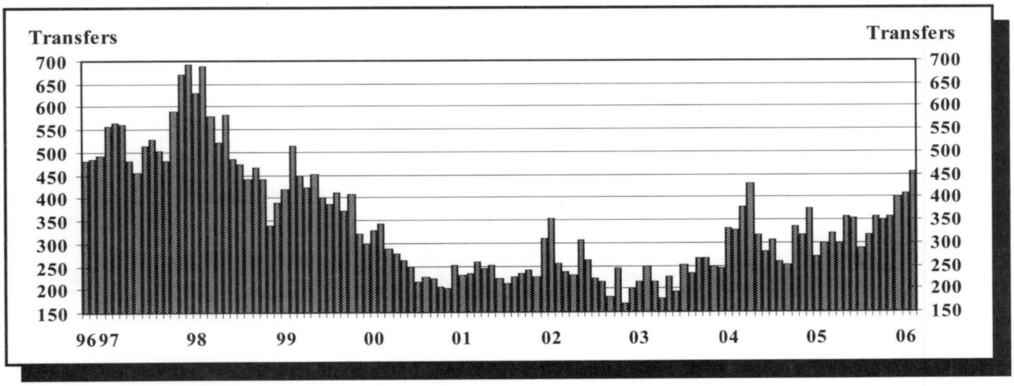

Trading Volume in the Futures Market

Annual Total, Through 2005. 2006 Annualized Through February.

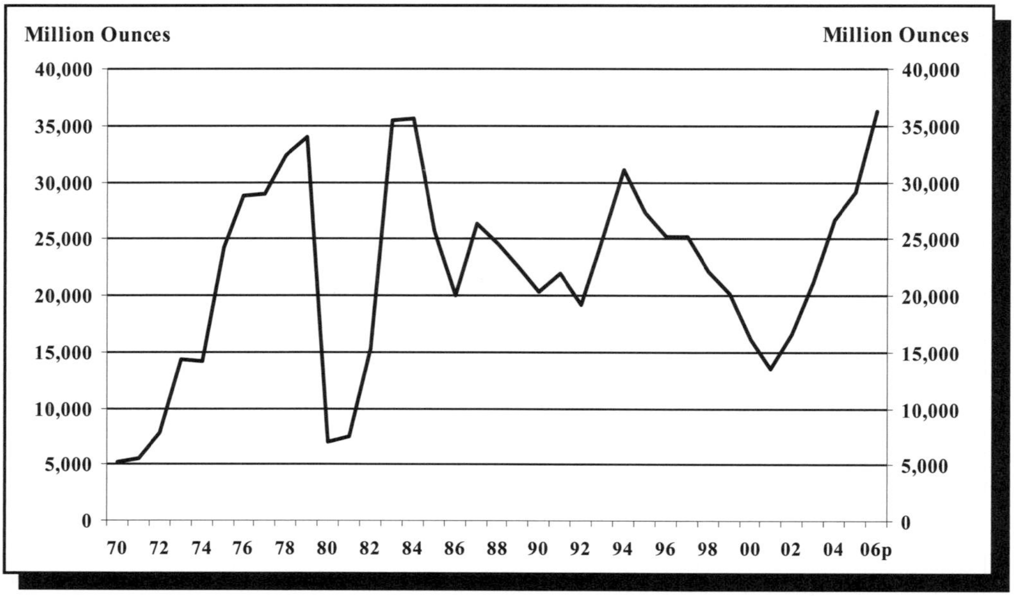

Open Interest in the Futures Market

Year-end, Through 2005. 2006 Through end-February.

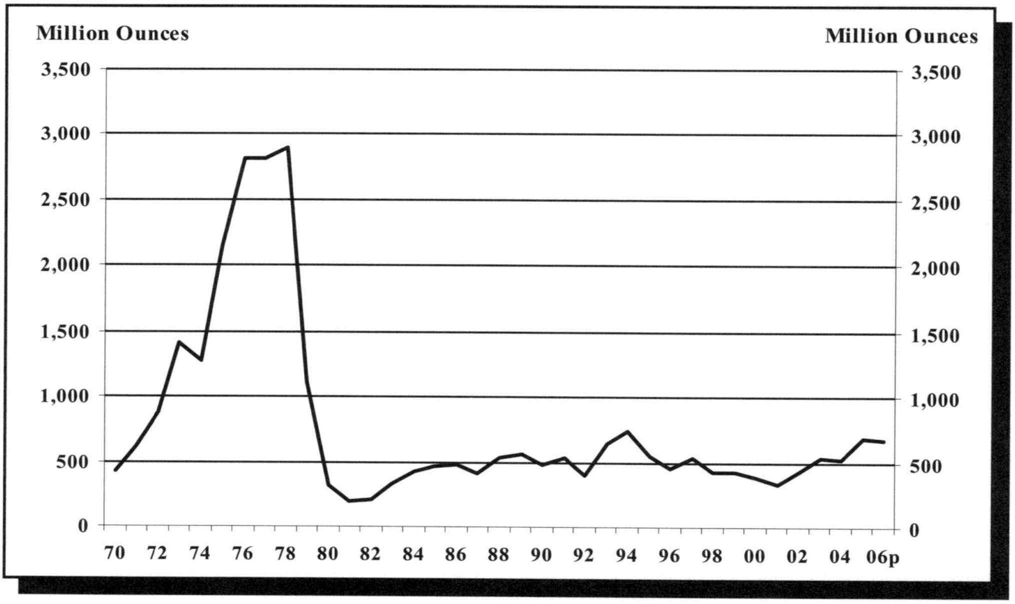

Trading Volume in the Options Market - Puts and Calls

Annual Total, Through 2005. 2006 Annualized Through February.

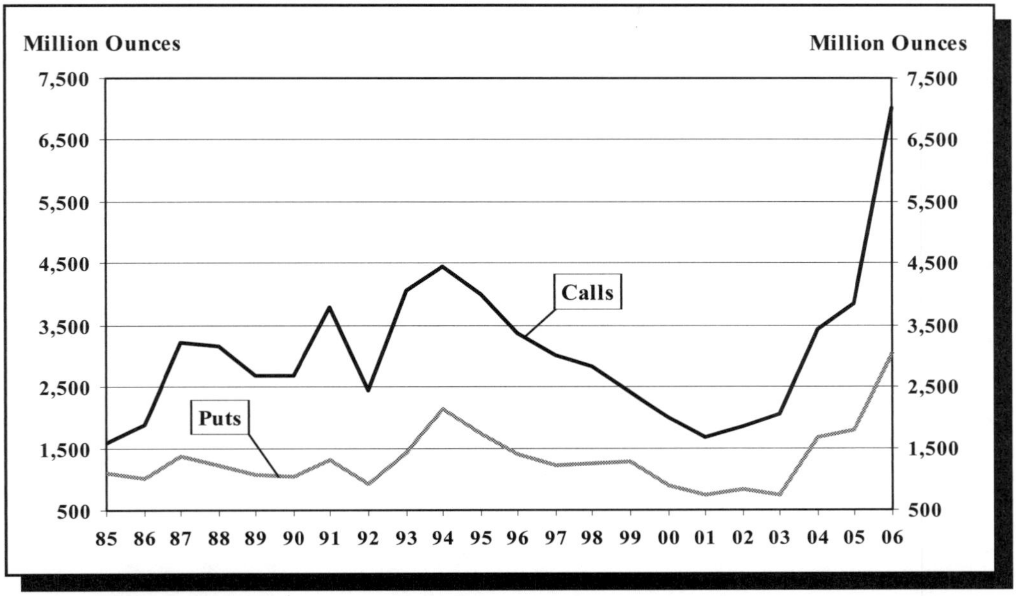

Open Interest in the Options Market - Puts and Calls

Year-end, Through 2005. 2006 Through end-February.

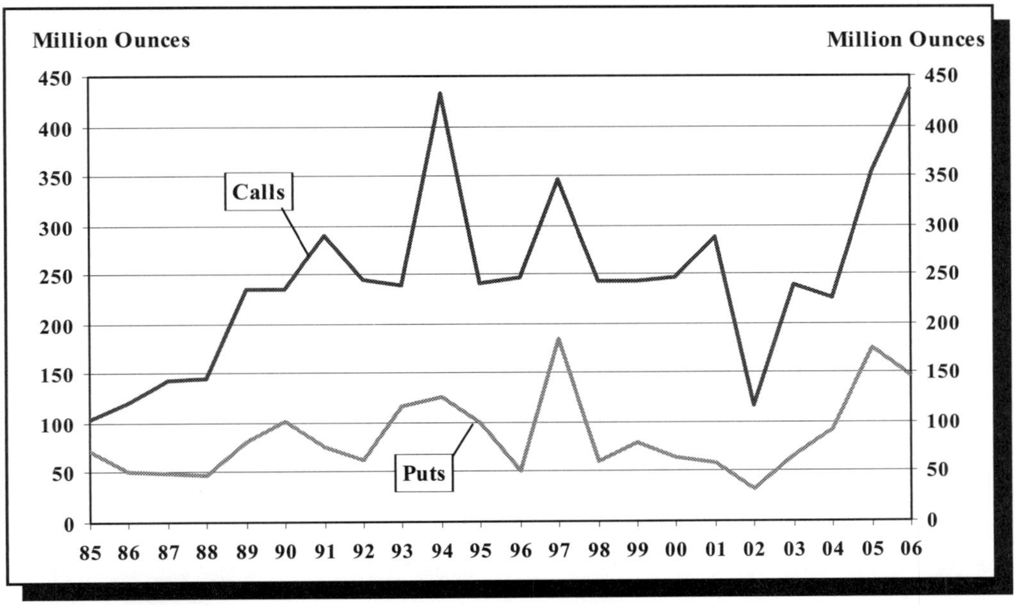

Silver Futures Exchange Activity
Million Troy Ounces

	Trading Volume			
	Comex	CBT	Tocom	Total
1970	3,468.5	1,813.1	—	5,281.6
1971	3,081.2	2,520.5	—	5,601.7
1972	4,074.5	3,770.2	—	7,844.7
1973	6,189.3	8,153.0	—	14,342.3
1974	6,829.6	7,314.0	—	14,143.6
1975	14,511.6	9,763.5	—	24,275.1
1976	18,709.5	10,055.2	—	28,764.7
1977	17,700.2	11,285.3	—	28,985.5
1978	19,110.4	13,289.2	—	32,399.6
1979	20,403.1	13,602.9	—	34,006.0
1980	5,293.7	1,705.2	—	6,998.9
1981	6,203.6	1,257.3	—	7,460.9
1982	14,188.1	1,163.6	—	15,351.7
1983	32,619.9	2,750.5	—	35,370.4
1984	33,712.5	1,887.3	—	35,599.8
1985	24,106.0	1,034.8	591.1	25,731.9
1986	19,248.4	511.2	227.1	19,986.7
1987	25,278.3	597.0	473.2	26,348.5
1988	23,323.3	502.4	740.2	24,565.8
1989	21,833.1	266.7	420.8	22,520.6
1990	19,568.5	192.0	486.4	20,246.9
1991	20,773.5	117.5	1,020.1	21,911.1
1992	18,941.6	55.1	223.6	19,220.3
1993	24,279.6	94.3	639.9	25,013.8
1994	29,971.7	139.8	1,005.2	31,116.7
1995	25,773.7	139.9	1,389.2	27,302.7
1996	24,354.0	42.1	726.3	25,122.5
1997	24,467.6	31.2	764.7	25,263.5
1998	20,473.1	35.5	1,620.1	22,128.7
1999	19,234.5	21.2	932.5	20,188.2
2000	15,585.2	12.6	538.9	16,136.7
2001	12,846.0	10.5	637.4	13,493.9
2002	15,677.8	8.1	897.9	16,583.8
2003	20,020.2	34.8	1,119.4	21,174.4
2004	25,030.6	266.2	1,421.1	26,718.0
2005	27,681.8	594.5	788.6	29,064.9
2006p	33,604.2	1,760.7	928.3	36,293.1

Notes: Trading volume is the total for the year. 2006 annualized Through February. Open interest is month-end. Sources: New York Commodity Exchange, Chicago Board of Trade. Tokyo Commodity Exchange
March 10, 2006

Silver Futures Exchange Activity

Million Troy Ounces

Open Interest				
Comex	CBT	Tocom	Total	
230.9	191.2	—	422.1	1970
245.5	366.7	—	612.2	1971
327.8	544.7	—	872.5	1972
428.0	981.6	—	1,409.6	1973
658.4	623.5	—	1,281.9	1974
1,276.4	864.5	—	2,140.9	1975
2,138.7	680.3	—	2,819.0	1976
1,404.9	1,409.8	—	2,814.7	1977
1,549.0	1,343.9	—	2,892.9	1978
636.8	468.7	—	1,105.5	1979
166.2	143.1	—	309.3	1980
140.0	56.3	—	196.3	1981
169.0	34.8	—	203.8	1982
301.7	32.4	—	334.1	1983
401.5	26.8	—	428.3	1984
430.7	18.5	17.6	466.8	1985
449.1	12.7	12.3	474.1	1986
371.2	11.2	24.8	407.2	1987
470.0	13.5	47.2	530.7	1988
474.2	9.7	80.2	564.1	1989
421.7	10.9	49.8	482.3	1990
488.8	6.1	38.0	532.9	1991
381.3	6.1	15.7	403.2	1992
578.9	7.0	62.1	648.0	1993
652.3	36.0	47.8	736.0	1994
492.8	2.5	51.9	547.2	1995
423.5	1.8	30.4	455.7	1996
494.5	1.2	42.5	538.2	1997
376.8	1.1	41.3	419.2	1998
381.9	1.2	35.6	418.8	1999
360.6	1.3	18.9	380.7	2000
315.5	0.3	15.4	331.2	2001
404.6	0.3	19.1	424.0	2002
511.3	1.4	21.0	533.7	2003
502.9	5.3	16.6	524.8	2004
656.1	10.8	16.3	683.3	2005
639.2	12.0	19.2	670.5	2006p

Comex - Trading Volume

Monthly, Through February 2006.

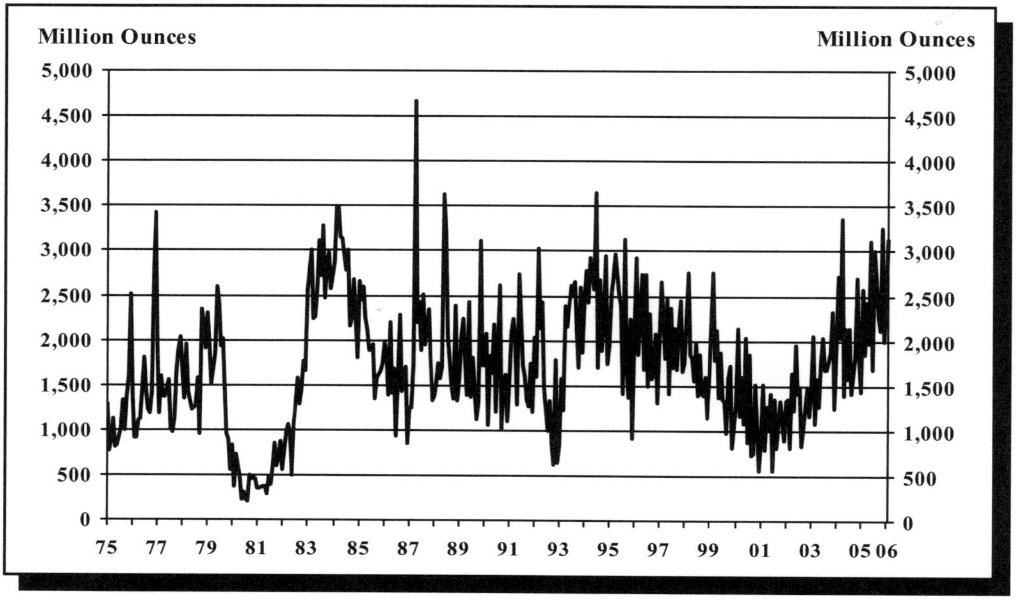

Comex - Open Interest

Month-end, Through February 2006.

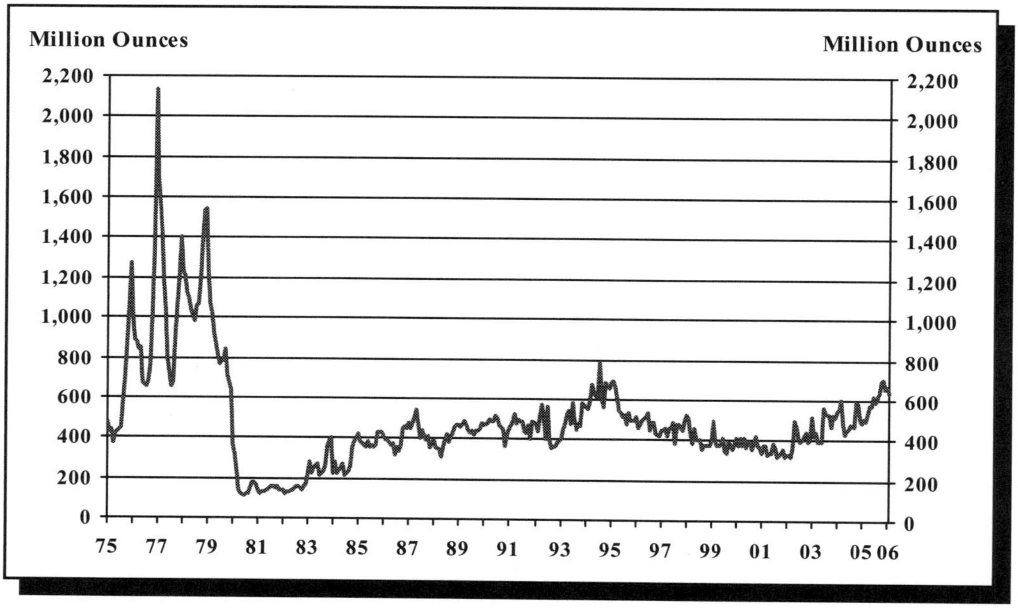

Tocom - Trading Volume

Monthly, Through February 2006.

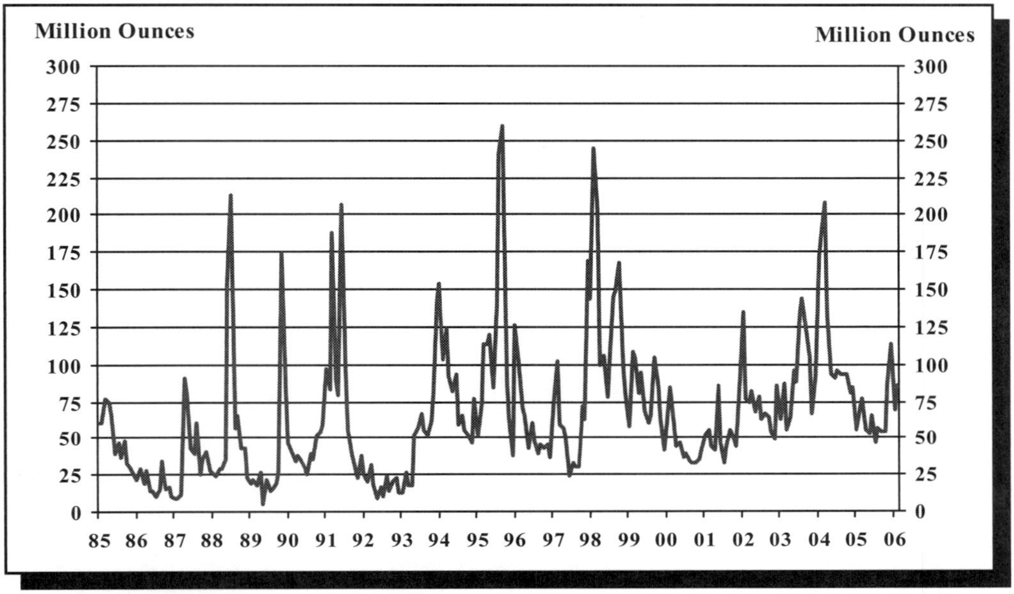

Tocom - Open Interest

Month-end, Through Febraury 2006.

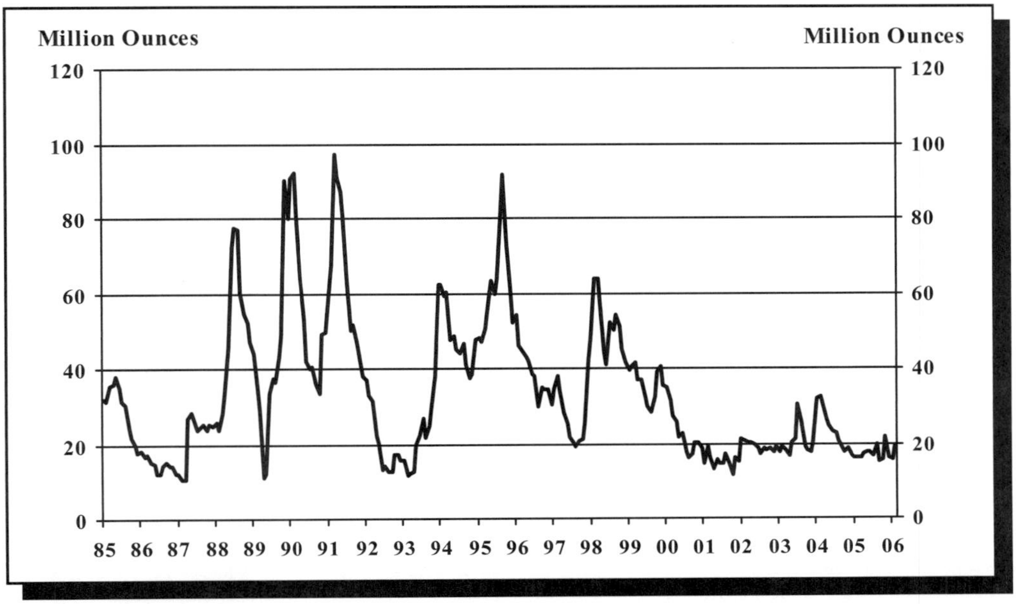

Comex Trading Volume

Thousand Ounces

	1975	1976	1977	1978	1979	1980
January	1,277,415	1,414,390	1,927,810	1,650,015	2,299,675	838,665
February	777,410	912,215	1,191,535	1,353,430	1,941,390	380,785
March	897,705	904,350	1,593,455	1,954,990	1,522,985	717,365
April	1,118,530	1,092,145	1,371,570	1,437,350	1,836,625	469,865
May	809,070	1,129,005	1,367,295	1,224,720	2,587,495	233,090
June	825,540	1,814,445	1,545,700	1,236,180	2,402,495	316,300
July	1,024,830	1,426,260	1,010,710	1,270,555	1,919,265	228,240
August	1,322,000	1,229,505	970,615	1,580,935	2,020,290	208,930
September	987,705	1,175,930	1,114,725	960,045	1,465,965	504,555
October	1,393,015	1,403,615	1,671,705	2,345,235	958,500	464,595
November	1,573,875	2,792,515	1,899,965	2,189,865	892,995	478,115
December	2,504,480	3,415,165	2,035,150	1,907,105	555,415	453,165
Total	14,511,575	18,709,540	17,700,235	19,110,425	20,403,095	5,293,670

	1981	1982	1983	1984	1985	1986
January	353,450	563,915	2,554,445	2,853,930	2,659,165	1,970,040
February	355,225	969,410	3,007,130	3,493,840	2,439,950	1,844,575
March	374,555	1,057,695	2,233,185	3,478,740	2,592,200	1,387,955
April	363,075	964,700	2,264,275	3,149,325	2,248,800	2,194,000
May	290,245	498,490	2,580,325	3,133,730	2,123,830	1,400,655
June	486,960	1,086,795	3,118,505	2,936,830	1,889,500	1,680,350
July	386,770	1,315,360	2,726,465	2,773,345	1,888,405	939,480
August	580,055	1,586,215	3,282,270	3,007,745	1,942,655	1,588,995
September	859,335	1,290,145	2,460,115	2,156,285	1,338,265	2,273,190
October	607,240	1,444,480	2,844,905	2,246,105	1,569,820	1,433,400
November	682,895	1,753,185	2,984,705	2,671,160	1,663,850	1,694,670
December	863,795	1,657,705	2,563,585	1,811,505	1,749,590	841,125
Total	6,203,600	14,188,095	32,619,910	33,712,540	24,106,030	19,248,435

	1987	1988	1989	1990	1991	1992
January	1,236,730	1,370,490	1,585,760	1,715,875	1,549,205	2,040,895
February	1,239,790	1,505,595	2,042,425	2,066,435	2,100,460	1,601,130
March	1,715,890	1,744,525	2,236,615	1,050,965	2,232,455	3,036,685
April	4,663,655	1,569,635	1,771,175	1,820,275	1,979,785	2,127,235
May	2,193,070	1,705,725	1,392,480	1,644,520	1,277,740	2,426,950
June	2,432,050	3,634,300	2,423,555	2,169,240	2,737,475	1,476,790
July	1,893,700	3,194,670	1,361,270	1,211,440	1,723,415	989,730
August	2,513,645	2,058,325	1,801,905	2,624,075	1,603,195	1,331,735
September	1,951,330	1,499,290	1,124,630	1,006,365	1,343,300	865,825
October	2,340,320	1,341,915	1,305,510	1,542,245	1,264,915	627,685
November	1,779,465	2,376,870	3,110,615	1,618,320	1,748,490	1,778,640
December	1,318,615	1,321,935	1,727,115	1,098,790	1,213,085	638,270
Total	25,278,260	23,323,275	21,883,055	19,568,545	20,773,520	18,941,570

Notes: Monthly total.

Source: New York Commodity Exchange.

March 3, 2006

Comex Trading Volume
Thousand Ounces

	1993	1994	1995	1996	1997	1998
January	836,005	2,445,275	1,952,265	2,079,005	2,009,975	1,763,440
February	1,579,580	2,775,680	2,507,270	2,918,835	2,652,570	2,754,000
March	1,214,870	2,420,670	2,709,035	1,840,875	1,804,355	1,840,635
April	2,382,770	2,925,290	2,963,100	2,738,145	2,469,995	1,800,650
May	2,167,300	2,581,980	2,502,610	1,674,865	1,402,680	1,550,650
June	2,619,805	3,647,070	2,382,405	2,748,155	2,361,530	1,969,855
July	2,519,675	1,696,490	1,403,255	1,484,525	1,701,225	1,393,870
August	2,658,860	2,678,610	3,131,785	2,303,430	2,127,355	1,836,285
September	2,141,830	1,887,700	1,720,910	1,581,830	1,677,000	1,417,375
October	1,690,945	2,225,245	1,361,810	1,608,905	2,151,985	1,400,330
November	2,602,955	2,946,100	2,235,475	2,077,205	2,440,120	1,596,080
December	1,865,025	1,741,615	903,775	1,298,265	1,668,810	1,149,910
Total	24,279,620	29,971,725	25,773,695	24,354,040	24,467,600	20,473,080

	1999	2000	2001	2002	2003	2004
January	1,575,825	1,290,265	875,130	1,328,865	1,455,600	1,925,425
February	2,751,355	2,129,550	1,510,175	1,356,465	2,048,685	2,724,695
March	1,777,795	1,156,680	778,290	819,490	1,083,300	2,042,235
April	2,124,110	1,593,760	1,262,430	1,629,445	1,576,200	3,355,885
May	1,370,010	1,084,690	1,022,760	1,217,375	1,255,480	1,393,515
June	1,868,310	2,037,275	1,409,230	1,948,990	1,762,820	2,127,505
July	1,342,400	876,175	564,780	1,406,070	2,039,655	1,581,320
August	1,336,625	1,853,695	1,338,555	1,482,895	1,677,540	2,139,865
September	968,140	730,035	801,645	822,685	1,677,540	1,408,685
October	1,591,280	746,260	1,051,330	1,046,245	1,867,965	1,820,790
November	1,721,445	1,518,365	1,330,385	1,464,305	2,321,220	2,706,830
December	807,170	568,435	901,280	1,154,990	1,254,175	1,803,875
Total	19,234,465	15,585,185	12,845,990	15,677,820	20,020,180	25,030,625

	2005	2006
January	1,427,245	2,478,245
February	2,568,085	3,122,455
March	1,851,690	
April	2,429,160	
May	1,960,780	
June	3,108,235	
July	1,674,515	
August	3,004,805	
September	2,275,165	
October	2,124,860	
November	3,264,585	
December	1,992,630	
Total	27,681,755	5,600,700

Comex Open Interest

Thousand Ounces

	1975	1976	1977	1978	1979	1980
January	475,905	995,275	1,705,165	1,236,140	1,226,220	365,205
February	426,820	886,325	1,560,845	1,208,870	1,067,780	318,680
March	443,215	883,435	1,413,210	1,127,325	1,018,345	243,685
April	372,680	844,265	1,175,485	1,091,580	928,155	136,080
May	425,065	849,795	1,035,510	1,043,645	871,710	119,275
June	427,075	676,175	792,900	985,085	771,940	114,845
July	447,710	652,680	650,945	1,059,995	785,475	125,395
August	578,225	684,615	675,750	1,067,020	789,760	121,190
September	698,145	771,720	895,200	1,184,620	838,615	149,920
October	880,275	1,035,445	1,053,655	1,394,035	712,765	174,300
November	1,055,395	1,399,210	1,204,240	1,536,055	670,490	180,660
December	1,276,405	2,138,745	1,404,875	1,548,985	636,765	166,160

	1981	1982	1983	1984	1985	1986
January	142,830	136,765	221,475	308,785	421,865	409,745
February	119,310	127,025	276,220	326,170	383,330	395,040
March	129,055	146,315	221,295	364,160	376,670	392,030
April	129,650	142,810	255,600	321,500	352,650	369,340
May	143,370	136,755	269,870	332,050	382,365	376,080
June	149,690	141,355	214,205	286,280	359,550	322,390
July	156,200	141,575	223,320	326,660	364,700	356,190
August	154,930	135,575	234,185	299,945	352,415	338,690
September	145,315	126,370	263,985	323,620	369,640	369,475
October	158,600	145,060	257,130	359,480	428,955	449,990
November	140,845	156,335	281,440	385,260	426,830	454,760
December	140,005	169,040	301,670	401,500	430,700	449,110

	1987	1988	1989	1990	1991	1992
January	478,360	397,350	470,890	464,460	448,630	481,715
February	447,190	355,010	459,550	476,570	483,065	438,035
March	503,755	343,540	486,585	493,760	526,675	518,290
April	544,410	311,780	469,245	482,715	475,815	568,620
May	469,015	355,415	435,830	487,845	494,445	513,940
June	403,725	397,155	428,945	511,780	485,810	401,915
July	441,385	419,795	441,760	500,960	482,645	561,920
August	411,800	384,350	420,060	467,520	439,900	397,630
September	392,865	409,515	440,555	459,035	434,090	359,445
October	414,900	430,450	443,810	447,070	468,735	365,230
November	355,845	455,520	452,395	368,535	405,200	362,335
December	371,165	469,950	474,215	421,715	488,835	381,320

Notes: Month-end data.
Source: New York Commodity Exchange.
March 3, 2006

Comex Open Interest
Thousand Ounces

	1993	1994	1995	1996	1997	1998
January	404,500	560,010	679,610	518,975	449,660	525,760
February	447,180	548,910	690,380	462,005	453,520	509,935
March	473,365	592,320	662,620	480,960	456,620	429,930
April	522,800	676,560	606,420	493,065	425,875	384,410
May	547,515	641,145	542,205	504,065	459,665	457,855
June	473,075	617,190	531,150	517,960	456,385	399,490
July	577,030	609,295	514,280	532,645	485,215	405,720
August	497,920	782,415	523,800	451,485	388,125	404,915
September	453,315	609,710	479,905	490,550	477,945	358,895
October	481,785	564,990	530,310	483,890	473,355	373,610
November	464,030	682,760	494,645	430,240	450,630	373,790
December	578,860	652,255	492,775	423,465	494,530	376,765

	1999	2000	2001	2002	2003	2004
January	404,975	411,470	333,090	327,300	517,550	546,340
February	494,770	370,350	374,600	327,400	421,010	552,890
March	391,300	411,940	376,770	319,525	443,555	601,640
April	376,640	372,965	325,305	368,090	391,685	489,325
May	378,675	413,250	339,770	496,100	394,355	428,480
June	381,370	366,485	335,610	463,950	395,780	445,665
July	412,285	394,065	388,080	412,065	560,055	459,250
August	347,410	389,285	361,180	389,720	531,255	476,150
September	339,055	359,970	322,815	405,850	527,710	466,045
October	397,525	424,205	338,720	436,010	471,745	586,640
November	357,870	374,150	359,835	394,870	520,610	584,790
December	381,935	360,605	315,505	404,600	511,250	502,930

	2005	2006
January	483,325	666,295
February	508,190	639,195
March	496,255	
April	536,320	
May	566,790	
June	575,105	
July	621,890	
August	586,780	
September	633,980	
October	690,690	
November	704,540	
December	656,145	

Tocom Trading Volume

Thousand Troy Ounces

	1985	1986	1987	1988	1989	1990	1991	1992
January	60,287	21,080	8,997	26,654	18,755	46,351	96,887	25,596
February	60,308	29,469	8,553	24,096	21,235	39,883	83,567	20,471
March	76,384	18,465	11,568	29,009	17,754	34,587	187,591	32,075
April	73,794	28,215	90,571	28,551	26,398	38,128	89,526	17,447
May	66,243	14,395	82,387	34,931	5,208	34,139	79,162	8,981
June	38,716	13,697	43,302	154,434	20,843	28,381	206,990	15,890
July	46,170	10,392	38,845	212,471	13,688	25,326	93,472	10,531
August	36,881	14,802	60,997	56,233	15,669	39,002	55,688	24,277
September	47,415	33,814	24,700	65,511	18,566	35,046	39,417	13,272
October	32,279	15,460	35,049	42,711	26,164	52,113	28,101	19,571
November	28,872	16,901	40,719	43,175	174,388	54,194	22,404	22,865
December	23,739	10,440	27,509	22,473	83,680	59,288	37,271	12,662
Annual Total	591,087	227,130	473,199	740,247	442,347	486,439	1,020,075	223,638

	1993	1994	1995	1996	1997	1998	1999	2000
January	13,031	153,885	51,637	126,413	73,756	144,202	57,563	55,006
February	26,421	102,995	73,714	102,148	102,339	244,629	108,836	84,051
March	17,538	124,089	113,865	70,336	59,463	203,117	104,147	58,938
April	17,434	92,452	113,422	66,005	56,609	100,016	80,435	43,725
May	51,215	81,909	120,048	43,418	50,990	106,201	94,430	46,490
June	56,594	92,995	84,000	60,082	24,073	77,664	67,622	35,983
July	66,842	59,589	141,165	47,497	32,765	103,742	60,101	38,714
August	55,091	65,357	241,263	38,772	30,247	144,509	65,534	34,491
September	51,530	55,610	259,723	45,365	30,597	149,036	104,080	32,413
October	62,037	52,196	89,288	43,452	71,609	167,862	85,676	32,373
November	80,212	47,042	63,417	45,900	63,421	98,538	62,396	34,787
December	142,004	77,088	37,653	36,893	168,846	80,539	41,716	41,974
Annual Total	639,949	1,005,209	1,389,196	726,279	764,715	1,620,055	932,536	538,945

	2001	2002	2003	2004	2005	2006
January	52,224	135,362	63,255	171,313	55,719	69,479
February	55,453	77,411	86,947	185,212	70,914	85,235
March	43,761	74,575	55,581	208,210	76,459	
April	41,433	81,626	63,980	132,987	55,254	
May	86,240	67,522	95,955	93,337	53,457	
June	46,066	78,295	88,802	90,302	64,927	
July	33,287	62,822	133,415	96,282	46,041	
August	43,711	67,067	143,118	93,117	56,455	
September	55,282	64,419	124,166	93,154	54,704	
October	49,464	53,678	104,828	92,821	54,078	
November	43,949	48,995	67,067	80,157	87,010	
December	86,546	86,086	92,276	84,203	113,598	
Annual Total	637,417	897,859	1,119,389	1,421,096	788,616	154,714

Notes: Monthly total.
Source: Tokyo Commodity Exchange.
March 9, 2006

Tocom Open Interest

Thousand Troy Ounces

	1985	1986	1987	1988	1989	1990	1991	1992
January	32,081	18,424	12,141	25,931	43,845	90,795	55,759	36,758
February	31,384	16,535	10,851	23,938	34,474	92,016	67,521	32,821
March	35,193	17,039	10,489	28,131	28,894	80,726	97,007	31,148
April	35,981	14,962	26,807	33,494	11,208	63,777	91,167	22,321
May	38,086	14,879	28,590	45,741	12,048	53,238	86,944	20,200
June	34,687	12,147	26,846	72,179	33,433	42,022	80,315	12,931
July	31,613	12,156	23,987	77,375	37,394	39,830	63,273	13,960
August	30,309	14,148	24,707	76,950	36,279	40,426	50,039	12,553
September	24,405	14,980	25,512	60,474	42,976	35,808	51,783	12,839
October	21,588	14,268	23,596	54,930	48,627	33,393	46,960	17,226
November	19,989	14,148	25,181	52,071	90,100	49,366	41,240	17,050
December	17,612	12,154	24,757	47,181	80,200	49,750	38,012	15,718

	1993	1994	1995	1996	1997	1998	1999	2000
January	15,729	62,094	48,006	54,321	34,438	47,484	39,450	34,846
February	11,407	59,259	46,867	45,997	38,046	63,737	40,312	31,209
March	11,920	60,269	50,513	44,758	34,061	63,623	41,701	27,387
April	12,840	47,360	55,028	43,178	28,225	56,866	36,965	26,057
May	19,850	48,373	63,228	41,934	25,216	44,005	36,977	21,759
June	22,225	45,259	59,931	38,491	21,787	40,818	32,320	22,584
July	26,752	44,163	63,852	38,190	20,283	52,027	30,118	17,732
August	21,648	46,568	81,741	30,010	19,261	50,166	28,467	16,123
September	24,739	41,173	91,636	34,937	20,886	54,207	32,367	17,417
October	29,524	37,475	72,928	34,628	21,463	51,103	38,768	20,040
November	38,215	38,259	60,329	34,289	25,863	45,299	40,513	20,437
December	62,113	47,813	51,925	30,419	42,479	41,326	35,628	18,864

	2001	2002	2003	2004	2005	2006
January	14,717	21,284	17,619	31,866	16,347	15,546
February	19,070	20,969	19,050	32,393	16,166	19,245
March	16,165	20,315	18,180	30,192	16,317	
April	13,169	20,286	16,723	26,468	17,000	
May	15,645	19,723	20,053	24,897	17,743	
June	14,891	18,668	21,053	23,359	17,656	
July	14,602	17,259	30,437	22,533	16,676	
August	17,454	18,840	25,878	20,943	19,611	
September	14,546	18,069	19,320	18,924	15,285	
October	11,773	18,532	18,237	17,468	15,863	
November	16,228	17,910	17,802	18,913	21,727	
December	15,398	19,071	20,981	16,594	16,298	

Notes: Month-end data.
Source: Tokyo Commodity Exchange.
March 9, 2006

Trading Volume on Comex and Tocom

Annual Totals Through 2005.

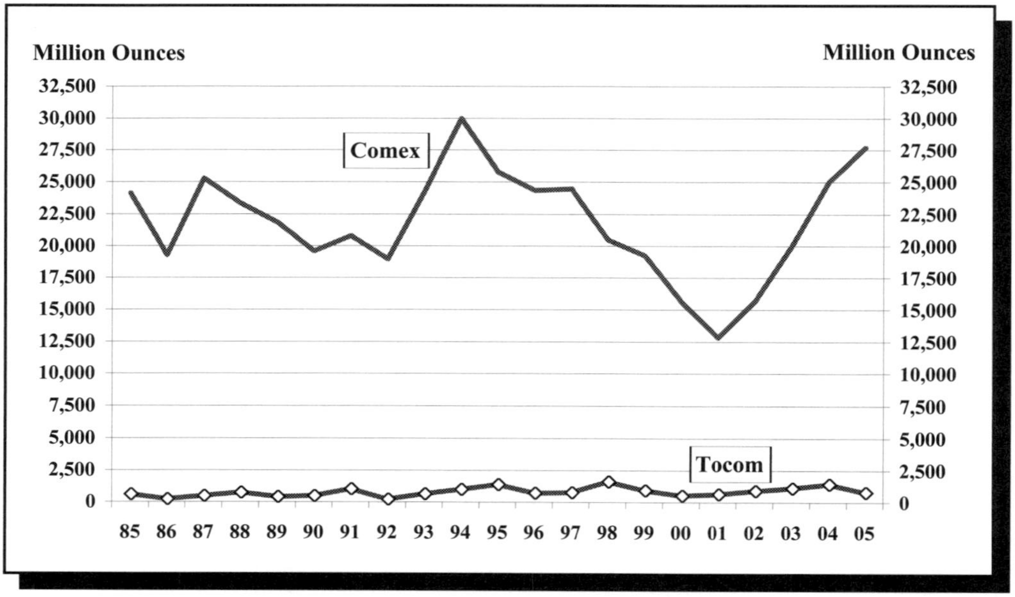

Open Interest on Comex and Tocom

Year-End, Through 2005.

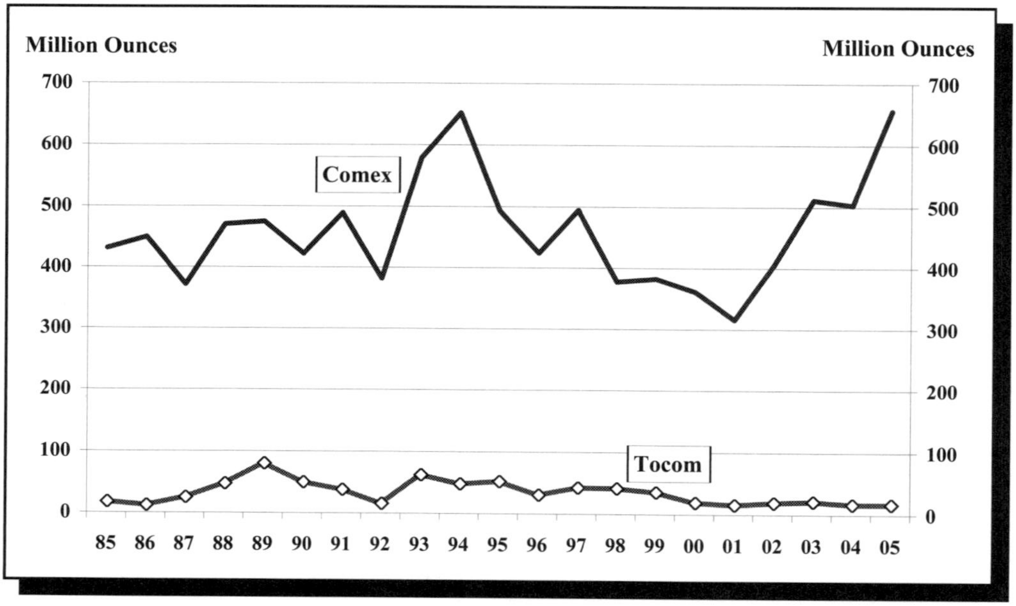

Trading Volume in Comex Silver Options

Monthly Total, Through February 2006.

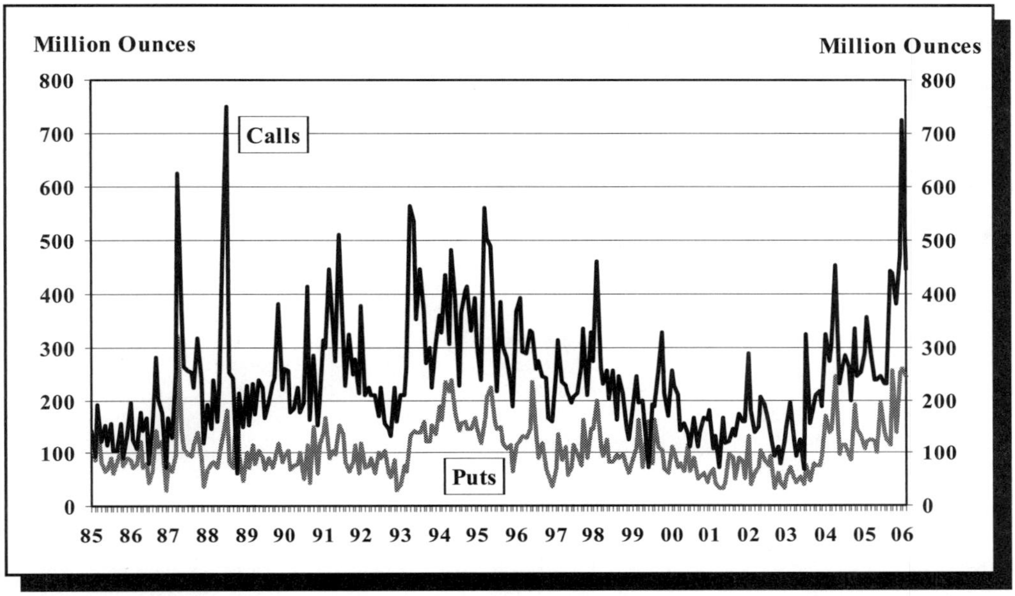

Open Interest in Comex Silver Options

Month-end, Through February 2006.

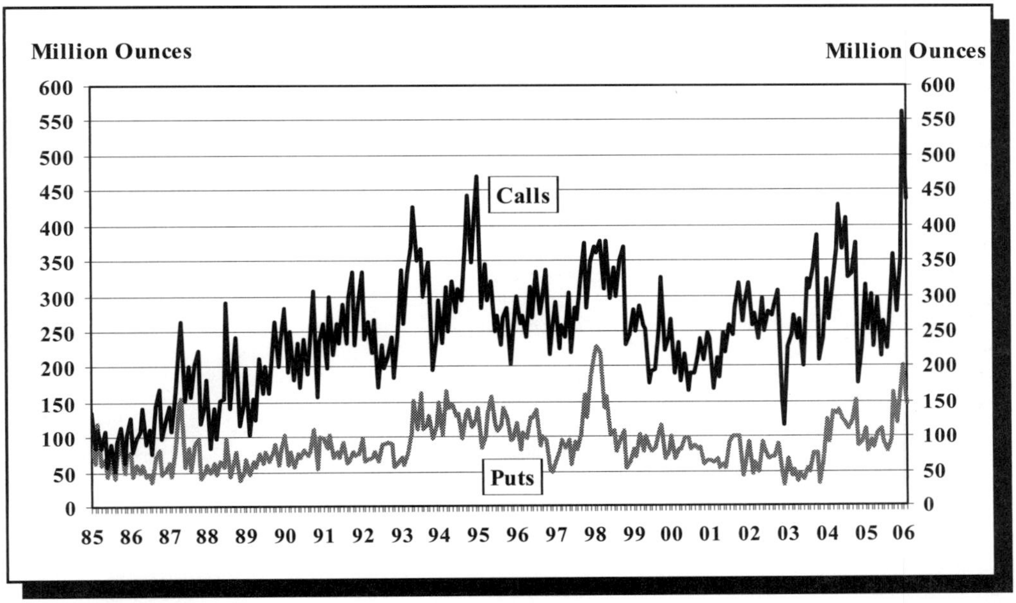

Annual Silver Options Activity
Troy Ounces

	Trading Volume		
	Puts	Calls	Total
1985	1,095,955,000	1,563,237,744	2,659,192,744
1986	1,018,975,000	1,878,150,000	2,897,125,000
1987	1,373,015,000	3,217,305,000	4,590,320,000
1988	1,211,685,000	3,148,845,000	4,360,530,000
1989	1,070,900,000	2,692,325,000	3,763,225,000
1990	1,040,990,000	2,696,505,000	3,737,495,000
1991	1,292,890,000	3,802,575,000	5,095,465,000
1992	930,160,000	2,452,555,000	3,382,715,000
1993	1,424,615,000	4,048,895,000	5,473,510,000
1994	2,145,140,000	4,438,110,000	6,583,250,000
1995	1,722,725,000	4,009,840,000	5,732,565,000
1996	1,385,065,000	3,361,130,000	4,746,195,000
1997	1,216,195,000	2,998,420,000	4,214,615,000
1998	1,252,370,000	2,837,895,000	4,090,265,000
1999	1,280,270,000	2,407,960,000	3,688,230,000
2000	900,820,000	1,994,605,000	2,895,425,000
2001	735,975,000	1,680,955,000	2,416,930,000
2002	825,100,000	1,851,020,000	2,676,120,000
2003	753,045,000	2,047,045,000	2,800,090,000
2004	1,678,040,000	3,433,700,000	5,111,740,000
2005	1,797,130,000	3,861,815,000	5,658,945,000
2006YTD	508,610,000	1,171,750,000	1,680,360,000

	Open Interest		
	Puts	Calls	Total
1985	72,470,000	103,565,000	176,035,000
1986	50,745,000	121,025,000	171,770,000
1987	48,825,000	143,570,000	192,395,000
1988	47,830,000	145,455,000	193,285,000
1989	81,520,000	235,390,000	316,910,000
1990	100,935,000	235,110,000	336,045,000
1991	74,975,000	290,255,000	365,230,000
1992	62,745,000	244,670,000	307,415,000
1993	116,695,000	239,840,000	356,535,000
1994	126,165,000	433,525,000	559,690,000
1995	99,035,000	240,585,000	339,620,000
1996	50,115,000	246,480,000	296,595,000
1997	184,180,000	347,110,000	531,290,000
1998	61,145,000	243,145,000	304,290,000
1999	78,820,000	242,225,000	321,045,000
2000	64,570,000	247,515,000	312,085,000
2001	57,815,000	287,930,000	345,745,000
2002	31,180,000	116,650,000	147,830,000
2003	65,580,000	238,745,000	304,325,000
2004	93,095,000	225,090,000	318,185,000
2005	174,560,000	353,105,000	527,665,000
2006YTD	146,000,000	437,560,000	583,560,000

Notes: Trading volume is through February 2006. Open interest is month-end through February 2006.
Sources: New York Commodity Exchange.
March 3, 2006

Comex Options Trading Volume

Thousand Troy Ounces

	1985	1986	1987	1988	1989	1990	1991	1992
January	266,155	283,135	243,530	260,255	326,100	351,820	455,335	496,310
February	179,250	195,970	190,630	225,560	221,965	360,135	467,925	283,225
March	362,940	183,260	347,870	321,835	345,745	243,400	538,570	297,650
April	206,795	299,430	945,225	232,870	252,785	260,485	440,300	299,875
May	216,150	215,220	506,820	324,425	344,900	302,005	370,280	271,110
June	182,095	247,170	372,460	645,510	312,370	279,455	664,690	271,725
July	244,780	120,225	354,450	933,410	236,075	247,270	456,225	311,570
August	161,630	213,200	348,845	338,190	283,860	527,835	309,320	260,655
September	187,605	423,115	339,310	313,690	303,620	206,060	390,850	207,155
October	261,770	314,195	455,155	263,655	327,215	434,325	332,210	186,370
November	163,820	302,435	333,900	305,765	502,655	213,035	395,445	310,170
December	223,585	99,770	152,125	195,365	305,935	311,670	274,315	186,900
Annual Total	2,656,575	2,897,125	4,590,320	4,360,530	3,763,225	3,737,495	5,095,465	3,382,715

	1993	1994	1995	1996	1997	1998	1999	2000
January	252,505	548,670	452,490	483,725	317,940	420,735	270,725	366,635
February	286,850	492,030	358,520	517,680	447,155	661,555	358,085	330,765
March	327,035	674,380	725,320	426,195	323,710	371,550	360,525	283,655
April	696,420	526,010	710,335	417,865	341,010	323,130	269,575	221,300
May	677,550	721,560	715,680	479,015	269,430	383,405	261,070	224,230
June	492,825	563,825	458,570	566,080	268,035	284,010	231,560	249,495
July	583,330	369,530	366,635	393,025	320,655	339,270	272,945	174,000
August	528,445	520,840	533,140	364,485	309,160	260,295	353,350	254,810
September	390,540	565,350	421,810	365,725	337,060	333,590	366,300	161,705
October	420,030	561,175	390,415	309,060	501,140	310,510	430,410	191,215
November	378,770	481,075	349,335	226,845	301,360	218,150	281,820	231,040
December	439,210	558,805	250,315	196,495	477,960	184,065	231,865	206,575
Annual Total	5,473,510	6,583,250	5,732,565	4,746,195	4,214,615	4,090,265	3,688,230	2,895,425

	2001	2002	2003	2004	2005	2006
January	242,055	421,655	203,425	498,645	393,505	986,950
February	176,300	221,855	268,410	414,935	479,425	693,410
March	175,735	199,715	170,395	455,450	415,890	
April	103,170	219,640	132,650	698,660	361,955	
May	198,700	309,380	178,030	326,550	339,990	
June	161,660	280,275	109,695	366,240	440,205	
July	217,925	233,240	399,880	401,150	370,275	
August	236,630	228,620	205,265	356,115	356,755	
September	182,685	122,495	271,490	287,275	558,540	
October	265,120	171,205	286,150	526,985	696,855	
November	243,560	120,210	292,015	392,650	519,975	
December	213,390	147,830	282,685	387,085	725,575	
Annual Total	2,416,930	2,676,120	2,800,090	5,111,740	5,658,945	1,680,360

Notes: Trading volume is monthly total.
Source: Commodity Exchange.
March 3, 2006

Comex Options Open Interest

Thousand Troy Ounces

	1985	1986	1987	1988	1989	1990	1991	1992
January	219,055	204,515	207,985	242,625	266,925	385,315	358,125	431,075
February	148,085	120,100	151,910	131,335	149,570	252,850	283,280	304,560
March	231,150	156,565	238,970	204,905	219,330	328,815	400,995	332,460
April	142,695	156,265	377,555	144,165	181,185	239,710	285,830	290,010
May	174,595	200,845	418,485	216,535	289,250	310,815	337,185	346,090
June	99,180	132,485	210,490	211,685	226,145	242,260	305,360	235,335
July	157,860	159,270	283,145	388,425	280,305	320,725	379,515	320,485
August	91,515	112,365	207,630	186,240	229,415	261,730	294,955	287,775
September	161,095	215,180	292,925	273,145	311,650	303,570	365,130	306,585
October	206,415	252,110	320,620	319,745	353,130	419,310	411,695	331,025
November	113,150	143,105	160,320	155,965	259,805	212,025	304,455	241,035
December	176,035	171,770	192,395	193,285	316,910	336,045	365,230	307,415

	1993	1994	1995	1996	1997	1998	1999	2000
January	406,805	443,185	610,590	419,115	353,730	584,920	361,045	367,085
February	320,210	335,945	365,810	342,685	307,710	587,555	322,380	256,900
March	407,475	479,455	446,475	378,225	352,385	599,130	389,170	315,225
April	475,835	390,795	426,695	339,025	325,560	449,470	337,735	262,440
May	578,575	466,270	477,200	440,945	400,040	534,975	351,355	314,200
June	463,325	406,460	366,575	397,165	282,000	398,915	260,380	262,060
July	528,930	442,100	381,215	469,815	373,810	449,195	272,945	271,260
August	409,290	392,015	349,310	362,860	348,095	378,335	279,640	277,910
September	453,095	517,915	410,215	389,480	425,600	445,540	365,650	297,870
October	479,230	582,300	412,080	432,590	535,050	478,860	442,525	322,880
November	294,735	459,940	296,680	268,005	410,865	286,200	289,510	269,730
December	356,535	559,690	339,620	296,595	531,290	304,290	321,045	312,085

	2001	2002	2003	2004	2005	2006
January	304,155	410,015	297,640	449,970	427,405	763,120
February	231,015	305,145	287,330	356,735	329,865	583,560
March	277,320	336,555	323,630	451,915	396,300	
April	237,395	289,480	274,100	499,605	312,320	
May	306,720	387,385	311,185	567,325	402,720	
June	274,070	331,735	237,585	492,255	326,880	
July	349,560	344,750	376,705	528,925	355,515	
August	343,485	341,560	357,770	437,040	306,470	
September	384,070	355,545	415,155	454,810	403,430	
October	420,300	394,565	462,220	525,675	521,465	
November	307,070	202,600	242,925	263,175	395,530	
December	345,745	147,830	304,325	318,185	527,665	

Notes: Open interest is month-end.
Source: Commodity Exchange.
March 3, 2006

Comex Options Put/Call Ratio

Monthly, Through Febraury 2006.

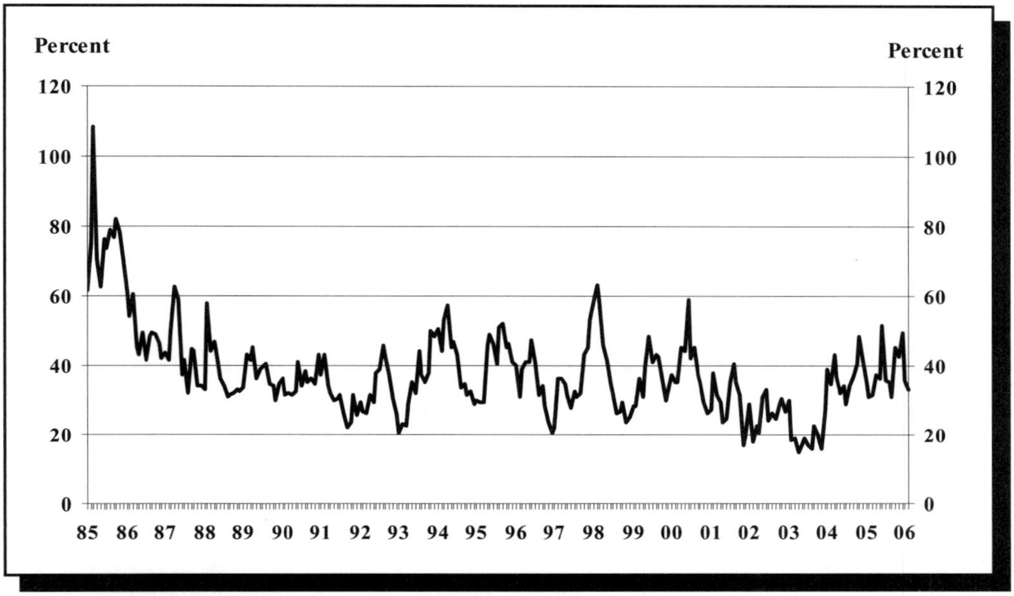

Note: Open interest of puts as a percentage of open interest of calls.

Prices

Prices

The price of silver averaged $7.35 in 2005(basis the nearby active Comex futures contract settlement price). This was up 9.7% from $6.70 in 2004, and marked the fourth year in a row in which annual average silver prices rose. Prices had reached a low annual average of $4.38 in 2001. Last year's price was 67.8% higher than that cyclical low, using annual averages.

Silver prices ranged between a low of $6.45 and a high of $9.10 last year. The low was reached on 7 January 2005 and a high of $9.10 on 9 December, again based on daily settlement prices. The intraday low for last year was $6.35 on 4 January, and the intraday high was $9.35, on 10 December.

The upward move in silver prices continued in the first three months of 2006. Silver traded between $8.85 and $9.36 for much of the first three weeks of 2006. After the U.S. Securities and Exchange Commission posted a notice of Barclays Global Investors' proposed silver exchange traded fund in the Federal Register, seeking public comment on the plan, on 23 January, prices rose even further. Silver settled at $9.073 on 23 January. It rose to settle at $9.228 the following day, and $9.605 by the end of that week. Prices continued to rise through February and into March, breaking above $10 on 2 March to settle at $10.208 that day. Silver reached $10.74 on Friday, 24 March, following the SEC's announcement earlier in that

Weekly Average Silver Prices

Comex Nearby Active Settlement, Through 24 March 2006.

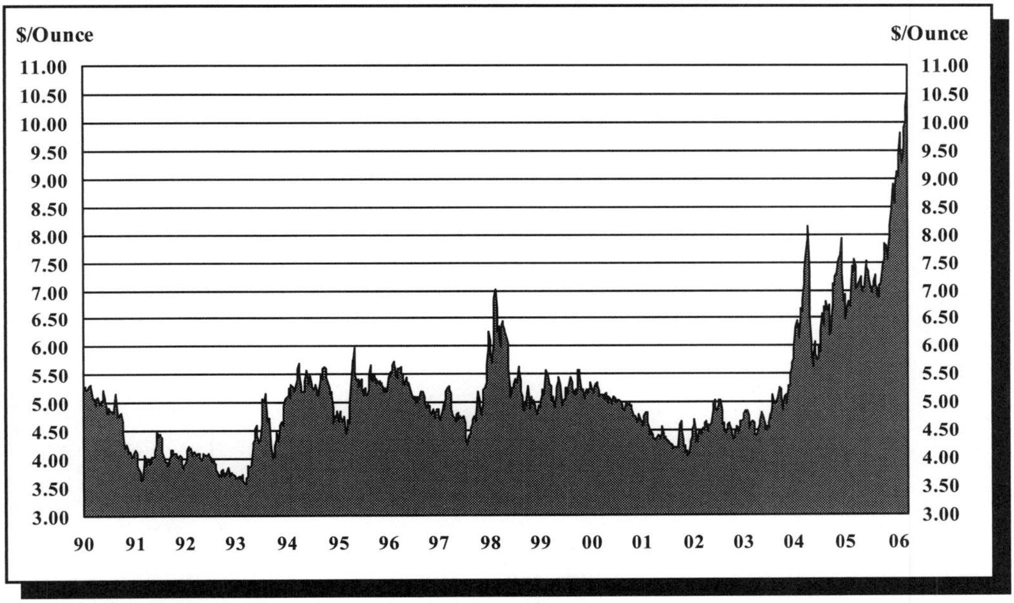

week that it had approved of the proposed silver ETF program.

While silver prices have been rising for the past four years, the volatility of prices has not been particularly high. There have been some spikes in volatility, but generally speaking the degree of variability in silver prices has been in line with that which was experienced from the late 1980s through the 1990s. The silver price has been less volatile than it was in the 1970s. This is in line with gold prices, which also have risen over the past five years without seeing a major increase in price volatility. The upward move has been more measured and consistent this time around than it was in either of the two periods of sharply rising prices in the 1970s.

Price Review

The price of silver began 2005 by falling 33 cents, from $6.837 on 31 December 2004 to $6.507 on 3 January. This was the culmination of a decline that had begun in early December 2004, when silver peaked at $8.235 on 2 December. Prices consolidated between $6.40 and $6.70 during January, dropping once more to $6.50 in early February. Prices then recovered, rising initially to $6.965 on 10 February. Prices continued to strengthen, and moved into a new trading range between $6.90 and $7.55 for most of the next seven months, from February through August. Prices rose as

High, Low, and Average Silver Prices

Annual, Comex nearby active settlement, 2006 Through 24 March.

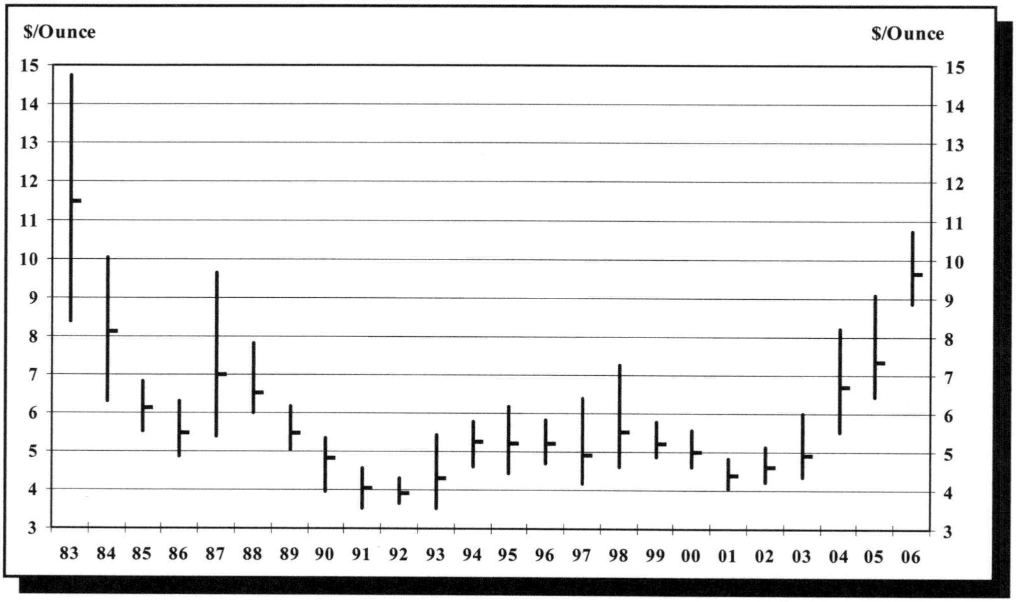

high as $7.75 during this time, on 9 March, but could not maintain that upward pace.

Silver weakened toward the end of August, in line with the prices of a number of other commodities. Silver dropped below its trading range, falling to as low as $6.63 on 30 August. That was the day that Hurricane Katrina hit the Louisiana coast, devastating the economy in that region and knocking out a sizable portion of U.S. oil and gas production, refining, and distribution. The prices of silver and most other commodities began rising sharply after that. Silver prices rose to around $7.50 by late September and then $7.90 by late October. Prices broke sharply higher in November and December, rising to $8.353 on 28 November and $9.095 on 9 December (touching $9.345 on an intraday basis on 10 December).

High, Low, and Settlement Prices in 2004-2006

Daily, Through 24 March 2006, Basis nearby active Comex contract.

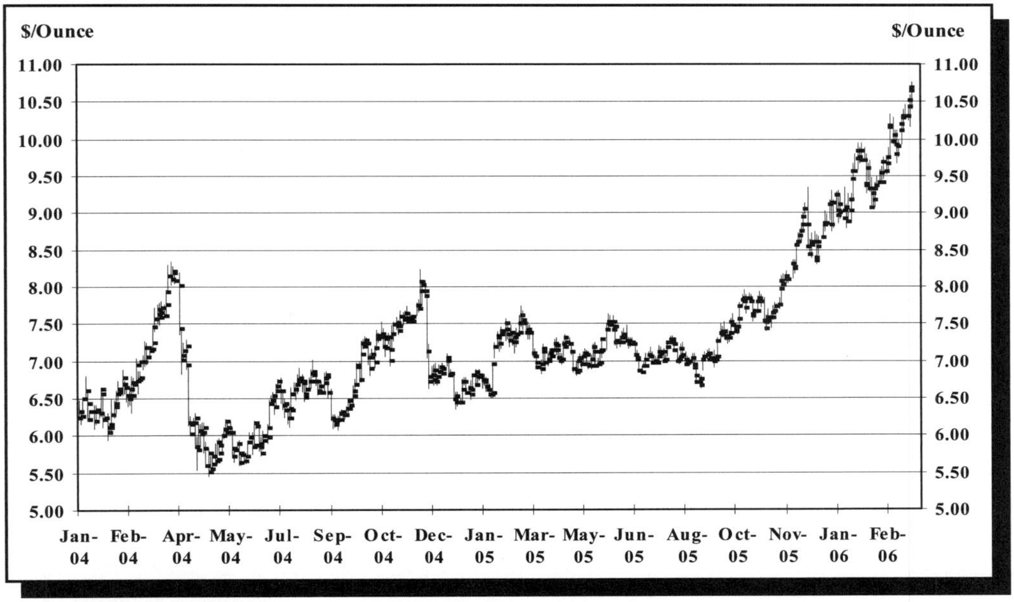

Silver Contango and Backwardation

Difference Between Comex nearby active and forward active prices.

Daily, Through 10 March 2006.

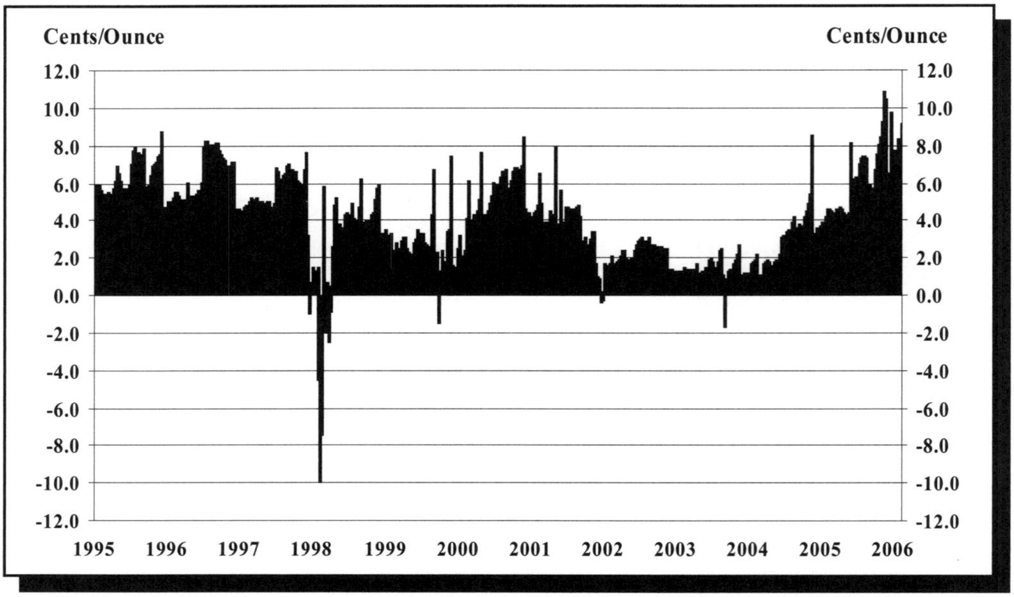

Monthly Silver Price Volatility

Through February 2006.

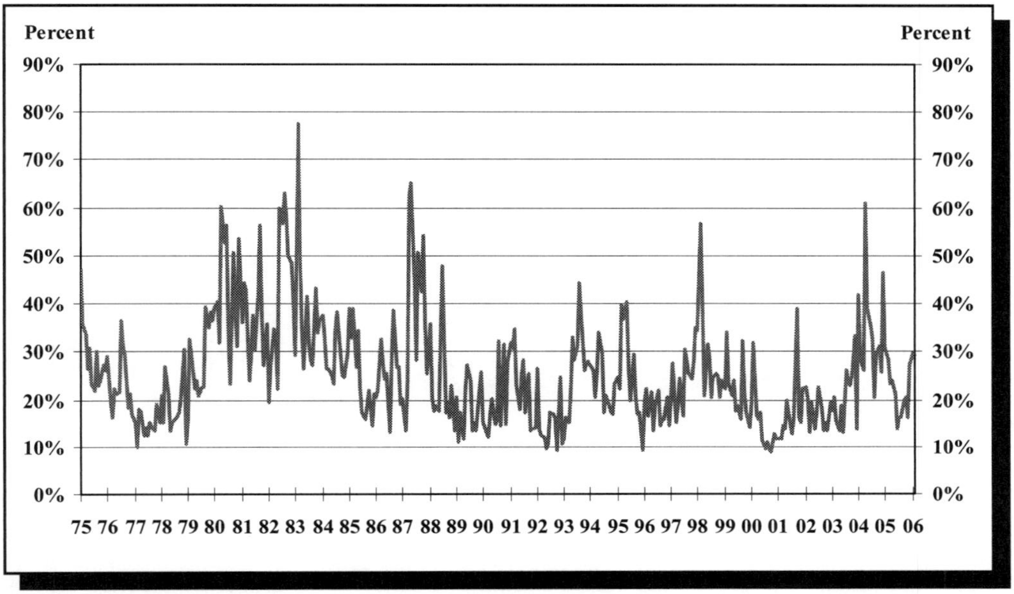

Histogram of Daily Silver Prices since 1975

Daily, Through 24 March 2006. Basis nearby active Comex contract.

Daily Gold and Silver Prices

Through 2 March 2006.

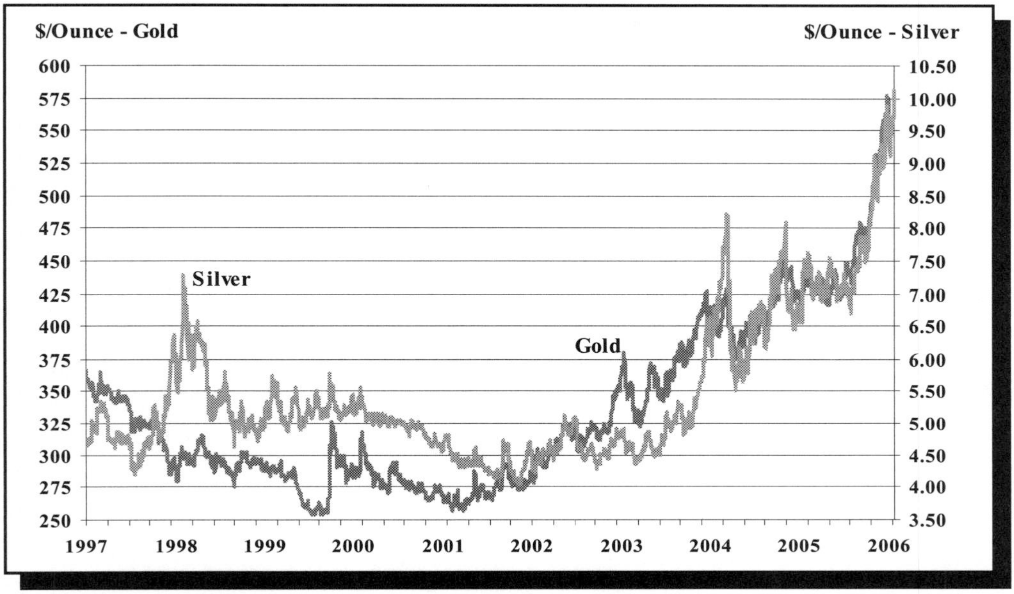

The Gold/Silver Price Ratio

Monthly, Through February 2006.

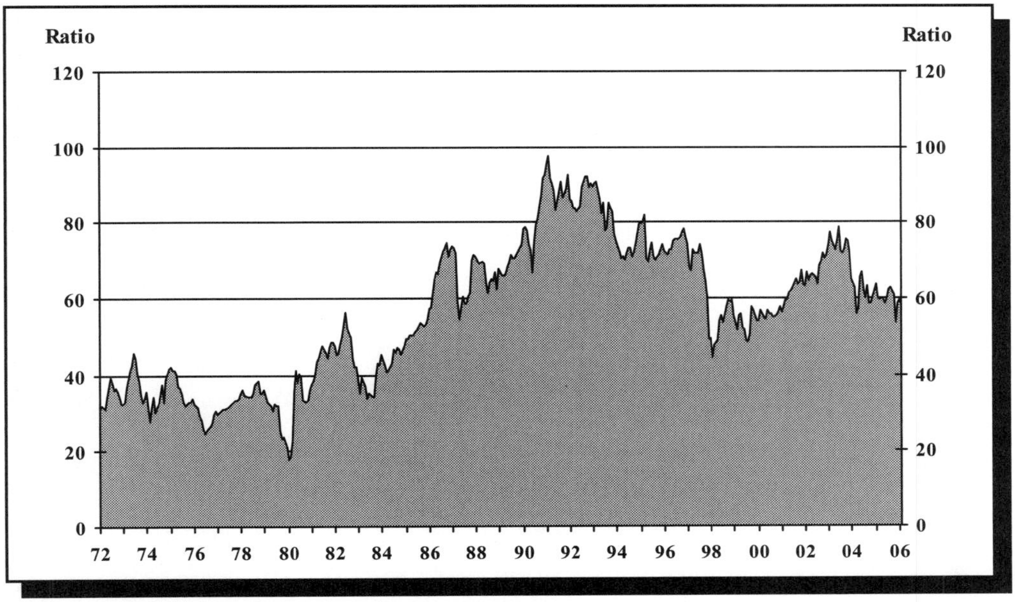

Quarterly Silver Price Volatility

Through Fourth Quarter 2005.

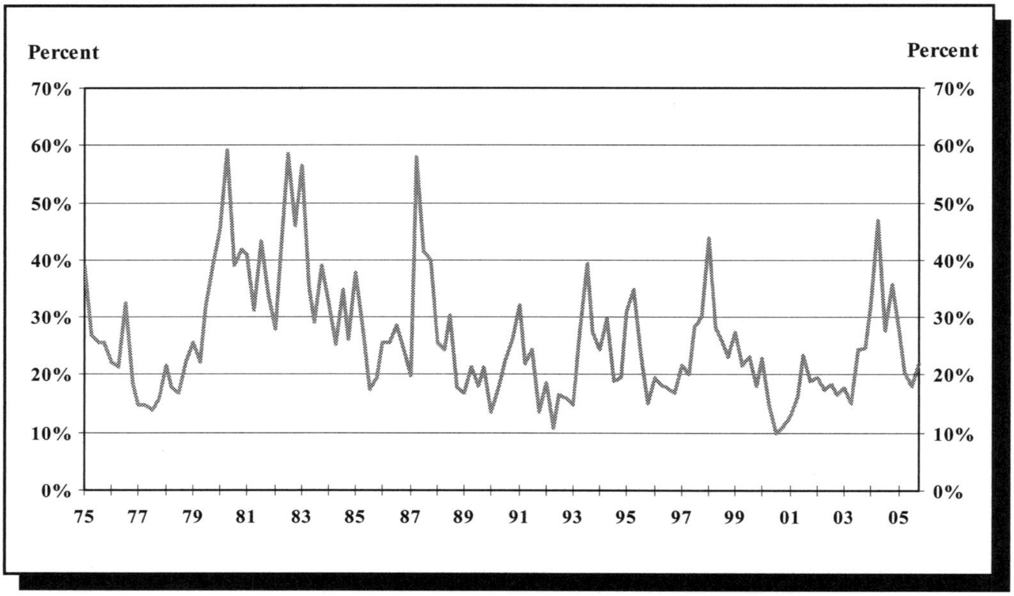

Annual Silver Price Volatility

Through 2005.

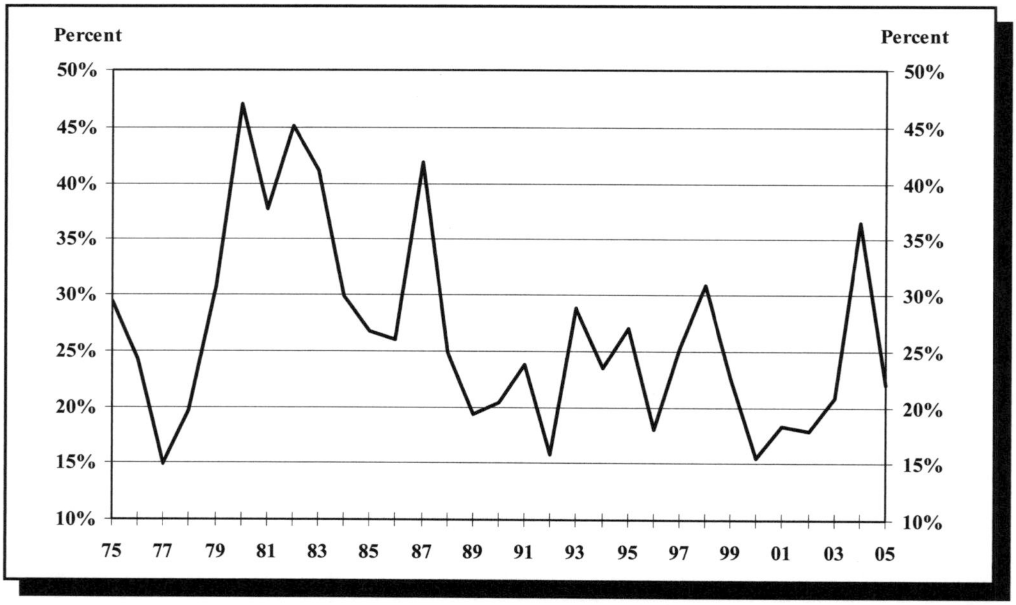

Implied Silver Lease Rates

Daily, Through 2 March 2006.

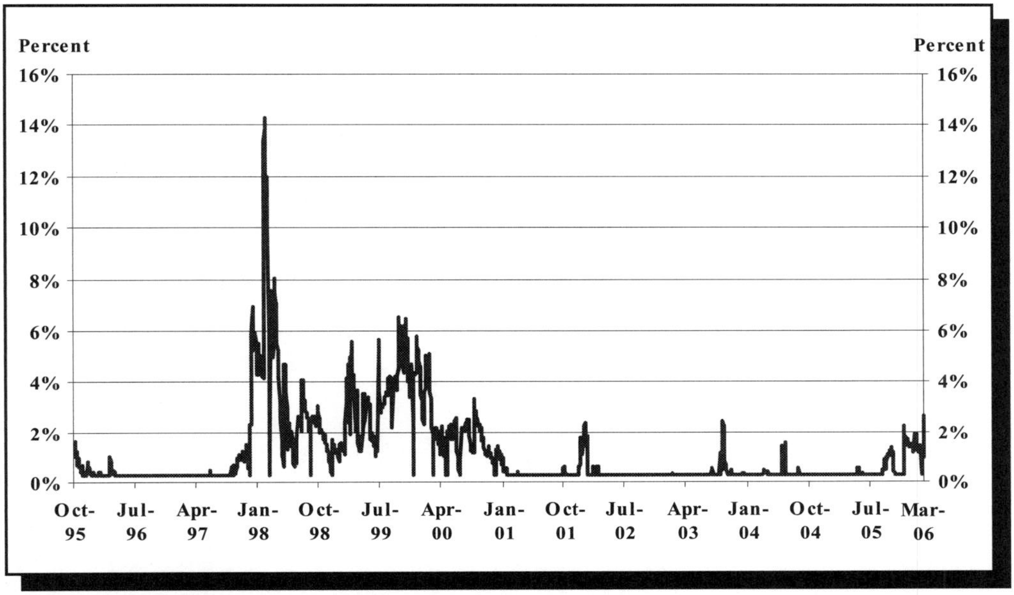

Quarterly Real and Nominal Silver Prices

Through Fourth Quarter 2005.

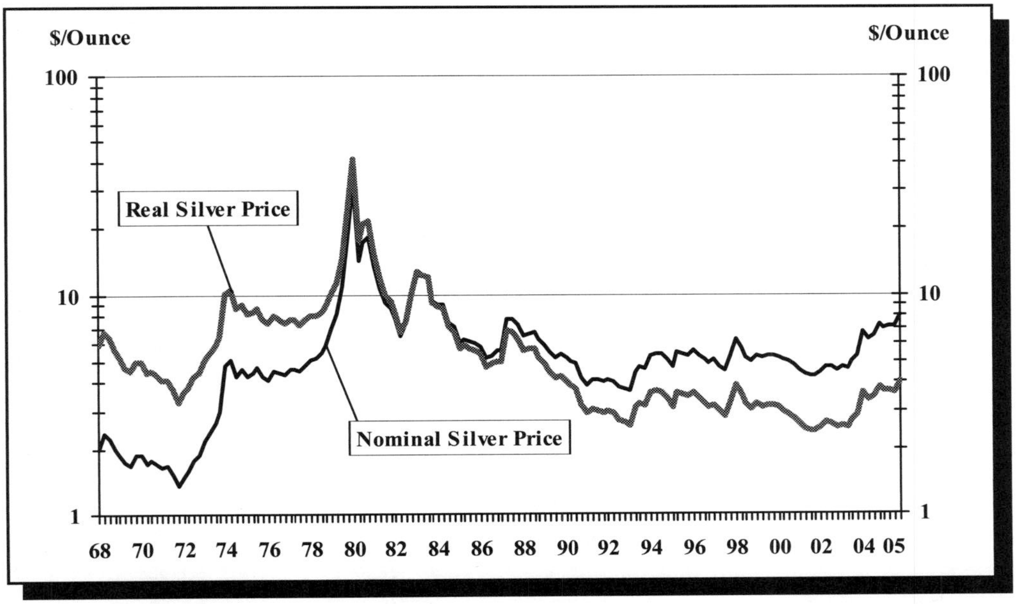

Silver and U.S. Inflation

Quarterly, Through Fourth Quarter 2005.

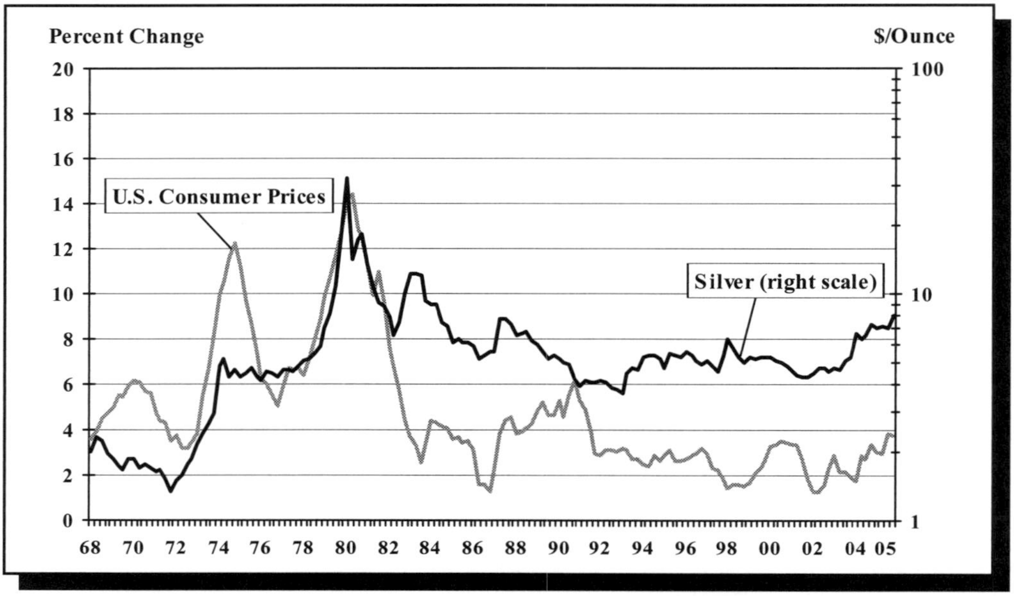

Interest Rates and Silver Prices

Quarterly, Through Fourth Quarter 2005.

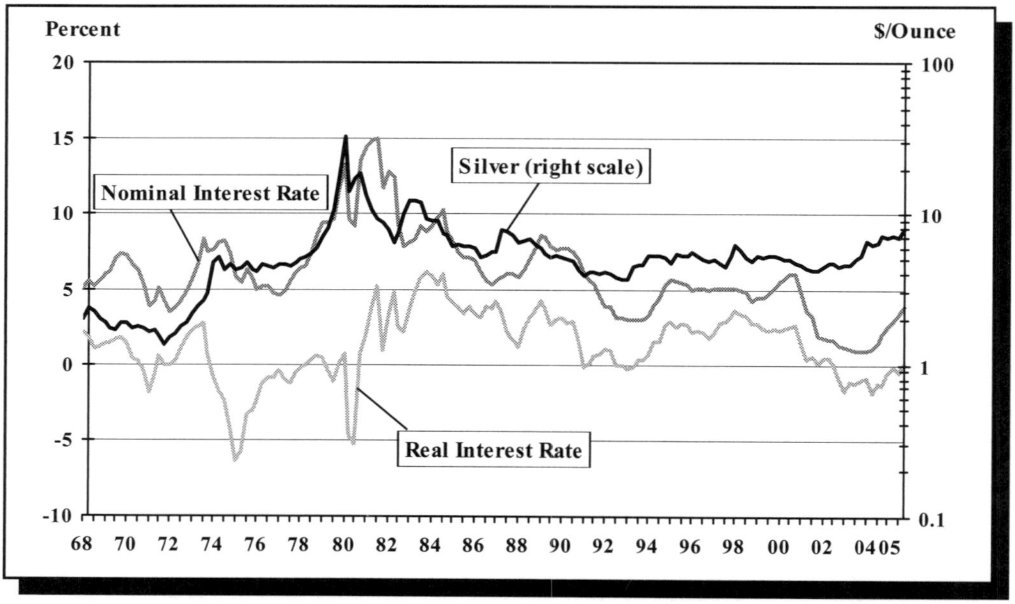

Silver and the U.S. Dollar

Quarterly, Through Fourth Quarter 2005. Dollar is the J.P. Morgan Index.

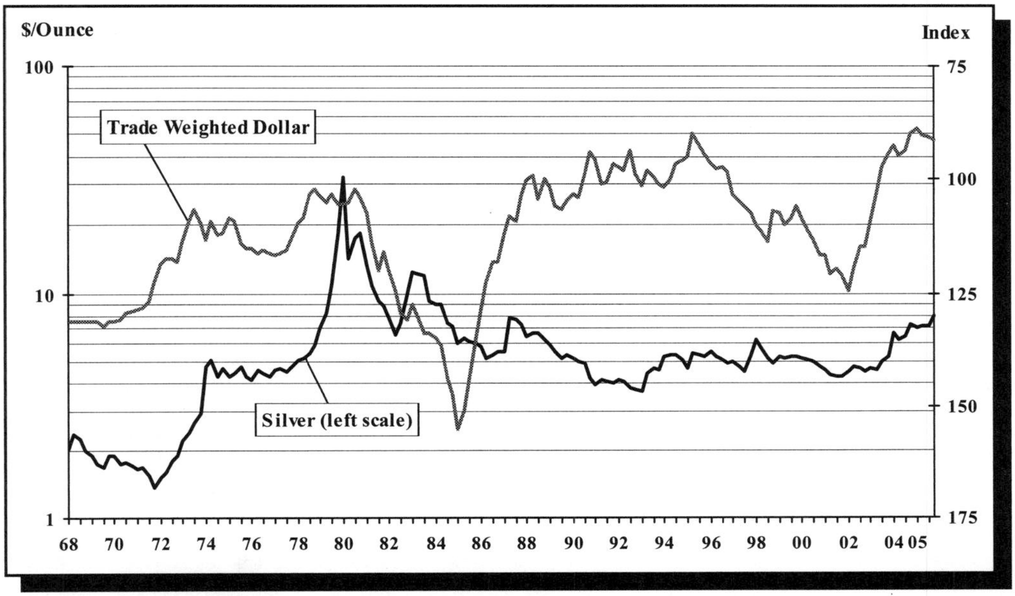

Silver and the 30-Year U.S. Treasury Bond

Monthly, Through February 2006.

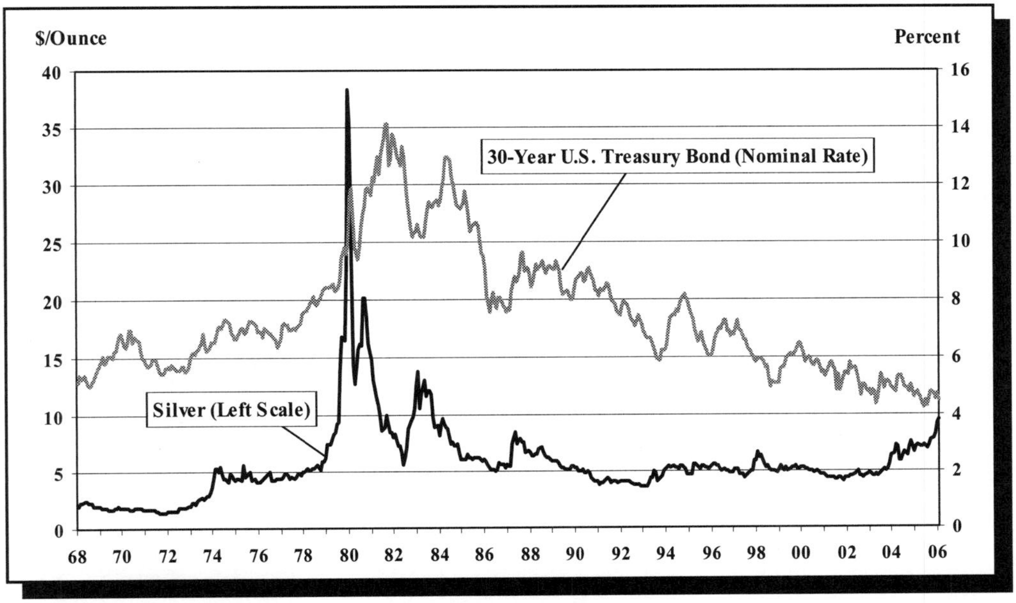

Monthly Average Silver Prices
Comex Settlement Price

	1963	1964	1965	1966	1967	1968	1969	1970
January	—	$1.29	$1.30	$1.30	$1.29	$2.06	$1.98	$1.87
February	—	1.29	1.29	1.29	1.29	1.98	1.82	1.89
March	—	1.29	1.29	1.29	1.29	2.25	1.83	1.88
April	—	1.29	1.29	1.29	1.30	2.24	1.78	1.84
May	—	1.29	1.29	1.29	1.39	2.40	1.76	1.66
June	1.28	1.29	1.28	1.29	1.70	2.44	1.63	1.63
July	1.29	1.29	1.28	1.29	1.75	2.31	1.61	1.68
August	1.29	1.29	1.29	1.29	1.73	2.20	1.65	1.80
September	1.29	1.29	1.29	1.30	1.68	2.22	1.78	1.79
October	1.29	1.30	1.29	1.29	1.80	1.96	1.87	1.75
November	1.29	1.29	1.29	1.30	1.97	2.01	1.92	1.74
December	1.29	1.29	1.29	1.30	2.11	1.96	1.79	1.63
Annual	$1.29	$1.29	$1.29	$1.29	$1.82	$2.16	$1.78	$1.76
Percent Change	—	0.0%	0.0%	0.0%	41.1%	18.7%	-17.6%	-1.1%

	1971	1972	1973	1974	1975	1976	1977	1978
January	$1.64	$1.47	$2.01	$3.65	$4.19	$4.06	$4.41	$4.94
February	1.60	1.50	2.24	5.27	4.39	4.09	4.54	4.94
March	1.67	1.54	2.23	5.34	4.34	4.17	4.85	5.28
April	1.72	1.57	2.18	5.02	4.22	4.35	4.78	5.11
May	1.66	1.58	2.38	5.41	5.55	4.49	4.69	5.13
June	1.60	1.57	2.60	4.89	4.49	4.81	4.44	5.31
July	1.58	1.75	2.68	4.41	4.72	5.00	4.50	5.35
August	1.58	1.85	2.63	4.41	4.92	4.22	4.45	5.49
September	1.42	1.77	2.67	4.04	5.00	4.30	4.54	5.57
October	1.33	1.81	2.88	4.80	4.31	4.22	4.77	5.19
November	1.32	1.82	2.86	4.64	4.32	4.37	4.83	5.88
December	1.39	1.97	3.14	4.39	4.08	4.36	4.71	5.93
Annual	$1.54	$1.68	$2.54	$4.69	$4.54	$4.37	$4.63	$5.34
Percent Change	-12.5%	9.1%	51.2%	84.6%	-3.2%	-3.7%	5.9%	15.3%

	1979	1980	1981	1982	1983	1984	1985	1986
January	$6.25	$38.28	$14.78	$8.03	$12.51	$8.20	$6.11	$6.07
February	7.43	35.28	12.97	8.29	13.83	9.17	6.07	5.86
March	7.42	23.95	12.35	7.23	10.66	9.69	6.03	5.64
April	7.49	14.45	11.48	7.28	11.76	9.24	6.46	5.22
May	8.40	12.69	10.90	6.66	13.02	8.97	6.27	5.11
June	8.54	15.82	9.96	5.61	11.73	8.73	6.18	5.15
July	9.18	16.15	8.63	6.20	12.13	7.41	6.11	5.05
August	9.40	16.00	8.99	7.15	12.14	7.65	6.26	5.21
September	14.02	20.20	10.05	8.74	11.89	7.28	6.20	5.69
October	16.85	20.18	9.27	9.51	9.85	7.30	6.20	5.67
November	16.59	18.61	8.54	9.82	8.88	7.50	6.13	5.57
December	22.81	16.28	8.47	10.62	9.14	6.65	5.88	5.37
Annual	$11.20	$20.65	$10.53	$7.93	$11.46	$8.15	$6.15	$5.47
Percent Change	109.7%	84.4%	-49.0%	-24.7%	44.6%	-28.9%	-24.6%	-11.1%

Notes: Comex nearby active silver futures contract prices.
Source: New York Commodity Exchange, Metals Week.
March 1, 2006

Monthly Average Silver Prices
Comex Settlement Price

	1987	1988	1989	1990	1991	1992	1993	1994
January	$5.54	$6.73	$5.98	$5.24	$4.03	$4.13	$3.67	$5.14
February	5.49	6.33	5.87	5.27	3.72	4.13	3.64	5.28
March	5.43	6.43	5.94	5.06	3.96	4.11	3.65	5.45
April	7.36	6.46	5.78	5.05	3.97	4.03	3.97	5.31
May	8.44	6.55	5.44	5.08	4.04	4.07	4.45	5.44
June	7.43	7.03	5.28	4.90	4.39	4.05	4.37	5.38
July	7.72	7.12	5.23	4.85	4.29	3.95	5.04	5.27
August	7.81	6.70	5.18	4.97	3.93	3.79	4.80	5.20
September	7.61	6.35	5.14	4.78	4.04	3.76	4.16	5.53
October	7.56	6.29	5.14	4.34	4.10	3.74	4.34	5.43
November	6.71	6.29	5.49	4.16	4.05	3.76	4.51	5.17
December	6.79	6.13	5.52	4.08	3.91	3.71	4.99	4.75
Annual	$6.99	$6.53	$5.50	$4.82	$4.03	$3.93	$4.30	$5.28
Percent Change	27.8%	-6.6%	-15.8%	-12.4%	-16.4%	-2.5%	9.4%	22.8%

	1995	1996	1997	1998	1999	2000	2001	2002
January	$4.75	$5.52	$4.79	$5.86	$5.17	$5.24	$4.71	$4.47
February	4.69	5.64	5.10	6.71	5.52	5.27	4.55	4.42
March	4.66	5.56	5.22	6.22	5.17	5.11	4.40	4.54
April	5.54	5.39	4.74	6.30	5.07	5.09	4.37	4.58
May	5.53	5.39	4.77	5.55	5.28	5.05	4.44	4.73
June	5.34	5.13	4.73	5.26	5.06	5.03	4.36	4.90
July	5.19	5.06	4.36	5.47	5.22	5.03	4.25	4.93
August	5.40	5.13	4.50	5.13	5.28	4.92	4.19	4.53
September	5.47	5.04	4.76	5.02	5.28	4.97	4.45	4.58
October	5.37	4.94	5.02	4.98	5.39	4.88	4.41	4.40
November	5.29	4.83	5.06	4.96	5.16	4.70	4.10	4.52
December	5.21	4.86	5.85	4.89	5.22	4.70	4.35	4.66
Annual	$5.20	$5.21	$4.91	$5.53	$5.23	$5.00	$4.38	$4.60
Percent Change	-1.4%	0.1%	-5.8%	12.7%	-5.3%	-4.5%	-12.4%	5.1%

	2003	2004	2005	2006
January	$4.84	$6.37	$6.65	$9.24
February	4.65	6.47	7.08	9.53
March	4.52	7.31	7.29	
April	4.52	7.06	7.13	
May	4.75	5.86	7.06	
June	4.53	5.85	7.32	
July	4.85	6.39	7.05	
August	5.01	6.70	7.02	
September	5.20	6.43	7.24	
October	5.02	7.17	7.72	
November	5.19	7.51	7.89	
December	5.67	7.14	8.29	
Annual	$4.90	$6.69	$7.26	$9.38
Percent Change	6.3%	36.6%	8.5%	36.8%